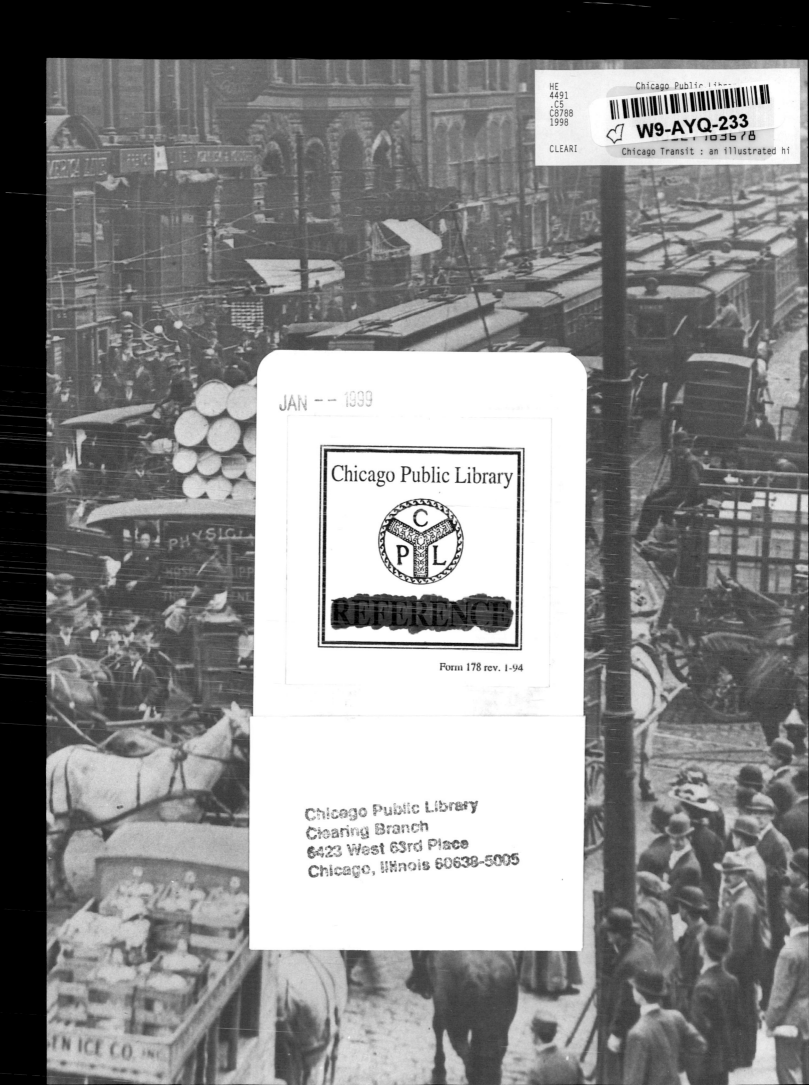

CHICAGO TRANSIT

CHICAGO
TRANSIT

AN ILLUSTRATED HISTORY

DAVID M. YOUNG

NORTHERN ILLINOIS UNIVERSITY PRESS

DeKalb 1998

Published by the Northern Illinois University Press, DeKalb,
Illinois 60115
Manufactured in the United States using acid-free paper
Design by Julia Fauci

Library of Congress Cataloging-in-Publication Data
Young, David 1940 Sept. 22–
Chicago Transit : an illustrated history / David M. Young
        p.   cm.
Includes bibliographical references and index.
ISBN 0–87580–241–9 (alk. paper)
1. Chicago Transit Authority—History. 2. Local transit—
Illinois—Chicago—History. I. Title.
HE4491.C5C8788 1998
388.4'09773'11—dc21

Maps created by Mapcraft, Woodstock, Illinois.

Photographs and illustrations provided courtesy of the
Antique Automobile Club of America, Michael Brown, the
Chicago and North Western Railway Company, the Chicago
Transit Authority, George Krambles, Metra, Bruce Moffat,
the Naperville Heritage Society, NAVISTAR, the Owls Head
Transportation Museum, PACE, Pullman Inc., David
Solzman, the Waukesha Historical Society, and the
Wisconsin Maritime Museum.

CONTENTS

Chicagoans have always faced transportation choices. This photograph of visitors leaving the 1933 Century of Progress fair (shown here on Lake Shore Drive looking north) illustrates two options, the streetcar and the automobile. While the streetcar faded into obsolescence with the passage of time, the car emerged as the most widely used mode of transportation in the twentieth century. (Krambles Archive)

PREFACE

This project started more than twenty years ago when I was assigned by the *Chicago Tribune* to cover the political furor that accompanied the creation of a regional transit agency in Chicago and I began to wonder how one of the world's largest and best transit systems could have gotten itself into such a mess. The voices of the transportation professionals were being drowned out by the politicians, whose agendas often seemed to favor narrow constituencies rather than the general welfare of the system. The transit system lurched from crisis to crisis until it was on the brink of insolvency. Like most reporters in similar situations, I began to look for a cheat sheet, some quick explanation, perhaps a good general history, that would provide the necessary background to understand what was happening to transit in Chicago; but there was none.

This book attempts to fill that void by telling the story of Chicago's mass-transit system from the city's inception on a muddy marshland to its maturity as one of the world's metropolises: from the stage-coaches that plucked local passengers off dusty streets to the bilevel trains that whisk fifteen hundred passengers at a time to distant suburbs and the hundreds of thousands of automobiles that each day creep bumper-to-bumper along the expressways. Despite the existence of one of the best developed rail and bus transit systems in the Western Hemisphere, eight out of ten commuters in the Chicago metropolitan area rode to work in a car in 1990.

Transportation historians over the years have tended to treat public transit and automobility as separate, antithetical phenomena, as if the straphangers who jammed the streetcars and Ls had no relationship to the people who sat behind the steering wheels of the highwheelers, an early motorized buggy built in Chicago. They were indeed the same commuters, and they switched from straphanging to highwheeling because in rapidly decentralizing Chicagoland the automobile was a better way to get to work. The auto very nearly destroyed America's rail transit systems because it fostered decentralization; it almost destroyed the nation's cities as well, at least those nineteenth-century cities built on the European model. This history treats the automobile as a mass-transit system and treats decentralization as a natural extension of the suburbanization phenomena that began with the railroads in the 1850s.

The project would not have been possible without the generous help of George Krambles, the retired executive director of the Chicago Transit Authority, who knows more about mass transit than possibly any man alive and who provided documents and photographs from his files as well as advice. Jeff Stern, Violet Brooks, and Bruce Moffat at the CTA also provided considerable assistance and access to documents and photographs, as did Chris Knapton at Metra and Joseph DiJohn at Pace, who allowed me access to an outline of suburban transit history prepared under his direction. Harry Bruce, now retired chief executive of the Illinois Central Railroad, let me peruse the early annual reports of that carrier, and officials of the Chicago & North Western Railroad let me rummage through their corporate archives. David A. Kolzow Sr. provided access to his antique Chicago-built cars and extensive files on the early automobile industry.

Michael Brown provided photographs, old and new; Ted Schuster gave me a copy of his history of west suburban transit; and John Allen was kind enough to furnish me with an early copy of his study on the chaotic years of the Regional Transportation Authority. Lyle Dorsett at Wheaton College offered some excellent suggestions that led to extensive revisions of an early draft. Robert Goldsborough, one of the best editors in the business as well as an author, and George Krambles both read the finished manuscript and offered a number of corrections and helpful suggestions.

A note on the terminology used in this volume is in order. Trying to keep up with all the name changes that have occurred over the years can be maddening. The Aurora Branch Railroad successively became the Chicago, Burlington & Quincy; Burlington Northern; and Burlington Northern Santa Fe. The Logan Square branch of Metropolitan West Side Elevated was later known as the Milwaukee Rapid Transit Line, the O'Hare Line, and most recently the "Blue Line." Other instances abound. Where I could I shunned newer designations to keep the names of the lines as simple, consistent, and geographically meaningful as possible. Appendix C lists many of the more common names of the transit systems over the years.

Financial terminology also has changed considerably over the 150 years of transit history. Earnings, for example, was once a synonym for gross revenues but now means net income, or profits. I have translated such terms to conform to contemporary financial reporting standards. Bureaucratese, such as "public funding requirement" as a euphemism for deficit and "light rail system" for street railway, also has been translated.

CHICAGO TRANSIT

Omnibuses became the first transit vehicle used in Chicago in the 1850s. Long after streetcars had replaced them in hauling commuters, they were used for station-transfer service. These Parmelee omnibuses are shown at the North Western station at Kinzie and Wells Streets sometime in the late 1800s. (Krambles Archive)

Part One

THE NINETEENTH CENTURY

♦ Chicago grew in less than one century from a frontier fort to one of the world's great industrial cities. At the time of the Fort Dearborn massacre of 1812 the outpost had less than 100 residents, 55 of whom were soldiers, but the population had increased to 1,698,575 by the end of the nineteenth century. Chicago was blessed by geography that made it the best canoe portage between the Great Lakes and the Mississippi River system and by the simultaneous arrival at midcentury of industrial, agricultural, communications, and transportation revolutions. Before the completion of its first canal, railroad, and telegraph line in 1848, Chicago was little more than a booming but isolated port in a remote corner of the Great Lakes. The canal and railroads extended the city's reach inland for more than one thousand miles, making it New York's economic satrapy in the American interior, "Nature's Metropolis," as William Cronon dubbed it more than one century later.

Although Chicago was destined by geography and technology to become the most important transportation center in the American interior, it could not have grown to the size it did without developing an internal transit system. Both the external transportation and internal transit systems were made possible not only by the development of mechanical traction but also by the business enterprises that capitalized on it. The horse slowly gave way to the steam engine and all its metamorphoses, from railroad locomotives to central generating plants, just as the family-owned enterprise yielded to incorporated joint-stock companies capable of financing and operating complex transit systems. In the frontier outpost of 1830s Chicago, the streets belonged to the animals. One of the first official acts of transportation control imposed by the young city was to ban wandering livestock, especially on the sidewalks. By antebellum times humans had generally claimed the sidewalks, but the streets, such as they were, still belonged to the horses. Anyone intending to use the streets generally rode on or behind a horse, probably in an omnibus or horsecar.

By the end of the nineteenth century, the horse was making its last stand. Chicagoans and their machines were taking over the streets, filling them with clattering, clanking trolley cars and even a few motor buggies. Where streets were too congested, Chicago in the last decade of the century simply built railways in the air. Chicago-area residents intent upon traveling for any distance, even to the suburbs, generally did so in trains pulled by steam locomotives, some of which were capable of speeds of up to 100 miles per hour. By this time both the steam engine and private enterprise were approaching their limits: steam engines could not efficiently power the small road vehicles that appeared, and private enterprise was finding it increasingly difficult to finance the expensive new urban transit systems.

1
THE CITY OF MUD

◆ When Jean Baptiste Point du Sable arrived at the southwest corner of Lake Michigan sometime after the Revolutionary War he found a marshland and prairie cut by a sluggish river that extended inland only a few miles. It was a site that not even the local Indians considered permanently habitable.[1] The native Potawatomis, with whom du Sable hoped to trade, generally lived on higher ground farther inland. The Indians held only a passing interest in the place as a nexus of trails that meandered around the south end of Lake Michigan and every direction from there, an excel-

lent canoe portage, and a fertile hunting ground. To them it offered little more.

The place had little utility to Neolithic cultures. The Potawatomi had no need of permanent settlements, even if they were capable of sustaining them, and the earlier and more advanced Mississippian society had built its fortified mound cities such as Cahokia (A.D. 900–1300) far to the southwest in the river valley that today is the site of modern St. Louis. Here the valleys offered the Mississippians game and good soil for farming, and the rivers provided an avenue for trade.[2] In contrast, the Great

In 1839 the city required property owners to provide sidewalks. Plank sidewalks elevated pedestrians above the quagmire caused by poorly drained streets. Even during the 1897 construction of the Northwestern L at Dayton Street, the popular sidewalks remained in place. (Krambles Archive)

Lakes could be dangerous for the primitive Indian canoes to navigate.[3] The Indians did not fully appreciate the fact that Chicago sat atop a low-lying continental divide that separated by only a few miles the Chicago River, which flowed east through the Great Lakes to the Atlantic Ocean, and the Des Plaines River, which flowed south via the Illinois and Mississippi Rivers to the Gulf of Mexico. This strategic alignment would not prove important until the Industrial Revolution abruptly supplanted the Neolithic Age.

The French explorers in the 1670s, one century before du Sable's arrival, first recognized Portage Chicagou as the potential location for a canal connecting the St. Lawrence and Mississippi Rivers watersheds. Since Louis XIV was not particularly interested in the colonization of the vast North American wilderness so far from Versailles,[4] Robert Cavelier Sieur de LaSalle abandoned those plans, and the principal interest of France in the Midwest became the fur trade, an industry that did not need a canal.

The French and British had been content to leave Portage Chicagou to the Indians, but the newly independent United States fortified the place to secure its tenuous hold on the vast interior—the old Northwest Territory—that it had acquired from Britain at the end of the Revolution. For two generations after du Sable built his cabin near the mouth of the Chicago River, where he became the place's first permanent resident, trade with the Indians and the soldiers who manned Fort Dearborn after 1803 sustained the economy of the primitive frontier outpost. By then the area had already acquired a reputation as an unhealthy place to live because workers building the fort had been plagued by "bilious fevers."[5]

When du Sable sold his trading post and left Chicago in 1800, walking and canoeing were still the principal methods of getting around in the wilderness. Within a few years, however, the horse and sail became the predominant engines of transportation.

Transportation was largely seasonal; the Great Lakes were frozen or too dangerous to navigate for up to four months each winter, and because of mud the Indian trails were largely impassable to horse-drawn wagons in the spring and fall.[6] Chicago in 1830 was small enough that residents could easily walk or ride a horse anywhere in the community. There was no need for local public transportation.

THE CANAL AGE

When William B. Ogden, the man destined to become Chicago's first mayor, arrived in 1835, Chicago was already booming. New York had opened the Great Lakes to development ten years earlier by building the Erie Canal to connect the Hudson River with Lake Erie, and Chicago at the far end of those inland seas represented a potential gateway to the Mississippi Valley and the vast interior beyond. Geography favored New York with the easiest route inland, and it won the race with the rival ports of Boston, Philadelphia, Baltimore, and New Orleans to establish economic hegemony in the American interior. Once New York gained access to the upper lakes, its influence could be extended as far as the Mississippi Valley by means of a canal that the earlier French settlers had talked about digging at Portage Chicagou.

Federal authorization for just such a ninety-six-mile canal between the Chicago River and the head of navigation of the Illinois River at LaSalle was granted even before New York completed the Erie Canal. Illinois's canal commissioners platted a new town at the eastern end of the canal where Fort Dearborn had been, and an assortment of adventurers, entrepreneurs, and speculators who flocked to the place in anticipation of the start of canal construction threw up a wooden shack town.[7] The boom occurred despite delays in obtaining financing for the canal, a cholera epidemic, and an Indian uprising. Indeed, the first steamship to visit

Chicago, the *Sheldon Thompson,* arrived in 1832 under government charter, bringing troops for the Black Hawk War.[8] It also carried cholera. By the time the Illinois and Michigan Canal belatedly opened in 1848, the telegraph had arrived and the city's first steam-powered grain elevator had set up business, paving the way for the bulk movement of agricultural commodities, which until that time had been loaded by hand in bags.[9]

The trading post that had survived the closing of Fort Dearborn by 1830 was barely able to support a population estimated between forty and fifty living on an area of less than half a square mile,[10] by 1850 the city covered just under ten square miles and was occupied by nearly thirty thousand residents. Aside from the ill-fated and uncompleted National Road that was supposed to link the then state capital at Vandalia with Baltimore, the I-M Canal was the Illinois government's most significant transportation project in the nineteenth century. Not only did it cause Chicago's first boom, but the problems Illinois encountered with financing it also strongly influenced state and local attitudes toward public financing of transportation for generations. Undoubtedly it was responsible for the general political philosophy that prevailed into the 1970s that public transportation should be paid for by its users.

Congress had authorized the canal in 1822, but because the new state that had come into existence only a few years earlier had no money with which to build it, Congress in 1827 enacted a land grant that stipulated Illinois could sell off excess lands not needed for the canal right-of-way to raise the $4.6 million needed for construction. The Canal Commission platted Chicago for that purpose in 1830 but found that revenues from land sales were insufficient. Ultimately the commission was forced to resort to financial markets in the East. The deal that was eventually cut with New York bankers who sold the bonds in Europe involved financing construction of the canal from future operat-ing revenues—a technique later used by local government to finance all manner of public works projects, including the acquisition of the city's transit system after 1945 and the building of airports and tollways in the second half of the twentieth century.[11]

Ogden, an investor who arrived in Chicago during its first boom, became an indefatigable booster and a promoter of its first railway. Despite the fact that the horse-drawn wagon was still the predominant form of land transport and that Chicago was the destination for nearly seventy thousand such wagon teams, the railway began service in 1848, the year that can conveniently be used to delineate the arrival of the Industrial Revolution in Chicago.[12] The Chicago railroads were also financed largely by eastern and European private capital, first by the sale of equity shares in incorporated joint-stock companies and later by bonds. That relieved Chicago of the need to commit public funds to attract railroads, as had been the case in other states and cities, including St. Louis, Chicago's principal rival at the time.[13] The Illinois Central Railroad, like the I-M Canal earlier, was given a federal land grant to generate construction funds, but when that proved insufficient it was forced to resort to the sale of stock and bonds for capital. By the middle 1850s, two-thirds of its investors lived in England and a committee of directors met regularly in London.[14] Chicago's street railways, which came on the scene just before the Civil War, also used the sale of stocks and bonds to generate capital, although by that time the city had accumulated sufficient private wealth to enable greater numbers of Chicagoans to buy stock in those ventures.

THE STAGECOACH STOP

In the early nineteenth century, with its rows of hurriedly constructed wooden buildings flanking dirt streets, Chicago looked a lot like the Wild West towns

Stagecoaches were used for intercity traffic, as shown in this painting by local historian and folk artist Les Schrader of a Temple Line coach stopped at Paw Paw (later the suburb of Naperville) in the mid-1830s. The route was downgraded to omnibus service after the railroads arrived. (Image provided by the Naperville Heritage Society with original painting on exhibition at Naper Settlement, Naperville, Ill.)

popularized in American movies.[15] Unlike the dusty Wild West towns in the movies, however, Chicago sat atop a poorly drained marshland. Rain and heavy traffic turned the streets into a quagmire of mud, garbage, and horse dung that gave rise to frontier humor. According to one tale, after a particularly rainy spell a passerby noticed a man's head protruding from the center of a muddy street and inquired if he could be of some help. "No, thank you. I have a good horse under me," replied the buried man.[16] Another popular story of the day told of a Frink & Walker stagecoach that had become mired in the street in front of the Sherman House, a hotel. Although the passengers and horses were rescued, the crew left the stage stuck in the muck overnight only to discover the next morning that a quick freeze made it impossible to extricate; it remained in place till the spring thaw.[17]

The senior partner of the Frink & Walker stagecoach company was John Frink, probably Chicago's first transportation baron, a businessman who was brusquely intolerant of failure by his

employees and was almost Machiavellian in his dealings with any competitor who dared to challenge his Midwest postal-route monopolies. He had collected these over the years by lobbying in Washington and greasing palms. Frink was also known to sneak his injured horses to the veterinarian after dark so the public or competitors would not know how severely he used the whip. "I find horses, I want you to find whips," he was quoted as telling one of his drivers who had lost a race with a rival stagecoach because he feared that driving his horses too hard would kill them.[18]

Frink, who arrived in Chicago in 1836 at age thirty-nine, had considerable experience on eastern stagecoach lines. He soon bought out Dr. John L. Temple's three-year-old coach line and began expanding. By 1850, it was reported that he held mail contracts in six midwestern states worth $128,000 per year. That success, however, had not come without a fight. In the mid-1840s, a competitor from Ohio won away many of Frink's mail contracts, and Martin O. Walker, his junior partner, fearful of the mounting losses, wanted to sell out.[19] Frink, however, decided that his new competitor, General Hinton, was undercapitalized and that a fare war was in order. So Frink cut his rates and Hinton followed his lead "until the rival lines became practically free, with meals thrown in for good measure."[20] The tactic worked against Hinton, who left town, but was useless against the railroads, which showed up a few years later. Frink sold his interest in the stage line to Walker and invested in the Galena & Chicago Union, Peoria & Oquawka (later Burlington), and Peoria & Bureau Valley (later Rock Island) Railroads as well as omnibuses.[21] He died in 1858.

THE MUD

Aside from ordinances banning the wandering of livestock and the dumping of animal carcasses on city streets, the first attempt to improve walking mobility in Chicago by the Common Council, as the City Council was called before 1875, was the passage in 1839 of an ordinance requiring property owners to provide sidewalks. The ordinance also empowered the street commissioner to build sidewalks at the expense of the property owner whose property they fronted. Typical planked walkways were a few feet wide and stretched along the front of the buildings. The sidewalks proved to be so popular that the city had to ban their use by equestrians,

The use of wooden planks, illustrated in Les Schrader's painting of the building of the Chicago-Oswego plank road near Naperville, was a common but unsuccessful technique used in the 1840s and early 1850s to provide a hard surface on rural toll roads and Chicago streets. (Image provided by the Naperville Heritage Society with original painting on exhibition at Naper Settlement, Naperville, Ill.)

Old wood-block pavement shows through asphalt in a paved alley on Chicago's South Side in 1997. (David Solzman)

lounging livestock, and teamsters.[22]

It was a relatively easy step for the city to try to adapt sidewalk technology to the streets, and in the 1840s Chicago began to experiment with planking them. Simple grading had leveled the surface of the streets until the next rain but did little to solve the drainage problem. Surfacing with cinders and stone had likewise proved unsuccessful, also because of poor drainage. It was therefore assumed that planking the streets, an idea developed in Russia and used widely in Canada, would solve the problem by raising the surface of the street above the quagmire. The plank road or street involved nothing more than laying parallel wooden timbers, or stringers, flat on the ground six to seven feet apart and placing a deck of planks three inches thick and eight feet long atop them. Lake Street was planked to a width of forty-eight feet from State Street to the south branch of the river in 1848, and an abortive gravity-flow drainage system was installed.[23]

Unfortunately, plank roads did nothing to solve the underlying drainage problem, so the city resorted to raising the elevation of streets from two to six feet, jacking up the adjacent buildings, and installing new foundations beneath them. Market (now Wacker Drive), State, LaSalle, Wells, and Madison Streets were then planked in the central business district. Elevating the city improved the drainage somewhat but did not solve the problems inherent to plank roads, including warped planks, rotting stringers, and rapid deterioration under heavy traffic. Despite additional experimentation with cobblestone and block limestone, Chicago was not quite ready to abandon the inherent cost advantages of wood technology.

In 1857 Chicago adopted a technique developed by Samuel Nicholson that consisted of surfacing a street with wood blocks similar to the way a parquet floor is laid. The Nicholson process consisted of excavating a street to create the proper subgrade, including a crown, then laying a subfloor of one-inch pine planks impregnated with hot tar. On top of the planks were placed six-inch-deep pine blocks laid side by side. The gaps between the blocks were filled with gravel, and the surface was coated with tar. The first pine block street proved so successful that by 1861 the city was ready to embark on its first major street program with four hundred miles scheduled for improvement. By 1871, Chicago had 56 miles of wood block streets, primarily in the heavily trafficked downtown, out of a total street inventory of 533 miles.[24]

The continuing street and drainage problems forced the city in 1861 to create the Board of Public Works, apparently the first public agency in Illinois with a professional staff dealing with roads. It continued to experiment with street-paving materials despite the success of pine block, which was still being used on some lightly trafficked streets as late as 1910.[25] Macadam, a crushed stone surface that is pounded into a hard surface by wagon traffic, was first tried in 1863 on Market Street between Madison and Van Buren; sheet asphalt was used on North Park in

1882; and brick was used on Lake Park Avenue between 29th and 31st Streets in 1890. Macadam surfaces were often used immediately outside the downtown area, cinder and gravel were used on lightly traveled streets, and dirt was used on roads in outlying areas. Concrete first appeared as a paving material in 1905 on Schlitz Avenue between 111th and 113th Streets.[26]

Financing the street improvements proved to be a problem. Toll roads were obviously impractical in a city, and the rural corvee of three days' labor, or its equivalent in cash ($1 per day), required of every male between the ages of sixteen and sixty each year failed to cover the cost of materials. The city attempted without much success to impose a road tax and later tried special assessments on adjacent property owners.[27] These proved vulnerable to corruption and long court challenges, including a suit that caused a two-year delay in the imposition of the first such assessment while the courts decided on its constitutionality. The use of the often cumbersome special assessment began to wane in the twentieth century as Chicago increasingly resorted to other taxes such as vehicle registrations and motor fuel levies.

Thus almost from the inception of Chicago government the streets became the responsibility of the public treasury. They proved to be a heavy load on the treasury, which is undoubtedly why a few years later the city was willing to adhere to common practice of the time and allow private enterprise to build and to operate its public transit system. In the fiscal year ending February 26, 1948, Chicago spent about 20 percent of its municipal budget on streets and alleys—$7,371 out of a total budget of $33,650.[28] Planking cost up to $2,000 per mile but was far cheaper than paving with stone; even so, the cost of planking in Chicago alone for the period 1849–1850 was $30,000.[29] Despite the fact that from 1857 until 1861 the city spent $234,000 in general funds on street improvements, it could not embark on a general street improvement program until it found a permanent source of revenue.

The new charter in 1863 allowed special assessments of up to 3 percent of the value of adjoining property to be imposed based on the assumption that the value of property fronting a street benefited from any improvement.[30]

The rapid development of street railways after the Civil War, especially following the introduction of the cable car system in 1882, became another impetus for paving streets. To protect their underground cable conduits from damage caused by heavy wagon wheels, the cable companies were forced to build concrete channels between the tracks. Brick came into use as a surfacing material late in the century, especially on streets containing trolley lines, but brick streets were expensive to build and to maintain. Many were resurfaced with a layer of asphalt after the trolley lines were abandoned.

Possibly the last transportation development of the old walking city, at least in its equestrian phase, was the boulevard. Initially developed by landscape architect Frederick Law Olmsted for New York's Central Park, the concept was brought to Chicago in the period 1869–1870 by Olmsted and Calvert Vaux, who began planning scenic parkways, or boulevards, to connect Chicago and south suburban Hyde Park.[31] Although Olmsted and Vaux had no way of knowing the impact the automobile would have on American society half a century later, the concept of the modern, limited access, landscaped express highway had its origins in the park boulevards. Lincoln Park Drive, begun in 1893, in fact evolved into Lake Shore Drive, Chicago's first expressway. By the time the boulevard came to Chicago, however, the city was already being transformed from a walking town into an industrial city dependent upon a transit system.

INDUSTRIALIZATION

The census of structures in 1837, more than the enumeration of population, provides insight into the preindustrial nature of Chicago. The census reported 4 warehouses, 29 dry-goods stores, 5 hardware stores, 3 drug stores, 19 grocery and provision stores, 10 taverns, 26 groceries, 17 lawyers' offices, 5 churches, and 398 dwellings.[32] The local economy was dominated by the retail merchants who depended on general merchants in New York for their goods; the existence of several warehouses indicates, however, that the city was becoming a center for assembling bulk cargos for shipment east over the Great Lakes and Erie Canal as well as for breaking down shipments of manufactured products destined for distribution in the hinterland.[33] The factory had not yet appeared in Chicago in 1837, and the little manufacturing that did exist was done in the homes of craftsmen.

The city's first manufacturing facility was a steam-powered sawmill built in 1834 on the north branch of the Chicago River near Clybourn Avenue. Cyrus McCormick's original 1847 reaper factory, on the banks of the river at Michigan Avenue, was powered by a steam engine and employed thirty-three persons. This early industry on the river was exceptional, however, as most of the earliest industrial growth in northern Illinois occurred outside Chicago, where rivers were available to power machines by means of water wheels.[34] Chicago had too severe a drainage problem and the Chicago River was too sluggish and too heavily used as a lake port to permit the construction of the weirs and mill races needed to power machinery.

Warehouses until late in the nineteenth century were typically located along the river and by modern standards employed large numbers of laborers, since cargos were loaded and unloaded by hand. Grain moved in sacks in two-hundred-ton lots on sailing schooners, even though steamships in the 1830s had captured most of the passenger traffic on the lakes. Land transport was expensive, unreliable, and slow, used only when no alternative was available. Farm produce moved by wagon to lake ports in the autumn; high-value manufac-

tured goods were sometimes shipped overland in winter; and passengers moved by stagecoach in the winter and by steamship in warmer weather. A great number of the poorer pioneers rode their own farm wagons to Chicago or simply walked.

As the young city continued to develop, the riverbank became lined with warehouses, factories, grain elevators, and lumber yards dependent upon the lake for transportation. The retail district was one block inland, along Lake Street west of the abandoned Fort Dearborn, and houses fanned out from there. Local merchants, who in addition to serving their walk-in trade increasingly acted as regional distributors of goods to stores in rural areas, still tended to live on the premises. Business in antebellum Chicago was largely a family affair, but as those enterprises grew in size and in complexity they were forced to hire bookkeepers, clerks, engineers, professional management, and salesmen. This trend established the beginning of a middle class that created the demand for mass transit.

By 1846, there were 177 manufacturing businesses in Chicago employing 1,400 persons, or 10 percent of the population of Chicago. An enumeration of employees suggests the nature of the city on the eve of the Industrial Revolution: 71 people worked in foundries; 50 in tanneries; 46 in barrel-making operations; 61 in wagon shops; 190 in shoe shops; 59 in saddle and harness shops; 44 in cap and fur factories; 121 in tailor shops; 83 in furniture shops; 16 in candle, soap, and oil factories; and 250 in packing houses.[35] Within one decade manufacturing employment exceeded 10,000, and by 1890 it was in excess of 203,000.[36]

Life in preindustrial Chicago, despite its reputation as a boom town peopled by every type of hustler, was less hurried than it would be later. A Chicago businessman sending a letter to a vendor in New York in 1830 could expect a reply in a minimum of six weeks, although by 1857 that time was reduced to four days by the railroads.[37] Stagecoach schedules were irregular because of the deplorable condition of the roads, and although lake steamship packet lines published schedules for the sake of competition as early as 1830, the majority of the Great Lakes fleet sailed only when they were able to fill their holds with cargo, a practice that could delay travelers for days.[38] The preindustrial attitude toward time began to change in the 1850s when the railroads arrived. Trains on the single-track railroads of that time had to operate on tight, published schedules to avoid conflicts and collisions, and the telegraph enabled them to do so. After 1848 in rapidly industrializing Chicago, time became money.

Population density was probably the most important single factor in the development of a market for public urban transportation. Because Chicago already had in place an omnibus transfer service designed to haul people between hotels and train stations, the city was poised to develop its transportation system to meet the demand of the market. Despite a tenfold increase in population in its first decade of existence, Chicago in 1840 had a density of only 417 people per square mile (see Table A1). In the next decade ending in 1850, the population density increased to 3,070 per square mile. Although the omnibus system began service shortly thereafter, it was not until the density had doubled to nearly 6,246 in 1860 that street railways became economically feasible to the extent that investors were willing to buy stock.

The growth in population and size of the city had a practical effect on the length of the commute necessary to get to and from work. Although statistics were not compiled in those days, it is possible to in-fer the impact of growth on transportation from Chicago's dimensions and density. In 1850, the city, slightly more than three miles square, could be walked from limit to limit in approximately forty-five minutes, and a worker commuting by foot from the edge of town to downtown could get to work in twenty to twenty-five minutes. By 1870, the city had grown to the point that a hike across town was six miles, and walking from the edge of town to downtown took forty-five minutes.

In preindustrial cities, Chicago included, workers lived relatively close to their jobs, and merchant families, craftsmen, and their employees often occupied the floors above their stores or workshops. The factory with its division of labor changed all that. The environment of smoke, noise, and grime became unacceptable first to managers, who moved to rural settings that became known as suburbs, then to the emerging middle class, the clerical workers and technicians, who followed the managers to the suburbs a few years later. The immigrant laborers who worked the factory floors generally continued to live as close to the factory as possible because they could not afford the cost of commuting. The increasing duration of the walk to work triggered a response in Chicago commuters, especially the middle class: they preferred to pay five cents to ride at five to seven miles per hour in a rattling, unheated, open, horse-pulled omnibus than to slog through the mud at a somewhat slower pace dodging drays and dung.[39] It was only a matter of time before entrepreneurs discovered there was a nickel to be made in that market.

HORSE POWER TO MACHINE TECHNOLOGY

♦ Although it seems as if the industrialization of Chicago occurred abruptly as the railroads arrived between 1848 and the Civil War, the process in reality developed gradually over a long period of time. The transportation system is a case in point: it took the better part of the nineteenth century for mechanical traction to supplant the city horse and for the steam engine to be adopted by other technologies to result in the conversion of the entire urban transit system to mechanical power. Each step in its development resulted in a progressively larger and more efficient system to cope with the explosive growth of Chicago in the last half of the century. By 1900 equine traction was a dying technology that survived in certain niche markets only because motorbuses and motor trucks were not yet on the horizon.

The steam railroads relatively early in their existence began creating the suburban commutation market, but the street transit system that evolved in Chicago at about the same time had to meet the demands of its urban market with the horse and coach. Stagecoaches relegated to obsolescence in overland transportation by the railroads gained a new, if brief, respite as omnibuses.

For three centuries prior to the development of railroads mankind had been breeding progressively larger horses and increasing the size of teams to accommodate larger and heavier vehicles. By the nineteenth century even those improvements were encountering limits imposed by the poor condition of streets and roads.[1] The condition of Midwest highways limited the size of Frink & Walker intercity stagecoaches to a vehicle that was pulled by four to six horses and was capable of carrying six to eight people at an average speed of no more than eleven miles per hour on open roads under optimum conditions. What we now call a stagecoach was known in its heyday as a Concord coach—a light, oval-shaped coach suspended above the frame by leather straps that enabled it to sway instead of bump as the vehicle negotiated primitive North American roads. European roads were in far better condition than those in America and allowed a much heavier coach than

was capable of negotiating the American wilderness. As was often the case in transportation, Americans simply adapted a European invention to local conditions.

It did not take Chicago transit operators long to abandon the Concord coach in favor of a vehicle more suitable to urban traffic—the omnibus,[2] a box-shaped vehicle that could seat twenty to thirty passengers and was pulled by a team of two horses. Speed was not possible on city streets because of the congestion, frequency of stops, and relatively short distances, so omnibuses plodded along at speeds slightly faster than a man could walk. The omnibuses operated on fixed routes on hourly or half-hourly schedules and charged fares as much as five cents, although competition often kept fares lower. In contrast, taxi drivers charged as much as fifty cents but would take the passenger from door to door. The increasing masses of travelers who flowed through Chicago between eastern and western railroads for

(facing page) The street transit system in Chicago evolved to meet the demands of its growing urban market. Streetcars powered by steam were the street railways' first attempt to replace horses with mechanical traction, though they ultimately proved unsuccessful as vehicles of mass transit. The locomotive on this North Chicago Railway train, pictured in the 1880s, was enclosed to look like a streetcar.

(Krambles Archive)

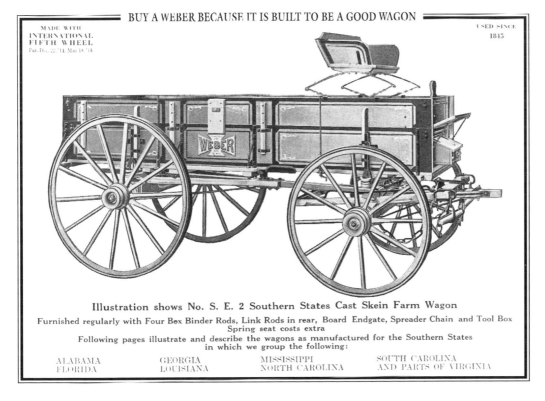

BUY A WEBER BECAUSE IT IS BUILT TO BE A GOOD WAGON

MADE WITH
INTERNATIONAL
FIFTH WHEEL
Pat. Dec. 22, '14, May 18 '16

USED SINCE
1845

Illustration shows No. S. E. 2 Southern States Cast Skein Farm Wagon
Furnished regularly with Four Box Binder Rods, Link Rods in rear, Board Endgate, Spreader Chain and Tool Box
Spring seat costs extra
Following pages illustrate and describe the wagons as manufactured for the Southern States
in which we group the following:

ALABAMA	GEORGIA	MISSISSIPPI	SOUTH CAROLINA
FLORIDA	LOUISIANA	NORTH CAROLINA	AND PARTS OF VIRGINIA

Wagons such as this one built by Weber carried goods on Chicago's streets from its earliest days well into the twentieth century. In 1904 International Harvester acquired Weber and employed it in manufacturing motor trucks. (Navistar) several years sustained the city's growing omnibus business. Hotels operated omnibuses as courtesy cars to the train stations, as did at least two dry goods stores.[3]

Except for Parmelee's deluxe railway passenger transfer vehicles, omnibuses were often open coaches and sometimes enclosed unheated coaches. Both were fitted with bench seats and the most rudimentary suspension systems that provided a ride endurable only because of its short duration. Omnibuses were predominantly a conveyance for the middle class, since the rich had personal carriages and the poor couldn't afford even the five-cent fare. Although the omnibus in transit service was replaced by the horse-drawn railway car within one decade, it continued to run well into the twentieth century in the station transfer business. Parmelee's company eventually converted to motorbuses and survived the decline of the railroads by shuttling passengers to the city's airports.[4]

THE HORSE-PULLED STREETCARS

By the end of the 1850s, the omnibus had developed into a more efficient vehicle called the horsecar. This was a lightly constructed wooden omnibus body placed on a set of flanged wheels that rode on rails laid in the streets. The light construction enabled a single horse to pull twenty passengers in what was known as a "bobtail" car,[5] although in Chicago the larger, two-horse cars with a passenger capacity of as many as thirty were more popular. Since horses in traffic plodded along at an average speed of only about three miles per hour, a pace a little slower than a person in a hurry could walk, the most immediate benefit of horsecars for Chicago commuters was that they no longer had to slog through the mud and snow.[6] Because the cars were unheated and dark, crews put a foot of hay or straw on the floor in winter to help riders keep their feet warm and placed coal oil–fired lamps at either end of the car. Though the horsecar, the culmination of equine traction, was considered a

"public necessity" soon after it appeared,[7] within a few years of its introduction the owners of the street railways already were casting around for more efficient mechanical traction systems to replace it. Until they found one in the 1880s, the horsecar had to do, and by 1890 there were about 150 miles of horsecar routes operating in Chicago, with the average Chicagoan riding 164 times during that year.[8]

As the system grew in size, its limitations became increasingly clear. Horsecars were adequate for Chicago in 1860, a city comprised of 17.5 square miles with a population of 109,000, but when it doubled in size and nearly tripled in population in one decade, both the horsecar system and the riding public began to feel the strain. By 1880, when Chicago had grown to nearly 180 square miles with a population of 503,000, the street railways had become the brunt of a great deal of public criticism, and an active search for a replacement began.[9]

Criticism focused not only on the rather poor economics of the horse as a traction engine but also on the substantial sanitation problem. The transit systems in Chicago owned more than 6,600 horses in the early 1880s, and as late as 1900, when the conversion of the street railway system to mechanical traction was well advanced, there were 115,260 nonfarm horses in Illinois out of a total equine population of 1.6 million in the state.[10] The public health problem that resulted from such a large urban horse population was substantial; the animals dumped an estimated one million pounds of manure and 25,000 gallons of urine on city streets annually. The necessity of disposing of approximately 7,000 horse carcasses left on city streets each year also posed a considerable problem.

Other health considerations also plagued the system. Horses carried diseases that were transmittable and fatal to humans, such as tetanus (the basis of mothers' long-standing admonition to their children not to go barefoot), and they were vulnerable to their own epizootics.

The Great Chicago Fire of 1871 devastated large parts of the central transportation system. Even waterborne transit was affected by the loss of docks and warehouses, as shown in this view of the Chicago River looking east from Wells Street. (Wisconsin Maritime Museum)

Urban horses were especially susceptible to influenza like epizootics, one of which decimated equine populations in the eastern United States in 1872, when about 2,250 horses died in Philadelphia and as many as 18,000 died or were incapacitated in New York City. The Great Epizootic, or a similar epidemic, hit Chicago that same year, killing much of what was left of the horse population that had survived the Chicago Fire one year earlier. Parmelee's transfer company suffered the loss of enough horses from the epizootic that it was forced to use oxen to pull its carriages. In 1901 Chicago's health commissioner publicly endorsed the automobile over horses as beneficial to the public health.[11]

The increased scale of industrialization after the Civil War put a great deal of pressure on the horsecar system, and the decentralization of population and industry following the 1871 Chicago Fire further eroded it. Coinciding with the rise of industrialization, steam railroads had created a system for mass distribution of goods throughout the nation; it was not long before manufacturers began to mass produce goods to fill that pipeline. Mass production meant larger factories built on cheap land far from the congestion of downtown Chicago. This trend resulted in the demise of the street railway system and the horsecar.

The meatpacking industry was Chicago's introduction to both mass distribution and mass production. Even during the Civil War the industry had begun the process of consolidating at a site remote from downtown Chicago and its rudimentary street railway system. The meat packers and railroads banded together beginning in 1865 to create the Union Stock Yard, a square mile of railroad tracks and pens for more than 125,000 animals surrounded by packing plants about five miles southwest of downtown Chicago.[12] The site had plenty of cheap land that could be assembled for industrial development; moreover, it was located some distance

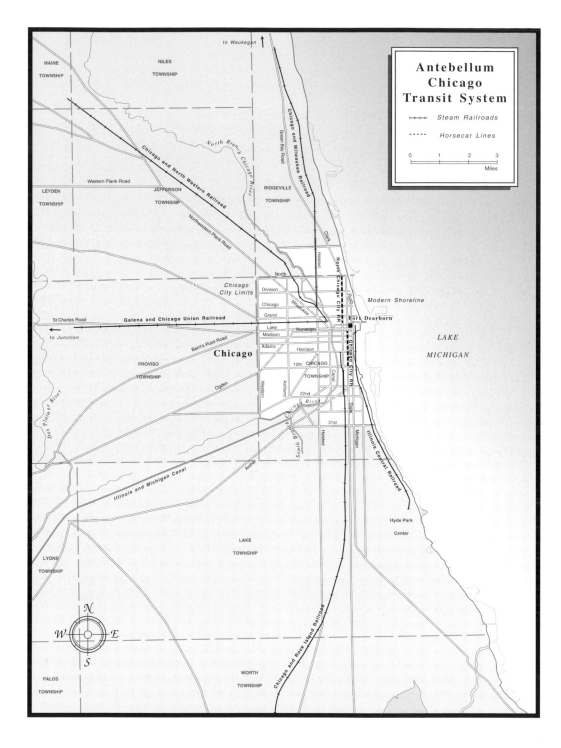

from populated areas that would find the smell of mountains of manure and rotting offal offensive. The thousands of low-paid workers generally moved into whatever accommodations they could find within walking distance of the stockyards or built a bungalow as close as they could to it. Higher-paid professionals and managers who wanted to live in more pleasant surroundings far from the stench created a market for horsecar lines and for the most part were still willing to endure long commutes, transfers, and multiple fares (since the city's street railway companies were franchised to serve specific areas and did not allow free transfers).[13] A four-mile ride

in a plodding horsecar could take the better part of an hour, depending on the traffic and the number of transfers necessary.

THE SEARCH FOR A REPLACEMENT

Shortly after the introduction of the horsecar in 1858, the city's fledgling transit industry began to experiment with mechanical traction as a replacement for the horse. The most obvious alternative was the steam engine. Since its development in England in the late seventeenth century as a device to pump water from mines, the steam engine had been progressively refined to power factories and ships. By 1825 it had been put on wheels for use as a propulsion system for land transport—the railroad locomotive. Early locomotives were capable of pulling a few Concord-style railway coaches seating fifteen passengers each at an average speed of fifteen miles per hour—probably about double what stagecoaches averaged year-round on Chicago-area roads.[14] By the time the railroads reached Chicago in the 1850s, their locomotives were pulling coaches seating more than fifty persons at speeds averaging thirty miles per hour for express trains. By the end of the century, passenger locomotives were capable of pulling trains of seventy-foot coaches seating sixty-six passengers each at speeds in excess of one hundred miles per hour, although the average speed was considerably less.[15]

The practical limitations on operating street railways in traffic made speed much less of a consideration than it was on the mainline carriers, but the ability to increase average speeds marginally and the passenger loads considerably was crucial to an industry that from its inception had fares limited by city government to five cents. Mechanical traction enabled the street railways to increase the capacity of their cars from twenty passengers in a horsecar to more than double that in an electric trolley car, or streetcar, as it was popularly known. Elevated railways built near the end of the century lifted public transit above the congested streets, resulting in greatly increased average speeds. They also affected passenger loads, enabling a single three-car train to carry 136 seated passengers.

By the time Chicago became the nation's dominant rail center before the Civil War, the locomotive had evolved from the British model to a heavier, more powerful version known as the American-style engine.[16] The most noticeable difference between early British and American locomotives, both of which were powered by four large driving wheels, was the appearance on the American version of four small, unpowered pilot wheels at the front to help the engine negotiate tight curves and rough track. This design also permitted a longer, heavier, and more powerful locomotive than was used in Britain. Passenger cars in democratic America were simply open rooms with a center aisle and rows of bench seats on either side, in contrast to the compartmentalized railway carriage in socially stratified Britain. American cars also rode on a pair of four-wheeled trucks that swivelled independently and allowed the car to negotiate tight turns, while the British remained content with their original arrangement of four wheels per car.[17]

The first railroad engine to arrive in Chicago, in 1848, was a vintage 1836 Baldwin Locomotive Works product that had four pilot wheels for stability but only two big drivers for traction. The Galena & Chicago Union Railroad's *Pioneer* weighed only ten tons—about one-third the weight of the small steam engines specially built for the Chicago elevated system more than half a century later—and as a result could pull a couple of cars at a maximum speed of about twenty-five miles per hour.[18] By the time of the Civil War, the Galena Railroad was buying American-class locomotives weighing in excess of thirty tons and rated at speeds of thirty miles per hour, although they probably could travel faster than track and operating conditions at the time would allow. *Samson*, an American-class locomotive with one of the fanciful names common among early railroads, was

Chicago's first steam locomotive in 1848 was a primitive 4-2-0 Baldwin called
the *Pioneer* by the Galena &
Chicago Union Railroad.
This locomotive, which now
belongs to the Chicago Historical Society, was a wood
burner. (Chicago & North
Western)

built for the Galena line in 1854, weighed
thirty-seven tons, and had tractive power
of 10,500 pounds.[19] The greater weight
contributed not so much to the speed of
the locomotive as it did to its tractive effort, a factor far more important to freight
operations than to passenger service, although in the 1850s locomotives typically
did double duty and trains often were a
mixed consist of freight and passenger cars.
In any case, an 1856 Galena Railroad
timetable indicates that a thirty-mile trip
from Aurora Junction, the site of the present-day suburb of West Chicago, to
Chicago took between one hour and forty-
five minutes and two hours and five minutes—an average of approximately fifteen
miles per hour.

As the mainline railroads developed
heavier and faster engines for long-distance
service, their older engines were downgraded to branch line or suburban commuter runs, where speed or the tractive effort to pull long trains was not as
important. The *Pioneer*, for example, was
consigned to work train service in the
1860s, and older American-style locomotives were a common sight on commuter
runs in the Chicago area. At about the
same time, the street railways, which often
ran parallel and adjacent to portions of the
suburban commuter lines, began to dabble
with the miniaturized steam engines, or
"dummies," as they were popularly called.

Even before the Civil War, the mainline
railroads had begun experimenting with the

idea of self-propelled cars, using small steam engines mounted in the front of the car to provide power for one-car trains on lines that did not have enough traffic to justify anything longer. This was an application of obvious interest to street railways even though they operated in a different environment with heavy traffic and frequent trains. However, the mainline steam cars were typically too large for the tight curves required of the street railways at intersections. The sixteen-ton, iron steam car operated as a test over the length of the Pittsburgh, Ft. Wayne & Chicago in 1860 was seventy-seven feet long—almost five times the length of the sixteen-foot horsecars in service at that time. It seated ninety-four passengers and carried three tons of baggage.[20]

In response to the need for small volume transport, the Chicago street railways took the small, four-wheel steam car locomotive and encased it in its own car body disguised to look like a horsecar.[21] Each locomotive typically pulled one or two unpowered cars, or trailers, in which the passengers rode. In 1867, the Chicago & Calumet Horse and Dummy Railroad was incorporated, received a franchise from south suburban Hyde Park, and operated dummy power there.[22] As late as 1891, traction magnate Charles T. Yerkes, who was always looking for ways to make his system more efficient, ordered a Belgian-built dummy, which was described at the time as a "steam tramway locomotive," for his North Chicago Railway Co. He also experimented briefly with gas motor-powered streetcars in 1892 but abandoned that project when all ten vehicles were destroyed in a car barn fire the following year.[23]

In 1899, when the electric streetcar had already become dominant, there were still seventy-five dummies in service in the United States, although the dummy was not particularly successful in Chicago.[24] They were criticized in local newspapers as early as 1859 before they even appeared on the scene; because of their noise and smoke and the danger of fire caused by

sparks from their smokestacks, the City Council restricted use of the dummies to outlying areas or to the suburban lines to Hyde Park, the stockyards, and Graceland Cemetery in Lake View.[25]

Small locomotives used to pull trains on Chicago's first elevated railways were logical outgrowths of the transit industry's experience with dummies, although these remained in service for only six years until they were overtaken by another advancement in technology, electrification. The Chicago & South Side Rapid Transit Railroad, which opened its first section between downtown Chicago and 39th Street in 1892 and its extension to the Columbian Exposition in Jackson Park the next year, bought forty-six small steam engines from Baldwin in Philadelphia to pull its coaches.[26] The Lake Street Elevated Railroad Company commenced service in 1893 with similar engines built by the Rhode Island Locomotive Works. It had thirty-five in service in 1896 when it electrified its system.[27]

The locomotives in use on mainline railroads had grown until they were far too large and heavy for use on elevated railways. The most common suburban commuter train locomotive in service when the first Ls were built was 60 feet long, including the tender that trailed the locomotive with a supply of coal and water, and weighed 110 to 120 tons—far too much for an urban elevated structure. Even a 0-6-0 steam switch engine, common in Chicago railroad yards in the 1890s, was 50 to 53 feet long, including the tender, and weighed between 80 and 90 tons.[28] Length was crucial because Chicago's elevated lines were built with a number of tight, 90-foot-radius turns above street intersections that could not accommodate a railroad car longer than about 50 feet.[29] By placing a small tender to carry coal and water on the rear of the locomotive frame, the engine builders in 1892 were able to compress the Chicago elevated locomotive into a vehicle about 28 feet long—about one foot shorter than a switch engine without its tender—that weighed only 29 tons. Those shorter tank engines were also favored by the elevated railways because they lent themselves to operation in either direction.

THE ELECTRIC REVOLUTION

As it turned out, the locomotives were obsolete before they pulled their first train. Although the South Side and Lake Street elevated companies balked at the cost of replacing them immediately, the Metropolitan West Side Elevated Railroad Company, originally intended to be a steam operation similar to its predecessors, switched to electricity in 1894, less than one year before it was scheduled to commence service. Its directors were favorably impressed by a demonstration electric elevated line operated at the Columbian Exposition in 1893, as well as by the conversion of some street railways to electric operation.[30]

This conversion was made possible by another offshoot of the steam engine—central power plants that could provide the energy to run an entire urban railway, first cable cars and later electric trolleys. The first practical application of the technology of transferring power from a central plant to multiple transit cars on the street was developed by a man named Andrew Smith Hallidie in 1873 in San Francisco, where steep hills made horse railways impractical on many routes. Large stationary steam engines were used to pull long underground cables to which transit cars were attached by means of devices called grips, and the cable car operator used the grip to clamp onto or to release the constantly moving cable as the need arose to start or to stop the car. The success of the San Francisco system was noticed by officials of Chicago City Railway Co., the progressive South Side street railway whose managers were looking for a mechanical replacement for the horse. Company President C. B. Holmes visited

San Francisco in 1880 and came home convinced that he had found an efficient replacement suitable for Chicago's flat terrain and severe winters. Cable cars were able to move passengers at twice the speed of horsecars and at half the cost.[31]

The immediate success of Holmes's cable car lines, the first of which opened on State Street in 1882, ended the question as to whether cable traction could work in a city vulnerable to heavy snowfalls that might, it was feared, clog cable channels beneath the streets. Despite the substantial capital investment of as much as $100,000 per mile to install a cable system and the lack of any hills to make them a necessity, Holmes quickly built one of the nation's largest cable systems. Within a few years the city's other two street railway companies began installing cable on the North and West sides.[32] Since cable could not be used on Chicago's bridges, which were moveable to accommodate ship traffic on the rivers, Charles T. Yerkes had to convince the city to allow him to expropriate existing but little-used street tunnels under the Chicago River to get his cable cars into downtown Chicago.

Eleven scattered power plants equipped with steam engines of up to 1,500 horsepower each operated the 41.2-mile Chicago cable system at speeds between 9.5 and 14 miles per hour. The network consisted of three independent systems (north, west, and south) operating eight separate car lines between downtown Chicago—where each line formed a loop around downtown streets—and Diversey Avenue on the north, 40th Avenue (Pulaski Road) on the west, and 71st Street on the south.[33] The powerhouses typically were located near the downtown area to operate the loops and halfway between the loops and the outer terminal.

Despite the complex mechanical apparatus necessary to run the system, cable traction proved to be far more efficient than horsecars, even in winter. The original Chicago City Railway cable system was able to replace about 1,000 horses with some 400 horsepower from the power-house, and within two years of its opening it was operating as many as 180 cable cars on a line that had been served by 60 horsecars.[34] By 1888 Chicago City Railway was able to operate 263 cars simultaneously from its three powerhouses; on a single day, October 23, 1893, the system reached its peak by hauling 700,000 people to and from the Columbian Exposition.[35] The major drawback to cable traction was its high capital cost, effectively limiting it to the highest density lines in urban areas. In outlying areas where it was not economical to lay cable, the horsecar continued in use. It was in those fringe areas still served by horses that the electric trolley car made its appearance in Chicago as an even less expensive alternative.

The conversion to electricity was abrupt, although it occurred at a somewhat slower pace in Chicago, where the street railways had a huge investment in cable systems, than in smaller cities, where horsecars, constituting the sole form of urban transit, could be converted to electric power simply by equipping cars with motors and stringing wire overhead. Even as Yerkes was trying to catch up with the Chicago City Railway Co. by converting his West and Northside horsecar lines to cable, the new electric technology burst on the scene in 1888 in Richmond, Virginia, where Frank J. Sprague developed the first practical electric streetcar.

An early Sprague rival was Charles J. Van Depoele, who arrived in Chicago in 1881 on contract to light Chicago's streets with a dynamo he had built. He remained in Chicago and began dabbling with electric traction. During the winter of 1882 he experimented with an electric railway that drew power from overhead wires; in 1883 he exhibited his results at the Exposition of Railway Appliances in Chicago. In 1884 he was contracted to develop a short electric railway in Toronto, through which he introduced the trolley pole—a fixture on

street railways that survives to the present. The flaw in Van Depoele's system was that he put his traction motor on the car platform, or floor, connected to the axle below by a chain drive. Sprague instead developed a way to mount the electric motor beneath the car next to the axle, which kept the electro-mechanical equipment conveniently out of the way and permitted maximum use of the floor of the car for fare-paying passengers.

The development resulted in an immediate and explosive growth of an electric railway industry. The traction motor made possible the electrification of horse and cable car lines, the construction of an extensive elevated and subway system in the cities, and thousands of miles of electrified interurban railways in the countryside. Indeed, the cable systems had begun electrifying their powerhouses, converting from steam-powered mechanisms to electric motors to pull cables even before they strung wire over the streets for the new trolley cars. Chicago City Railway replaced its coal fired steam engine with an electric motor in the powerhouse at 52nd and State Streets in 1895.[36] A system using central generating stations to provide power to electric traction motors slung beneath streetcars could be built at one-seventh the capital cost and operated at half the per mile cost of cable.[37] The power plants were relatively easy to convert because large stationary steam engines could be used to turn generators instead of cable wheels. The power was distributed throughout the system by means of overhead wires on the street railways and an electrified third rail on the elevated railways.

Although Chicago City Railway had begun electrifying new lines for trolley operation as early as 1893 and by 1905 had more miles of trolley lines than cable, Chicago did not complete conversion of its cable car lines until 1906, after the city mandated electrification.[38] In 1919 the city also required the Illinois Central Railroad to electrify its commuter lines to reduce pollution in the downtown area. The ordinance required electrification of the Illinois Central commuter line by 1927, downtown freight service by 1930, and intercity passenger service within Chicago by 1940. The commuter division was finished by 1926, but the Great Depression and World War II interrupted the progress of electrification before the rest could be completed. Dieselization of the railroads after World War II made the issue moot not only for the Illinois Central but also for every other railroad in Chicago.[39]

At the very end of the nineteenth century, the emerging electric technology resulted in quantum leaps in efficiency for the Chicago transit systems and somewhat more modest improvements for the riding public—the "straphangers," as Yerkes described them. Whereas the horsecars that appeared before the Civil War had provided relief for commuters on foot but had neither decreased commuting time nor offered any measure of luxury, forty years later it was possible to ride to work at an average speed of fifteen miles per hour aboard an elevated train that was not only heated in winter but also had sufficient illumination from its electric lights to enable riders to read a newspaper. Those apparent benefits were diminished somewhat by the enormous increase in transit ridership in Chicago that overloaded streetcars and elevated trains, causing deterioration of schedules.

The most immediate economic benefit to the street railways from the conversion to mechanical traction was a substantial increase in the size of transit vehicles and the lower operating costs that resulted. The horsecar was limited in size to what a two-horse team could pull—a vehicle of 18 feet in length and 7 feet in width, weighing 2.5 tons, with a capacity for seating 30. The earliest cable and electric trolley cars, because they were often converted from horsecars, were about the same dimensions.[40] Electric traction motors, however, permitted a growth in vehicle size that was

limited only by the operating environment—width of the streets and overhead bridge clearances—and the ability to negotiate 90-foot-radius turns at intersections. That effectively restricted the size of streetcars to a box 50 feet long (although most cars were a foot or two shorter) and 9 feet wide that seated 36 to 44 passengers.[41] In contrast, the commuter railroads, which were not plagued with as restrictive an operating environment, in the 1890s were using coaches that typically were 70 feet long, 14 feet high, and 10 feet wide, with a capacity for seating 66 to 80 persons.[42] Double-deck, high-capacity streetcars used in Europe were never popular with passengers in the United States [43] and were almost impossible to operate in Chicago because the ubiquitous railroad viaducts did not have sufficient clearance.

ELECTRIC TRAINS

A major advantage of the electric motor was that it enabled transit systems to operate entire trains without increasing the size of crews that had run horsecars. The electric elevated railroads in Chicago, including the Intramural Railway at the Columbian Exposition of 1893 and the Metropolitan West Side Elevated Railway that opened two years later, used heavily powered motor cars—coaches with the necessary electrical equipment slung beneath them that could seat forty passengers—to pull trains consisting of as many as two unpowered coaches with forty-eight seats each.[44] The motors could operate twenty-five one-car trains late at night when ridership was light, but at rush hour they could serve as locomotives pulling a train with a seating capacity of 136 passengers, or three times that of streetcars, which were operated as single units and rarely as trains.[45]

Short of using heavy-duty electric locomotives, as was done in London when that system electrified, there was no practical way to increase the length of elevated trains in Chicago to more than three cars unless some way could be found to put motors beneath every car and a system could be developed to enable the motorman to control them all from his cab. Sprague found the solution in New York, where he was working on the development of electric elevators after his trolley car company was absorbed by General Electric Co. He had developed a control system that controlled one or all of the elevators in the Postal Telegraph Building from a single master switch in the basement, and he realized the development could be adapted for electric railways. After he tried and failed to convince New York's Manhattan Railway to try it, he approached Chicago's South Side Elevated Co., which hired Sprague as a consultant for its conversion from steam to electricity. He persuaded the South Side Elevated line to electrify 120 of its fleet of 180 unpowered cars with his multiple-unit control equipment and by November 1897 had a test train of five cars running.[46]

Sprague's system involved installing small pilot motors on the electric throttles, or controllers, in every car and connecting them by cable so that when the motorman activated the master controller in his car the pilot motors automatically and instantly turned up the power on the controllers in every other car on the train. The system, the first multiple-unit control installed anywhere in the world, was such an instant success that Chicago's other two elevated railroads quickly converted their fleets to multiple-unit operation. Since every car provided its own power, the motors on the multiple-unit cars could be smaller—50-horsepower each (100 horsepower per car) as opposed to 125 horsepower motors (250 per car) on the motor cars. The practical operating effect was to increase the train capacity from 136 seated passengers on the three-car Metropolitan West Side trains to 230 on the five-car, multiple-unit South Side trains. Introduction of six- and eight-car trains later raised the seating capacity to 384 passengers and the standing room to probably more than twice that.

The private enterprises that built and operated Chicago's mainline, elevated, and street railways had benefitted from the continued development of the steam engine that through the second half of the nineteenth century had enabled them to increase substantially the size of their vehicles to accommodate ever more passengers. Chicago by 1899 was a city that ran on rails, and the influence of that industry on the city was pervasive.

3

DEVELOPMENT OF THE RAILROADS

♦ The first effort at transportation planning in Illinois during the 1830s was a political venture that turned into a financial fiasco. To a large extent this is why the state for more than one century afterward was quite willing to let private enterprise, primarily the railroads, handle the task of moving people and goods. The decision preserved the public purse but was not without drawbacks: within a few decades railroads became the single most influential industry in the state, affecting it in ways

that the rural, agrarian legislature of the 1830s could not have imagined.

In 1837, when Chicago was still a minor lake port, Abraham Lincoln and Stephen A. Douglas, the two men who were later rivals for the U.S. Senate and presidency, both served as members of the Illinois General Assembly and supported an ambitious state-financed public works program intended to accelerate the development of the still sparsely populated state. The $9.5 million Internal Improvements

Act, as it was called, empowered the state to issue bonds to finance the construction of eight railroads—none serving Chicago—as well as the Illinois and Michigan Canal—which had been proposed in 1822 but had languished for lack of funds until Governor Joseph Duncan in 1836 borrowed $500,000 to start construction. The overly ambitious Internal Improvements program collapsed after the Panic later in 1837, with a resulting failure of the state's credit.[1] The long-term consequence of the fiasco was that the state withdrew from the enterprise of planning and financing railroads until well into the twentieth century; it ventured back into it only to protect some lines during a period of railroad contraction. For more than one century, Illinois left the business of building and running mainline railroads, as well as street and elevated railways, when they finally appeared, to private enterprise.

The 1836–1837 legislature chartered sixteen private railroad companies, including one between Chicago and the lead-mining town of Galena in the northwestern corner of the state and another between Galena and Cairo at Illinois's southern tip where the Mississippi and Ohio Rivers meet. These companies suffered the same fate in the Panic of 1837 as did most of the publicly financed schemes: none of the ventures could raise the capital necessary to start construction.[2] Although the legislature just before the Panic of 1837 increased the capitalization of the Galena-to-Chicago railroad project to $1 million, ten times the amount in the original charter, and empowered the company to build a turnpike instead of a railroad, the only progress made before the project drifted into limbo was a survey of the route for several miles west of Chicago and the acquisition of a tract of land along the Des Plaines River.[3]

It was not the emerging industrialists of Chicago but the settlers scattered across northern Illinois who first proposed to revive the dormant Galena-to-Chicago rail-road project. They organized a convention in Rockford, nearly 90 miles northwest of Chicago on January 7, 1846. Among the 319 delegates who attended were 16 from Cook County, including William B. Ogden, the former mayor of Chicago, who had made a small fortune in land speculation and had become a tireless promoter of the city. He quickly grasped the project's potential and got himself elected president of the reorganized Galena & Chicago Union Railroad the following month. Ogden had no prior experience with railroads, although in a brief stint in the state legislature in his native New York he urged public support for construction of the New York & Erie (later Erie) Railroad. Despite the fact that he lasted only five years as president of the Galena railroad, resigning in 1851 after a dispute with other directors over his relationship with a firm from which the railroad bought construction supplies, he directed the fortunes of the venture during the crucial period in which the carrier solicited capital and began operations. Ogden, in spite of his early exit from the Galena railroad, could not stay away from railroads long, and he was quickly back in the business as a bondholder and director of the ill-fated Chicago, St. Paul & Fond du Lac Railroad. When it was sold at a bankruptcy receiver's auction in 1859, he organized and became president of the successor Chicago & North Western Railway that bought it. That same year he was one of the organizers of the North Chicago Street Railway, and in 1864 he engineered the consolidation of the Galena and North Western, one of the nation's largest railway mergers up to that time.[4]

Back in 1847, Ogden and a small group of Chicago business associates had bought out the New York investment firm that controlled the dormant Galena & Chicago Union Railroad for $20,000 in stock in the reconstituted railway, had induced the legislature to increase the capitalization to $3 million, and had set out to raise money for construction. That turned

(facing page) The explosive growth of the railroads transformed Chicago from a minor lake port into the largest and most important rail center in the nation by 1854. The American class 4-4-0 locomotive was the mainstay of power on U.S. railroads until well after the Civil War. The *Henry Keet* is pictured here in the 1860s. (Krambles Archive)

out to be something of an ordeal. Ogden and other organizers were able to raise from Chicagoans only $20,000 of the initial stock subscription of $365,000[5] and had no better luck with investors in the East or Europe, probably because of the Illinois and Michigan Canal's shaky financial history. They finally turned to the farmers and merchants in small communities along the route of the proposed line. Many of the original subscribers were farmers who pledged portions of future crops or, in the case of Du Page County farmer Warren L. Wheaton, a strip of land as a right-of-way for the railroad.[6]

Pledges were relatively easy to obtain, but cash was another matter. On April 5, 1848, in Ogden's first annual report to shareholders, seven months before the railroad ran its first train, he was reduced to pleading with subscribers to forward the money they had promised. He wrote, "Our subscription list, numbering over twelve hundred subscribers, it will be seen by the Secretary's report, exceeds in amount the sum required to complete the road with a plate rail to Elgin. Prompt payment by stockholders, generally, of all calls made to carry on the work, therefore, is all that is necessary to ensure the success of the road." He suggested that shareholders of limited means pay on the installment plan and stated that the railroad was even willing to borrow money in the interim until the fall harvest produced the remaining cash from stockholders.[7] Then Ogden took a big risk. With only $106,000 in cash on hand from the sale of stock—or less than one-third of the amount needed—he decided to proceed with construction of the first ten miles of the railroad to the Des Plaines River, on the assumption that the stockholders would keep their promise to pay up and that earnings from operations would cover the balance once the trains started running.

In the autumn of 1848, one month before it was ready to commence regular operations, the Galena & Chicago Union ran a special train for editors and dignitaries to publicize the ten-mile line. The inaugural train on November 20, 1848, consisted of a couple of baggage cars fitted with seats for one hundred guests. It was pulled by a small, third-hand locomotive that one month earlier had been brought to Chicago by ship, since at the time there was no rail connection to the East.[8] On the return trip from Oak Park, the train picked up a load of wheat and hides from a farmer and his wagon, apparently to demonstrate the freight capability of the new mode of transportation. The railroad was instantly profitable, earning $29,812 on revenues of $48,331 for its first full fiscal year of operation ending April 30, 1850.[9] Suddenly, investors were interested in all sorts of schemes to build railroads radiating to the north, west, and south from Chicago. The Chicago and Rock Island Railroad, which had been originally proposed in 1845 and chartered two years later to build a line parallel to the I-M Canal, was not able to sell enough stock to raise sufficient funds to start construction until November 1850.[10] The Aurora Branch Railroad (later Chicago, Burlington & Quincy) was a similar home-grown product that got its start after the Galena railroad began service and quickly wound up in the hands of eastern investors, in this case the Forbes family of Boston. Among the ventures, the development of the Illinois Central Railroad was unique because it had been mired in state politics dating from its inception as one of the unrealized Internal Improvements Act projects and because it became the beneficiary of a federal land grant—the first U.S. railroad to get one.

The Illinois Central Railroad was chartered in 1836 to cross the state from Galena in the northwest to Cairo in the south, bypassing Chicago by a wide margin. Therein politics came into play. Because a canal was scheduled to be built there, Chicago was bypassed for a railroad under the political compromise in 1837 that resulted in the Internal Improvements Act. The omission was not surprising at the time because northern Illinois was sparsely settled, but both Lincoln and Douglas, once they moved to Congress, tried to obtain federal land grants to revive the moribund project.[11] In 1850, Douglas engineered a compromise assuring southern votes by obtaining dual land grants for the proposed Mobile & Ohio Railroad as well as for the Illinois Central Railroad.[12] Equally important, Douglas also insisted that a branch of the I.C. run to Chicago, where he had moved and invested in land in 1847. By the time construction started on the I.C. in 1852, four other railroads were already providing service in or building toward Chicago.

Thus Chicago, which did not have a single railroad at the beginning of 1848, within six years was the largest rail center in the nation, serving as the terminal for ten different lines stretching for three thousand miles in almost every direction. Five lines headed west, three arrived from the East, and one, originally intended to bypass Chicago, detoured there once it became obvious the city was becoming an important railroad center.[13] By 1856, those railroads were operating fifty-eight passenger trains and thirty-eight freights per day to and from Chicago.[14]

THE CORPORATE MODEL

Because of railroads, Chicago grew from a minor lake port to the largest city in the U.S. interior within about half a century.[15] Railroads not only made mass production feasible by permitting the mass distribution of goods but also provided the emerging industries with a model for governance—the incorporated joint-stock company with its characteristics of pooled capital, separation of ownership and management, and operation by a professional staff. That model also was used repeatedly by private companies that were formed to build and to operate Chicago's public transportation system for the next one hundred years.[16]

The partnerships and family enterprises that dominated business in the first half of the nineteenth century for the most part either did not have the necessary capital to finance their ventures or were unwilling to risk it on a single venture, so incorporated joint-stock companies became a way to share the risk as well as to raise the huge sums necessary to start railroads from scratch.[17] The first ninety-two miles of the Galena railroad, a line that was entirely privately financed, cost an average $12,000 per mile.[18] Such ventures were too expensive for a single entrepreneur, who could get into the shipping business in the 1850s with an investment of $6,352, or $31.78 per ton, for a schooner or sloop and about $19,000, or $54.20 per ton, for a lake steamship.[19] The waterways on which these vessels operated were essentially free. Although the organizers of the Galena railroad did not invent the incorporated stock company, which dates from the sixteenth century in England as a way to promote overseas trade and colonization and was in wide use by railroads in the eastern United States by 1840, it was the first business in Chicago to employ the device.[20]

The dispersed stock ownership of the Galena railroad, and especially of the eastern- or foreign-owned railroads that followed, required a board or committee to oversee the interests of investors who did not have the time or the expertise to run a complex business extending over hundreds of miles. That, in turn, required railroads very early in their existence to develop professional managers, typically starting with an engineer hired to build the railroad. In 1847, for example, the Galena railroad hired Richard P. Morgan from the Hudson River Railroad at $2.50 per day to survey the route. In 1848, John Van Nortwick was hired as chief engineer to build the railroad and effectively became its general superintendent when trains started to run. By 1854 the railroad had also hired a freight agent and a general ticket agent for passenger service, and by 1857 nearly two thousand employees worked there.[21]

The railroad's original board included thirteen members, ten from Chicago, two from Galena, and one from New York, representing the investment of the prior owners, who had been paid in stock in the new venture. The board's role, at least in the early years, was primarily to raise the capital necessary to get the railroad built, but as the railroad continued to expand, it became increasingly difficult to finance such extensions with local stock subscriptions. The Galena railroad had to seek investors not only in New York and Europe but also in the emerging bond markets—a financing technique copied to excess by the street and elevated railway companies later in the century.[22] Investors, especially in Europe, often preferred bonds, which were secured by a mortgage on the railroad, although, unlike stocks, they conferred no voting rights to their holders. By 1854 bonds accounted for nearly $3 million of the $8.3 million in capital the Galena railroad had raised, and by 1880 the successor Chicago & North Western Railway had a stock-market capitalization of $36.5 million, although its bonded indebtedness exceeded $50.1 million.[23] The financial development of other early Chicago railroads evolved along similar patterns.

MASS TRANSIT ADOPTS THE RAILROAD MODEL

Public transportation in the mid-1800s was one of those emerging industries on which the railroads were most influential.[24] Not only did the railroads develop their own commuter services and provide the model for the emerging street railway companies, but some local transit companies were also effectively spinoffs of railroads. The street railways very early in their existence, like the railroads before them, were forced to adopt the incorporated joint-stock company to raise capital.

Franklin Parmelee might have been able to finance and to operate his omnibus service as a partnership, but he quickly found himself unable to do so with street railways, which required an up-front invest-ment in excess of $1,000 per mile to lay the necessary track. When Parmelee's partnership failed to survive a court challenge on another issue, the principals incorporated as Chicago City Railway Co., with a capital stock authorization of $100,000, and sought a street railway charter from the state. At about the same time, Ogden and John B. Turner, both veterans of the Galena & Chicago Union, obtained a state charter as the North Chicago Railway Co., a corporation with a stated capitalization of $500,000.

Turner (1799–1871), more than Ogden, was typical of the railroad men who built Chicago, although he worked much of his career in the shadow of his famous friend and associate. A native of upstate New York, Turner worked in a number of businesses, some unsuccessful, before drifting into railroad construction with contracts to build portions of the Ransom & Saratoga and Erie Railroads. He made enough money in canal and road construction in New York to retire comfortably in the Chicago area, where he raised sheep and devoted himself to civic enterprises. Following his retirement, Turner was attracted to the proposal to build a railroad, and he became involved as an investor and acting director, serving as Ogden's resident expert on the building and running of railroads. Turner succeeded Ogden as president of the Galena railroad in 1851 and became the first chairman of the managing committee of the merged North Western in 1864.[25]

By the time the city's third major street railway came into existence in 1861—the Chicago West Division Railway Co.—a pattern had clearly emerged. The street railway was organized as a corporation with a claimed capitalization of $1.25 million, which actually was little more than an authorization to issue stock with a face value of that amount. The incorporation of street railways became commonplace after the Civil War. Some were organized by real estate developers who believed the existence of street railways would enhance

property values, and others were simply ghost corporations assembled by corrupt politicians intent upon shaking down legitimate railway operators with the threat of competition.[26] Thomas R. Bullard, in his unpublished encyclopedia of local traction, counted 126 street-railway companies incorporated in Chicago between 1860 and 1895 before the state was finally forced to raise the corporate registration fee from $25 to $1,000 per million of capital stock.[27]

RAILROAD TRAFFIC

Conventional wisdom in the 1840s held that the Great Lakes were the city's great avenue of commerce to the East. Railroads were simply an extension of the those lakes, a way for the New York–Chicago financial hegemony to broaden its reach inland to Iowa and beyond and to interdict the Mississippi River traffic flowing through St. Louis and New Orleans. The railroads as originally proposed and built

failed almost altogether to contemplate significant local passenger traffic. The Illinois Central Railroad, for example, did not build a station between Chicago and Thornton, which was located 23.5 miles to the south.[28] While intercity passengers were considered an important source of revenue, the builders of the earliest railroads assumed that freight traffic alone would support their ventures. The earliest estimates of potential passenger revenues for the Galena & Chicago Union ranged from less than 20 percent of total revenues for a 41-mile line between Chicago and Elgin to almost 50 percent for a 181-mile carrier between Chicago and Galena.[29] John Van Nortwick's projections in early 1848 for the Galena railroad's first full year of operation put passenger fare receipts at less than $17,000 out of total railway revenues of more than $110,000.[30] When the results of the first fiscal year were finally tallied, however, passenger revenues at $22,802 were surpassed only slightly by freight revenues at $25,529.

The horsecar on rails was a common sight on Chicago streets for nearly half a century. This West Division car was photographed in the 1870s. (Krambles Archive)

Absent from the first annual report, and even subsequent annual reports, of the Galena & Chicago Union was any mention of "commutation" or "accommodation" passengers, as commuters then were commonly known. The phenomenon of commuting, although it existed in New York and Boston at the time,[31] was unknown in Chicago in 1848. Even after such traffic began to develop in antebellum times it was not considered consequential enough to mention to stockholders. Finally, about one decade after the Galena railroad ran its first train, the term "commutation fare" appeared as a footnote in the annual report of the Illinois Central Railroad, but this mention was only in reference to the revenues at the new station at Hyde Park.[32] Pioneer conductor Charles B. George, in the reminiscences of his forty-year career on several Chicago-area railroads published in 1887, used "suburban," "commutation," and "accommodation" interchangeably to describe the local service in 1855 on the Chicago & Milwaukee Railroad, which later became part of the North Western system. He comments, "It was thought a great thing when the first train was put on to accommodate the little towns along the lake shore." According to George, when the railroad directors considered discontinuing the money-losing train in 1856, he was called before the board and asked his opinion because of his "experience in carrying commutation passengers in Boston." The board accepted his recommendation to continue the service. George writes, "The wisdom of their decision has been proved by the vast increase of suburban traffic."[33] The railroads, of course, created Chicago's suburbs.

As might be expected of a city that billed itself as the nation's railroad capital, the effect of those institutions on the pattern of development was substantial. The sheer size of the railroad plant was itself a major factor in Chicago's development. Chicago originally had refused permission for the Galena & Chicago Union and Illinois Central Railroads to enter its corporate limits. In the case of the I.C., however, Chicago allowed its trains to enter over a railroad-built causeway in the lake that also served the city as a breakwater. An 1851 state law forbade eastern railroads from entering Chicago except on the tracks of Illinois-chartered lines, but by 1856 the tables had turned and it was the needs of the railroads that dictated the city's development. By the time Chicago began to reexert control in the final decade of the century, the city was already covered with railroad tracks.[34] The 400-square-mile Chicago switching district, an area about twice the size of the city proper, contained 5,710 miles of railroad serving 5,000 industries, 160 freight yards, and 76 freight stations.[35] By 1889, 6 million freight cars passed through Chicago, pushed and pulled by 300 switch engines and another 100 locomotives assigned to interline transfers.[36] By the turn of the century 650 freight trains arrived in or left Chicago daily on 30 railroads.

Despite Chicago's efforts in the 1840s and 1850s to exclude railroads within its boundaries, a substantial amount of trackage in the nineteenth century ringed its downtown area, since the railroads needed access to the city's port facilities for such things as grain elevators and lumber yards along the Chicago River. That situation, in turn, contributed to the early decentralization of the city by consuming prime land near the rapidly concentrating downtown area and by forcing residential development to move out to remote locations and to concentrate in wedges between industrial strips that hugged the railroads radiating from the city.[37] Even the sites for Chicago's parks were selected on the basis of their proximity to railroads so that the public could reach them.[38]

As the city continued to grow in the last decades of the nineteenth century, the railroad plant became such a constricting factor, especially on street traffic, that after 1890 the city forced the railroads to elevate hundreds of miles of lines so that street traffic could pass beneath them. The resulting railroad moraines, pierced occasionally by viaducts, cut the city into pieces and effectively defined neighborhoods until the coming of the expressways chopped it up even more. Increasingly the railroads were forced to build circumferential belt lines and yards on the fringes of the metropolitan area to reduce congestion as much as possible.

Because Chicago became a junction at which all railroads met but through which none passed, a well-developed hotel industry emerged. Chicago early on attained status as a convention center, dating from the 1860 Republican National Convention that nominated Lincoln.[39] The pattern and timing of the arrival of the railroads, as well as their competition for passenger traffic, created a problem that the railroads and the city never quite solved—an overabundance of passenger terminals. Although the railroads were able to build a consolidated Union Stockyards and various belt railways that permitted the through-routing of freight cars, all passenger trains terminated in Chicago and travelers often had to change not only trains but also depots to continue on their trips.

By 1888 there were six intercity passenger terminals in Chicago. In 1848 the Galena & Chicago Union was the first to construct a depot, which was located west of the downtown area at Canal and Kinzie Streets. On top of the depot Ogden had built a cupola to enable the railroad's staff to spot approaching trains. It was the first of a continuum of six stations occupied by the Galena railroad and its successor, the North Western. That was followed by the construction of the LaSalle Street Station, built by the Rock Island and Michigan Southern on the south edge of downtown in 1853; the Great Central (later Central) Station, built by the Illinois Central along the lakeshore in 1856; Union Station, built by the Pittsburgh, Ft. Wayne & Chicago (Pennsylvania Railroad) west of downtown in 1858; the jointly owned Dearborn Station in 1885; and Grand Central Station, built by the Wisconsin Central in 1888 but later acquired by the Baltimore & Ohio. The six stations combined served as many as 270,000 passengers on 1,500 weekday trains in 1920.[40]

Of the depots, only the Dearborn Station, owned by the six railroads, and Union Station, which at its maximum served as many as five of the city's twenty five railroads offering intercity service, succeeded as joint ventures. Union Station was the sole surviving intercity terminal in the last years of the twentieth century. By then, the stations of the Illinois Central, the Rock Island, and the North Western were devoted exclusively to commuter service. The Grand Central Station and Dearborn Station, which in its final years was used by the Atchison, Topeka & Santa Fe intercity trains, were abandoned with the advent of Amtrak. Chicago tried repeatedly to consolidate its depots, but consolidation occurred only when rail passenger travel had shrunk to the point that the federal government created the National Railroad Passenger Corporation (Amtrak) to take over the service in 1971. At that time, the government consolidated all intercity operations in Union Station.

The mainline railroads and depot consolidation was the least of Chicago's transportation problems in the second half of the nineteenth century, however. The street railways and their offspring, the Ls, in trying to emulate the financial success and power of the railroads, ran afoul of public opinion and became the locus of a political controversy in Chicago.

4

EVOLUTION OF THE STREET RAILWAYS

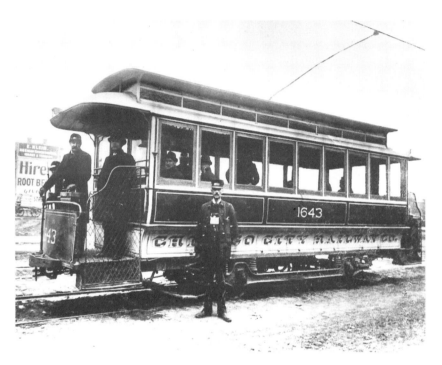

♦ Chicago's mass-transit system evolved not from any demand to move commuters but to enable long-distance railroad passengers to transfer between stations. The arrival of four railroads in 1852 and their construction of depots on the fringe of the city created an instant market. Shortly thereafter it became a relatively easy matter for the station transfer coaches to pick up local passengers along their routes when they had empty seats and then to assign some spare coaches to handle those commuters. It proved to be such a profitable business that within a few years the omnibus operators were able to afford to

spike tracks on top of the city's plank streets and to buy horse-drawn streetcars to handle the growing traffic.

The city's increasing population density and industrialization drove the commuter market. Two years after beginning production at his new harvester plant on the north side of the Chicago River in 1847 Cyrus McCormick employed 120 people.[1] More typical of the new enterprises that sprang up as Chicago made its industrial transition were companies that set up shop to distribute products or raw materials from elsewhere. In 1842 Joseph T. Ryerson opened a store in a rented, two-story building along the river at Clark Street to sell Pittsburgh-made iron. A couple of years later Alonzo Richmond founded a distributorship for Onondaga (New York) salt in the lakeside docks near the mouth of the river. In his first year he received 36,656 barrels of salt, shipping most of it west on the I-M Canal.[2] Between 1850 and 1860 the city's population more than tripled to 109,000. The banks of the Chicago River and its two branches became lined for miles with factories, elevators, warehouses, lumberyards, and railroad tracks.

The linear nature of that development, as much as the jump in population, helped create a market for public transit, although Chicago's early practice of restricting railroad terminals to outlying areas of the city seems to have been the precipitating factor in the development of a public transportation system. The Common Council in 1848 denied the Galena & Chicago Union Railroad access to a right-of-way inside the city limits, except to build a temporary track to the river to obtain its first locomotive by ship, so that its first station became located west of the river at Kinzie and Canal Streets.[3] The Illinois Central Railroad, which had purchased part of the old Fort Dearborn reservation, was given access to it in 1852 only by means of a three hundred-foot-wide right-of-way of submerged lakefront land, on which it was forced to build a trestle.[4] When it approached Chicago in 1852, the Chicago & Rock Island Railroad could get no closer than 22nd Street to establish a site for a terminal; by 1867, however, the line had advanced farther north to Van Buren Street.[5]

Railroad depots located on the edge of town caused long-distance passengers to travel as much as three miles across the city to change trains and created a market for some sort of transfer service as well as for transportation to local hotels and businesses. Franklin Parmelee (1816–1904) seized that opportunity on May 9, 1853, with thirty horses, twelve employees, and six "Concord wagons" adapted for Chicago's muddy conditions, all presumably equipped with broad-rimmed wheels.[6] Parmelee was an inventive, restless entrepreneur who could easily make the sort of changes necessary in his business to move with the times. Born in the upstate New York hamlet of Byron, Parmelee left home at the age of twelve to learn the transportation business, first working as a stage relay boy, then as a driver. In 1833, at age seventeen, he began working as a cabin boy on the *James Madison*, a vessel that sailed between Buffalo and Chicago. Eventually he became a clerk and settled for a short time in Will County southwest of Chicago in 1850. Three years later he entered into a partnership in Chicago with two other men in the new business of transferring railroad passengers, presumably using as omnibuses second-hand Concord coaches bought from over-the-road operators put out of business by the railroads. A few years later Parmelee started the city's first street railway; he later sold it during the Civil War to concentrate on the railway transfer business.[7]

Although the historical record is conflicting, the continuous operation of public transit in Chicago can be traced to Parmelee's 1853 omnibus transfer line despite the fact that John Frink in 1852 was operating hourly omnibus service between the Lake House, a hotel at Rush and North Water Streets, and the Michigan Southern Railway station at 16th Street.[8] Since that route approximated a section of the Frink & Walker stage route that connected Chicago with the railroad being extended west across Michigan, it is possible it developed into an omnibus line as the stagecoach crews sought the transfer business from the long-haul customers that had deserted them for the railroads. It is also probable that they began accepting crosstown fares from pedestrians to fill empty seats.

The omnibus business in the 1850s was quite competitive and largely entrepreneurial, and the amount of capital required to buy vehicles and teams was not excessive. Two of Frink's principal rivals in the omnibus business were his former partner, Martin O. Walker, and Walker's brother, Samuel. Warren Parker operated a rival service from his downtown livery stable, and Parmelee, who had experience in stagecoach operations before coming to Chicago, bought out the omnibus services of several hotels to get his depot transfer line started in 1853. By 1854, a few years after the omnibus appeared in Chicago, 18 carriers provided 408 daily trips on eight routes totaling 22 miles in length.[9] The following year, Parmelee started an omnibus line on State Street that traveled as far south as 12th Street; that transit route, now a subway, appears to be the city's oldest in continuous service.

(*facing page*) Chicago's increasing population and industrialization along the Chicago River drove the growth of its commuter market. One of the earliest electric streetcars in Chicago was this Chicago City Railway car, photographed in the 1890s. (Krambles Archive)

Largely unregulated and often cut-throat, the omnibus business was the subject of few complaints, since the alternative to taking an omnibus for five cents was slogging on foot through Chicago's muddy streets, paying thirty cents for a hack ride, or renting a one-horse carriage for $3 per day from a livery stable.[10] When he began operating half-hourly service with converted stagecoaches on State Street between Randolph Street and 12th Street in competition with the Walkers, Parker offered a discounted commutation ticket of twenty-five rides for a dollar—the first documented use of commutation fares in Chicago. The regular fare was a nickel. Frink operated hourly service two blocks away on the parallel Clark Street. This service ran from the Lake House, just north of the river, along the lake to the Michigan Central depot on the southern edge of the city. In 1853 Parmelee took over Parker's business and enlisted Liberty Bigelow, a Boston capitalist, and David A. Gage, proprietor of the Tremont Hotel, as partners.

HORSECAR LINES

Although both the railroad and the omnibus were developed in Europe, America combined them into the horsecar.[11] The first horsecar line, which opened for service in 1832 in New York City, for the most part was an extension of the New York & Harlem Railroad, connecting its terminal at Fourteenth and Prince Streets on the edge of town with the central business district. Although New Orleans built a 4.5-mile horsecar line to the suburb of Carrollton in 1835, the fledgling street railway industry seems to have been largely confined to those two cities until 1852, when Alphonse Loubat, a French engineer working in the United States, developed an improved rail for street use. Loubat's new design featured a grooved rail, the top of which was flush with the street pavement, that could take the pounding of heavy vehicle traffic typical of cities.

Omnibus service was far from satisfactory, largely because of the poor condition of city streets. It could take crews of men working with ropes and planks two days to rescue an omnibus that had slipped off the planking and into the quagmire.[12] Since service even on planked roads such as State, Madison, and Clark Streets had to be suspended in wet weather, Chicagoans began to look to the possibility of street railways to provide all-weather service.[13] In 1854 Charles B. Phillips, probably with the support of Stephen A. Douglas and several other owners of land south of the city, petitioned the city for permission to build a horse railroad. The Common Council took no action on that proposal, but on May 26, 1855, it approved a general ordinance authorizing franchises for street railways for a tenure of twenty-five years with option for the city to purchase the system after that time. The ordinance also imposed a maximum fare of five cents for each trip of a mile or less and ten cents for longer trips. The ordinance also required the street railways to plank or otherwise to pave the streets on which they operated.[14]

The condition requiring prospective street railway operators to pay for the street paving that the city could not afford proved to be too onerous. When there were no takers, the 1855 ordinance was repealed on February 7, 1856. Three weeks later the city approved another ordinance that eliminated the street planking requirement but substituted another requirement calling for the consent of owners of property fronting the proposed transit line. The latter requirement set an unfortunate precedent that plagued transit systems and lead to corruption for the rest of the century. Roswell B. Mason, an engineer who built the Illinois Central Railroad and was later the mayor during the Chicago Fire, and Phillips then sought a franchise for horsecar lines on State Street between Randolph and 22nd Streets and north of the Chicago River. They were unable, however, to raise the necessary capital, and

Mason sold out to Phillips. The Panic of 1857 put an end to the project entirely.

A group of investors assembled by Parmelee, including Bigelow, Gage, and Henry Fuller, a railroad contractor, applied for the expired franchise in 1858. It was granted on August 16 of that year, but not before Parmelee bought four horsecars from Heaton, Gilbert & Co., of Troy, New York, shipped them to Chicago, and put them on display at State and Randolph Streets to show a dubious Common Council he meant business.[15] Because of popular sentiment against monopolies, the Common Council was reluctant to grant Parmelee a franchise that would exclude competition,[16] and some property owners on State Street were opposed to the project. The owners successfully challenged the city's August 16, 1858, franchise ordinance in court on the grounds that the city did not have the statutory authority to franchise a railway.[17] That forced Parmelee and his partners to seek a charter from the state legislature. Their Chicago City Railway Co., the seminal business from which the transit system in Chicago can directly trace its corporate existence, was approved by the state on February 14, 1859. As had the earlier city ordinance, the state charter required the approval of the owners of two-thirds of the property on State Street between Randolph and 12th Streets before the company could install a second track.[18]

Parmelee and his partners failed to form a monopoly, however. Soon after the charter bill was filed for the Parmelee group, it was amended to include an application by another group, headed by railroad executives Ogden and Turner, for a charter for the North Chicago City Railway to serve the North Side of the city. The final bill covered both charters so that two street railways came into legal existence on the same day; because Parmelee was further along in his planning, he was able to get his State Street line running two months after the state authorized it. By the expedient method of spiking rails to the city's planks covering Clark Street, the Ogden-Turner group was able to get their first line operating between the river and northern city limits later that same year.[19]

A third line, the Chicago West Division Street Railway, was chartered in 1861 but did not begin operating horsecars until July 29, 1863, when the City Railway sold its West Side operations. Thus by 1863 the three corporations that were to dominate Chicago's public transportation for most of the remainder of the century were in place: City Railway, a corporation in which downtown merchants had a considerable investment after buying out Parmelee, operated from downtown to the South Side; West Division, controlled by a group of Galena investors, was dominant on the West Side; and North Chicago, controlled by principals in the North Western Railway, operated on the North Side.

FARE WARS

The omnibus lines put up a brief but spirited fight, and a fare war broke out as soon as Parmelee began operating his first horsecar line on State Street. The Walker brothers were already operating on that route, and William Young and Z. I. Pratt quickly opened what they called a "Zip Line" down parallel Wabash Avenue. Omnibuses often dashed down the streets to get fares ahead of the plodding horsecars.[20] Although he was authorized by his franchise to charge a nickel, Parmelee had to cut his fare by offering a twelve-ride ticket for fifty cents to meet a forty-rides-for-a-dollar offer by one of the omnibus operators.[21] The West Division as late as the 1870s was forced to charge as little as three cents per ride to meet omnibus competition. Since Parmelee also operated an omnibus line on the sections of State Street that did not have tracks, however, he could offer riders a transfer between the two modes. By 1860 the Walkers knew they had been defeated. They ceased omnibus service on both State and Randolph Streets, although they continued to run omnibuses on streets without horsecar

lines. That was the pattern for the few remaining years of the omnibus in Chicago;
they continued to operate until the horsecars appeared on their streets. Parmelee in
1863 sold his interest in City Railway,
which included some omnibus service, to
concentrate on his railroad transfer service,
and Samuel Walker sold his horses to the
West Division and shut down in 1864.[22]
The three remaining street railway companies continued to operate without serious
competition.

THE STREET RAILWAY ERA

The last half of the nineteenth century
in Chicago belonged to the street railroads. Even before the Philadelphia syndicate headed by Charles Tyson Yerkes in the
late 1880s bought the West Division and
North Chicago railways and eventually
merged them, there was little competition
among the three systems. They all nevertheless refused to accommodate the passenger by offering free transfers between
the systems. They had grown in size to the
point that shortly after the Civil War each
was large enough to buy out potential
competitors that sprouted at the edge of
the city and wealthy enough not only to
bribe politicians to maintain their geo-
graphic monopolies but also to pay off political shakedowns that occurred when
politicians created shell street railway corporations for the sole purpose of such extortion. They were sufficiently profitable
to pay substantial dividends to shareholders, to finance the expensive conversion of
many of their lines to cable car operation
in the 1880s, and to replace within a
decade the cable cars with electric trolleys.
They also financed construction of much
of Chicago's elevated railway system.

During this time, the street railways became the target of increased public dissatis-
faction. The riders complained of poor service, surly employees, overcrowding,
smoking on cars, and drunks and rowdies.
The newspapers editorialized against the
monopolistic transit systems, and the re-

formers griped about corruption. Drivers
and conductors, who became disenchanted, organized unions in the 1870s
and declared a strike in 1885 on the West
Side and in 1888 on the North Side. By
1880 mass transit in industrial Chicago
had become a public convenience and necessity, although technologically it had not
yet emerged from the horse and buggy era.
Supervisors and technicians who operated
increasingly complex machines of mass
production and middle managers who ran
those companies rode to work in horse-
drawn carts.

Although Parmelee began his mile-and-
a-half, single-track operation with only two
horsecars in 1859, City Railway by 1885
had grown into an 87-mile system, and the
West Division operated 75 miles of track.
The North Chicago system, plagued by
poor access to downtown Chicago over
bridges that were frequently open to allow
river traffic to pass, was somewhat smaller.
By then the street railways were sizeable
companies in their own right. The West
Division, for example, owned 655 cars and
3,733 horses, employed 2,200 persons,
and operated 3,029 daily round-trips.[23]

THE CHICAGO FIRE
AND THE AGE OF BOODLE

The Chicago Fire of 1871 that leveled
much of the city had the same effect as a
massive urban renewal project. Almost
overnight a wooden city was destroyed;
over the next few years it rebuilt itself with
brick and stone. The fire not only rekin-
dled the city's entrepreneurial spirit but
also simultaneously resulted in both a substantial increase in density of the warehouses, stores, and offices in the central
business district and the decentralization of
manufacturing industries, which could not
afford the real estate there.

In view of the destruction of 17,450
buildings in a swath one mile wide and
four miles long, the city's economic engine
surprisingly survived with relatively little
damage. The meatpacking industry on the

southwest side was out of harm's way, the lumber and milling industry along the south branch of the river escaped with little damage, two-thirds of the grain elevators survived, and, most important, the railroads remained intact.[24] Though several downtown terminals burned, the railroads continued to operate through the fire, evacuating some victims and bringing relief supplies as the embers cooled.[25] The street railway system, which was still rather small in 1871, also escaped complete devastation. Chicago City Railway on the South Side and the West Division Railway Co. on the West Side primarily lost their down-

town trackage. The North Side railway system, however, had most of its track, cars, and horses destroyed in the flames.[26]

From the time of the fire until the end of the century, Chicago was the world's fastest growing city. Immigrants from Europe poured in to work its assembly lines, railroads, and slaughterhouses, and the descendants of the pioneers from New England and the Middle Atlantic states who had arrived a generation earlier had graduated to the middle class or had ascended into positions of management. The new immigrants unskilled in the English language or the traditions of government, the

Heavy traffic became a problem in downtown Chicago long before the automobile appeared, as this scene at Clark and Randolph Streets in the 1880s shows. (Krambles Archive)

city's boomtown entrepreneurs, and the new class of wealthy robber barons who controlled the economy combined to create an atmosphere of corruption. The word that came to describe the corruption was "boodle," and in the long run that corruption proved to be far more damaging to the city than the fire had been.

Boodle was common from just after the Civil War until after the turn of the century, despite successive reform efforts to put an end to it. After rebuilding from the fire, the three street railway companies had aggressively added or extended lines to accommodate or to encourage growth. The requirement that they get prior approval of the owners of the majority of the property along each route to build or to expand lines resulted in the common practice of overextending lines into rural areas, where property owners were eager for development, in order to counterbalance opposition in populated areas. The influence of land speculators and corrupt politicians, however, often pushed street railway lines into unprofitable situations that also encouraged boodle.[27] Embroiled in a thicket of corruption, property owners demanded bribes to approve extensions past their front doors, politicians engaged in dummy franchise shakedown schemes, and companies extracted quick profits from unsuspecting investors by watering stock—the situation in which the value of the stock sold exceeds the company's worth. Even the sanctimonious reformers contributed to the boodle by enacting reform legislation that unintentionally encouraged it.

The principal characters in the first wave of corruption were James Hildreth, who was first elected to the Common Council in 1869 and served intermittently until 1888, and Edward F. Cullerton, who was elected in 1872 and served, except for a six-year period between 1892 and 1896, until his death in 1920. The documented corruption began in 1872 when four other aldermen were convicted of soliciting and taking bribes, but that did not stop Hildreth and Cullerton two years later when

Chicago City Railway Co. sought a franchise for Wabash Avenue one block east of its State Street line. Several other competitors of uncertain backgrounds, also seeking the franchise, had offered generous payments to the city for use of the street. Chicago City Railway president Silas B. Cobb at first refused to pay any bribes to Common Council members but apparently relented and finally acquired the franchise after doling out $30,000. Cullerton had originally sponsored an ordinance granting the franchise to one of the other companies, but eventually he played a role in steering the award to Chicago City Railway. The proposed competitors disappeared without a trace.[28]

In 1875 the Hildreth-Cullerton ring struck again by getting the City Council to enact a franchise for a company called the Metropolitan City Railway Co., whose officers were relatives of Hildreth, on the West Side in competition with the West Division. The scheme collapsed after Hildreth was convicted of defrauding the federal government of whisky tax revenues in an unrelated scheme and fled to Canada. He returned to Chicago and was back in local politics in 1880. By that time the City Council was divided into factions called "The Big Four"—including Cullerton—and "The Little Four," which between them controlled twenty-three of the thirty-six votes on the City Council.[29] By 1883, the council had become so corrupt that the aldermen were demanding $30,000 to approve an elevated railway franchise, but the promoters were unwilling to pay even half of that.[30] By then, however, there was a potential for bigger money, since the city's original, twenty-five-year street railway franchises were scheduled to expire.

Although Cullerton continued to hold his seat, a somewhat different cast came to dominate the City Council in the 1890s—the infamous "Gray Wolves." They included John J. "Bathhouse John" Coughlin, who served between 1892 and 1938 and received his nickname because he once worked as a bathhouse attendant; Michael

"Hinky Dink" Kenna, a South Side saloon owner who served between 1897 and 1921; and John Powers, who from 1888 represented the West Side saloon and the gambling interests of Michael C. McDonald, the man who made a fortune on a proposal to build an elevated railway on the West Side. Coughlin and Kenna continued the practice of using phony franchises to shake down street railways.

Before the state raised the filing fee for corporations to $1,000, the Gray Wolves got a $25 charter for the General Electric Railway Co. to run on several South Side streets with a line downtown. Shortly thereafter they induced the City Council to pass the necessary franchise ordinance and to override Mayor George B. Swift's veto.[31] Coughlin and Kenna then engaged in a bidding war with Chicago City Railway to obtain property owners' consent to build their General Electric lines along Wabash Avenue south of 22nd Street, where the Chicago City Railway line involved in the 1874 shakedown scheme had its terminal. The bidding drove up the bribe price for property owner consent from $4 to $12 per front foot, paid in an equivalent value in stock.[32] Back on the West Side, Mike McDonald, who earlier had been involved in several street railway shakedowns, acquired the 1888 charter for an elevated railway to be built above Lake Street. By 1892 he had watered the stock to the point that the railway capitalized at $17 million held only $4 million in assets. He visited New York City early that year, ostensibly to seek additional capital, and within days he sold the line, which was still under construction, to a group of investors there for slightly more than $2 million.[33]

Political corruption had become so pervasive at the end of the nineteenth century that the Gray Wolves were attempting to shake down virtually every utility dependent upon the city for a franchise, not just the transit systems. A clique that in 1895 included Roger P. Sullivan, later the state democratic chairman; George Brennan; and former mayor John P. Hopkins ob-

tained a liberal franchise for their Ogden Gas Co., ostensibly to provide competition to the existing People's Gas Light & Coke Co., but actually for purposes of greenmail to force the utility to buy them out to continue its monopoly.[34]

The clique's next target was Samuel Insull's Chicago Edison Co. electric utility. Sullivan first approached Insull to find out how much he would pay to prevent the formation of a competitor, and after Insull refused the invitation, the Gray Wolves created the Commonwealth Electric Co. Insull, meanwhile, had bought up the exclusive rights to electrical equipment from every U.S. manufacturer, and when the conspirators found they could not buy dynamos, they sold their company to him for a paltry $50,000.[35] The Chicago Telephone Co., later Illinois Bell, apparently was the final target when the Gray Wolves obtained a franchise for their Illinois Telephone & Telegraph Co. (IT&T) in 1898. One of the principals in that venture was Albert G. Wheeler, an earlier promoter of the General Electric Railway, which Coughlin and Kenna used in their shakedown of the Chicago City Railway.[36] The IT&T franchise required that its cables be buried, and after digging some cable tunnels the company after 1900 converted them into the city's underground freight railway system.

Corruption was not the only hindrance to development of transit in Chicago in the nineteenth century. The modernization of Chicago's transit system was also inhibited by a strange municipal inertia—a reluctance on the part of the general public and its government to allow new technology. The problem may have been rooted in the general distrust of the "monopolistic" transit companies or the outstretched palm, the "where's mine?" mentality prevalent among the populace and politicians at the time, but it became an impediment to normal progress. Dummy streetcars were banned in most areas,[37] and an attempt by Chicago City Railway to cut operating costs by introducing "bobtail" horsecars that could be operated by one

Cable cars successfully replaced horse-drawn cars but were too expensive to build on any but the most heavily used routes. State Street, pictured here in the 1880s, had both horse and cable service. (Krambles Archive)

man serving as both driver and fare collector ran afoul of public opposition. A citizens' group was formed to protest the new vehicles, and its members refused to pay fares. The company finally resorted to putting special agents on the cars to evict the deadbeats, but the City Council got involved and on November 29, 1875, passed an ordinance mandating two-man crews.[38] In one instance the street railways actually benefitted from the city's technological inertia. The proposed elevated lines were sufficiently controversial, probably because of their noise and obstruction of sunlight, that Chicago not only imposed property-owner consent restrictions on their construction[39] but also for a time refused to allow them to be built in the downtown area, a policy that left the unpopular street railways with a monopoly.

The cable car system was a distinct improvement in speed, efficiency, and sanitation over the horsecar lines, and when Chicago City Railway applied for permission on December 27, 1880, to convert its State Street horsecar line to cable, the City Council concurred within three weeks. The local property owners began objecting only after construction started. The opposition to electric traction a few years later was severe; indeed, the city's first trolley line franchises were initially granted by suburbs and were grandfathered into the city's statutes only after the two communities were annexed in 1889. Thereafter, the city allowed electrification of existing lines only gradually and with opposition at every step. Much of the concern over the new technology involved safety: trolley cars traveled faster than horsecars or cable cars, and there was widespread concern over electrocution of riders or bystanders.[40]

In 1892 the City Council finally bowed to pressure from Chicago City Railway and allowed it to electrify three crosstown lines, none of which came closer than 3.5 miles to downtown. In 1894 the City Council relented by allowing Yerkes to electrify 210 miles of outlying trolley lines, though with the stipulation that none of the lines would run downtown. That exception created an absurd situation wherein street railways had to tow their electric streetcars through the downtown area behind horses or cable cars or make passengers switch to horsecars. On July 15, 1895, the City Council allowed Chicago City Railway to electrify its remaining horsecar line downtown on Clark Street, except for one three-block stretch that continued to be served by horses for another four months. The following year it allowed the two Yerkes systems to begin downtown electrification. Finally, in 1905, the city required the electrification of both cable and horse lines by the end of 1906.[41]

Despite the corruption, lack of coordinated transit planning, and reluctance of the city to embrace new technology,

Chicago's street railway system was relatively progressive by the standards of the day. Chicago City Railway serving the South Side was the best of the lot, a well-managed corporation that attracted investors of considerable importance. Its relatively progressive chief executive, C. B. Holmes (1840–1922), was typical of the early street railway executives in that he drifted into the business from other lines of work. Originally from Springfield, Vermont, he moved west to work as a teacher and farmer near Belvidere, Illinois, before becoming a coal merchant in Chicago in 1863. Within ten years he had become the superintendent of the former Parmelee system on the South Side.[42] For one decade after Parmelee sold it the company did not expand much beyond downtown Chicago and a single, five-mile line to the South Side on State Street as far as 39th Street and Cottage Grove Avenue. Shortly after the fire, Chicago City Railway began an aggressive expansion southward, first with a line on Wabash Avenue as far south as 22nd Street, built in 1875, and then another on Halsted Street beyond the city limits, laid in 1877. The State Street line reached 55th Street in 1881 and 63rd Street, about 5.5 miles south of downtown, in 1882, the same year Holmes began converting much of his system to cable.

Chicago City Railway, which in 1885 had eighty-seven miles of track in operation, was predominantly a locally owned company that Holmes was able to expand into a national traction syndicate through its National Railway holding company. Chicago City Railway had on its board such wealthy and influential Chicagoans as Samuel N. Nickerson, president of the First National Bank; Board of Trade dealer Benjamin P. Hutchinson; capitalist Silas B. Cobb; meatpacker Samuel W. Allerton; dry goods merchant Marshall Field; and real estate tycoon Levi Z. Leiter. They were the nucleus of the investors in Holmes's national syndicate that was organized to buy—and often to convert to cable operation—street systems in such places as Indianapolis; Rock Island,

By the beginning of the twentieth century streetcars such as this one at Van Buren and Kedzie, photographed about 1904, had developed into the optimal size and form their operating environment allowed. (Krambles Archive)

Illinois; Houston; Memphis; Madison, Wisconsin; St. Louis; and, in 1889, Los Angeles.

Chicago City Railway was consistently profitable from 1860 through the end of the century. In the 1890s it paid out on average almost 30 percent of its revenues in stock dividends, an exceptional record by modern standards and the best financial performance of any of the three street railways in Chicago at the time.[43] It was sufficiently profitable that in 1889, the same year the Holmes syndicate began building a cable system in Los Angeles, it was able

to buy $500,000 in bonds for the proposed South Side elevated, a line for which the developers were having a difficult time raising capital. Chicago City Railway eventually increased its stake to more than $3 million and became the majority stockholder in the venture, although it ultimately disbursed its shares in the Alley L to its stockholders.

Holmes's downfall in 1891 resulted from his leading the syndicate into a bad investment in a cable system in Los Angeles and running afoul of two of his investors over the issue of street railway access from the West Side to downtown Chicago, where they maintained their businesses. Although Holmes was one of first individuals to recognize the advantages of cable over horsecars, he continued building capital-intensive cable systems after less-expensive electric traction had rendered them obsolete. The end of the Los Angeles land boom, rains that flooded the cable powerhouse there, and unexpected high debt of the horsecar franchises that Holmes's syndicate had acquired undermined the value of his Pacific Railway Corporation. He had also alienated Field and Leiter when he tried to prevent Charles T. Yerkes' West Division Railway from installing a cable car line on State Street parallel to the original Chicago City Railway line. Field and Leiter both wanted residents of the West Side to have access to their businesses in the Loop.[44]

Chicago's other two street railway systems, the West Division and the North Chicago, proved to be somewhat less profitable than Chicago City Railway and less innovative as well, which may have contributed to the ease with which a Philadelphia syndicate represented by Yerkes took them over in the 1880s. Although Chicago City Railway after 1870 consistently paid dividends equal to 10 to 15 percent of revenues, the North Chicago system generally paid about half that rate on a substantially lower revenue base.[45] Until the takeover, neither the West nor the North system bothered with the expense of cable, despite Chicago City Railway's success with the technology.

Both companies seemed complacently happy with the status quo and had little turnover in either the executive suite or the board room. While the Chicago City Railway had eight presidents and thirty-two different directors between 1859 and 1885, the West Division Railway, controlled by a Galena syndicate, for all intents and purposes had only one chief executive, J. Russell Jones, and ten directors over the same span.[46] The North Chicago Railway similarly had only two presidents between its inception and 1885, and during that time seventeen individuals sat on its board, most with ties to the North Western Railway.[47]

North Chicago was the smallest of the three systems, the one with the worst access to the downtown area because of heavy traffic on the Chicago River, which its cars spanned on public bridges. It was also the system that suffered the heaviest damage in the Chicago Fire. Nevertheless, by 1975 it operated six miles of double track and four miles of single track.[48] It was the North Chicago system that the Philadelphia traction syndicate of Peter A. B. Widener and William C. Elkins, at the suggestion of Yerkes, chose as its first acquisition target in 1886, while the local Holmes syndicate on the South Side was preoccupied with expansion and cable conversions in other cities.

Given the high profitability of Chicago's street railways and the lack of adequate laws governing business in the nineteenth century, it was probably inevitable that corruption was endemic and that the transit systems eventually would be subjected to the same forces of consolidation that were at work on the mainline railroads. The potential for high profits at low risk also attracted some new players—local versions of the railroad robber barons.

5

THE TRACTION BARON AND STRAPHANGERS

Charles Tyson Yerkes was the single most influential developer of Chicago's transit system in the nineteenth century. Many features of his controversial system, including the elevated railway, continue to impact present-day commuters.

♦ Unexpectedly superimposed on Chicago's tumultuous mass-transit system in the 1880s was a character who seemed to have been sent by central casting. In his two decades in Chicago Charles Tyson Yerkes was excoriated by his detractors as an unscrupulous robber baron, although in recent years there has been some rehabilitation of his reputation.[1] By his proponents he was hailed as a far-sighted man who made noble efforts to modernize and to improve Chicago's transit system, albeit with some tactics that were not always ethical. Whatever he was, by the end of the nineteenth century Yerkes had become the lightning rod for a controversy over mass transit that had been brewing in Chicago since 1858—one-quarter century before he arrived on the scene.

"It is the straphangers [standees] who pay the dividends," he was quoted as saying when questioned about why he did not run more streetcars to relieve overcrowding at rush hour.[2] Yerkes, an expatriate from Philadelphia, began the consolidation of Chicago's transit system and was blamed for a great deal of the corruption of the Chicago City Council and Illinois General Assembly during the 1890s. When he arrived in 1881 it was with the intention of running a bank, not a street railroad. Like a number of captains of American industry, Yerkes was an assembler of syndicates, a businessman who acquired at minimum risk to his investors a group of independent companies with similar interests. The acquisitions were highly lever-

aged and they collapsed soon after he left, but while he was in the executive suite Yerkes proved to be an adept manager of both the money and the railway systems.

Yerkes grew up in a Quaker family in Philadelphia. He apparently acquired his business skills in his youth. As he related to his sanctioned biographer, as a twelve-year-old boy he once overheard a grocer say he was willing to pay as much as nine cents per pound for a brand of soap he sold at retail for twelve cents. Yerkes located the brand at a nearby auction, bought twenty-five cases at less than six cents a pound, and quickly resold them to the grocer at the agreed nine cents.[3] By the time he was twenty-two in 1859 he had set himself up as a stockbroker in Philadelphia. He was successful enough at that to have accumulated enough money in three years to buy a banking business in which he specialized in the purchase and sale of government, state, and city bonds. When the bond market collapsed after the Chicago Fire of 1871, he ironically was unable to meet the monthly payment due on the City of Philadelphia's account with him, and he was financially ruined. He was convicted of embezzlement and sent to jail but had served only seven months of his thirty-three-month term when some prominent Philadelphians intervened and persuaded the governor to pardon him.

Although he went back to banking and rebuilt his fortune, that conviction later was used by his detractors in Chicago, including Mayor Carter Harrison Jr., to paint him as a crook who could not be trusted, especially with the corrupt Gray Wolves in charge of the City Council. "Trained in the public utility school he saw a roseate future ahead for the first man who would apply eastern methods of official corruption to the crude half-way measures so far practiced by the novices in Chicago's best financial circles," wrote Harrison years later.[4] The sentiment apparently was mutual. It is an oft-repeated anecdote that when Harrison's newspaper, the *Times,* persisted in attacking Yerkes's railways, Yerkes strode unannounced into Harrison's office one day and said, "Carter, I always did know you were a scoundrel. Good Day, Sir," then closed the door and left before Harrison could utter a word.[5]

After his pardon in Pennsylvania, Yerkes resumed his brokerage business and made some "fortunate stock speculations that put him in a position of financial independence again."[6] One of those investments was in the Elkins-Widener Continental Passenger Railway in Philadelphia, which he spotted at $15 per share and watched quickly rise to $100 per share. When he finally settled in Chicago in 1881 after a fling at real estate in Fargo, North Dakota, he opened a branch of his Philadelphia bank. Like many of the monied easterners who emigrated to Chicago before him, however, Yerkes soon became intrigued by the great opportunities for profit-making ventures, and it was not long before the conservatively operated street railways on the West and North sides caught his eye.

The Chicago that Yerkes first visited in 1880, before making it his home a year later, consisted of 35.6 square miles inhabited by slightly more than half a million people, about 380,000 of whom were concentrated within a three-mile radius of downtown. The 1889 annexations of portions of the towns of Lake, Jefferson, and Cicero; the City of Lake View; and the village of Hyde Park added overnight more than 125 square miles and 225,000 people.[7] By then plans were well under way for a great fair to commemorate not only the fourth centenary of Columbus's discovery of the western hemisphere but also Chicago's emergence as a major city. In fact, Chicago was growing so fast that its laws, especially those governing its transit system, could not keep pace.

RUNAWAY GROWTH AND ARCHAIC LAWS

When public transit companies began to appear in Chicago prior to the Civil War, the body of law that was supposed to govern them dated from before the Industrial Revolution, and the principal political body in Illinois was a relic from a frontier, agrarian society. Most power in the state was vested in three large committees of elected representatives—the two houses of the Illinois General Assembly, as the state legislature was called, and occasional constitutional conventions that met four times between 1818 and 1870. Chicago's Common Council, another elected committee, had some control over local matters, although powers not specifically delegated by the General Assembly and constitution were reserved to the state. The vesting of such power in legislative assemblies often meant that in times of rapid change the law trailed technology and the evolving economic system by many years.[8]

The General Assembly until 1870 dealt with problems of growth on a piecemeal basis, and almost every local action from municipal incorporation to chartering corporations required a special act. As a result the two principal regulatory mechanisms governing the construction and conduct of street railways often were conflicting. The state sometimes granted street railway corporate charters for as long as ninety-nine years, but the municipal franchises for use of their streets usually specified only twenty years. Neither mechanism proved adequate to deal with growing Chicago, the population of which increased fifteen-fold in the last four decades of the century. Over the same span the street railway system expanded from 1.5 miles of track on which four horsecars operated to 718 miles of track and more than 3,000 vehicles by 1907.[9]

The state charter was a legal device that created a variety of public and private corporations, including railroads; conferred to them some state powers, such as eminent domain; regulated them, albeit minimally; and in some instances, limited competition. In the 1860s, six groups of promoters sought street railway charters from the legislature, but only three were granted, including one later ruled illegal by the courts and one to a nonfunctioning subsidiary of North Chicago City Railway Co.[10] As a practical matter, the charter was the only device available to the state for the first fifty years of its existence to regulate transportation companies. The constitutional convention tried to solve some of the resulting problems in 1870 with a provision requiring the legislature to pass general incorporation laws that made the formation of corporations an administrative matter. The result of this solution after 1872, however, was a proliferation of 120 new transit companies, some of them created for the sole purpose of extortion by unscrupulous politicians, until the legislature in 1895 raised the incorporation fee.[11]

The convention also laid the groundwork for a more effective regulatory mechanism. The state legislature, under pressure from the growing Granger movement, in 1871 created the Railroad and Warehouse Commission to regulate those interrelated industries—the first such agency in the nation with powers of economic regulation of common carriers.[12] Because they were considered a local problem unique to Chicago, however, the legislature made no effort to regulate street railways similarly until the very end of the century, when the railways themselves unsuccessfully sought such legislation.[13]

The underlying problem of regulation was that the complex financing mechanisms developed to feed the mainline and street railroads' gigantic appetite for capital were beyond the comprehension of the rural legislature, the ward healers who ran Chicago's City Council, and the general populace. It cost an average of $10,914 per mile to build a horsecar line, $57,399 for a cable car line in 1888,[14] and as much as $65,040 per mile for an electrified streetcar line in Chicago in 1896,[15] which made it necessary for public transportation companies to turn from public stock subscriptions to bonds to generate the necessary capital. Indeed, two bodies of law were needed: one to create a sophisticated agency to regulate the street railway companies as utilities, to strike a balance between the convenience and necessity of customers and the needs of transit owners to make a return on their investment; and the other to regulate the transit corporations to protect their investors. In nineteenth-century Chicago, those two separate and distinct issues were often blurred in the controversy over stock watering and overcapitalization that dominated the transit debate.

The 1848 constitution directed the General Assembly "to encourage internal improvements by passing general laws of incorporation for that purpose."[16] This led to a complex system of government unique in its persistence in Illinois—the special taxing district. The political theory that local citizens could vote in referenda to tax themselves to solve local problems led to thousands of special taxing districts to support libraries, sanitation projects, pest control, forest preserves, drainage, hospitals, and eventually mass transit, ports, and airports. Nearly one century later, special taxing districts were the method used to transfer the Chicago area's mass-transit system to public ownership.[17]

The 1848 constitution lasted only twenty-two years. By the time it became obvious that a new one was needed, the part-time legislature, still dominated by rural interests, was being overwhelmed by the problems brought on by growth.[18] Illinois, which had begun its existence in 1818 with 34,620 residents, less than the 40,000 required for statehood, by 1860 had 1.7 million inhabitants and was the fourth most populous state in the union. Incorporation of municipal and private enterprises, however, was possible only by a special act of legislature and, as in the case of a public corporation such as Chicago in 1833, usually was done to confer powers of taxation, public debt, and public works. In contrast, railroads incorporating as joint-stock companies needed the state-granted power of eminent domain to acquire rights-of-way.

The street railway issue became mired in a legal quagmire almost from the start. When the promoters applied to the city for a franchise for a horsecar line, they were forced to take the issue to the General Assembly when the courts held that the city did not have the legal power to franchise railways.[19] The legislature then chartered the street railway but with many of the same conditions the city had imposed in its franchise, including a five-cent fare cap and property owner consent.[20] Limits on fares were never really a subject of dispute in the nineteenth century, but the tenure of franchises was.

The original Chicago franchise of 1855 and state charter of 1859 both stipulated a duration of twenty-five years, which was later reduced to twenty years, but because of increased difficulty in funding capital projects with short-term financing, the street railways on several occasions sought to have that lengthened by the state legislature.[21] Banks were reluctant to make a twenty-five-year mortgage to a company with only nineteen years remaining on its franchise, so the traction companies in 1865 asked the state legislature to extend their charters by ninety-nine years. The legislature complied over a gubernatorial veto, and the resulting public furor led to the reform movement that plagued transit into the next century.

CHICAGO GETS REGULATORY POWER

The constitutional convention in 1870 was dominated by reformers, and the new constitution included a provision that pro-

hibited the legislature from granting a street railway charter without the consent of local government, effectively shifting the power of regulation from the state to the city.[22] As a result, the Cities and Villages Act of 1872 and the Chicago municipal charter of 1875 both limited future franchises to no more than twenty years; in 1883 the city also extended the existing franchises to twenty years. As a practical matter, the twenty-year franchise limitation simply meant street railways had to refinance their bonds every two decades. The practice of paying only interest on bonds and rolling over the principal was endemic in the industry in the nineteenth century.[23] Besides continuing the five-cent fare limit, Chicago also negotiated a new factor into the franchises—taxation. The companies agreed to an annual $50 car license fee.[24]

Yerkes, by then the dominant figure in Chicago traction, controlling two-thirds of the street railways and about half of the elevated system, in 1897 induced the legislature to pass the Allen Law (after Representative Charles Allen, of Hoopeston), which extended street railway franchises to fifty years.[25] The resulting furor was probably a major factor in the decision by Yerkes, whose street railway franchises were to expire in 1903, to sell out and leave town.[26] By then, the franchise as a mechanism to regulate traction systems was rapidly obsolescing, although Chicago continued to use it to increase its regulatory powers.[27] It took the city and traction companies several lawsuits and four years to negotiate the next round of franchise extensions—the so-called Settlement Ordinances of 1907, which also had a twenty-year duration. It was not until after the street railways were hopelessly mired in bankruptcy in 1930 that Chicago—three years late—negotiated new franchises for an indefinite period, the so-called terminable franchise.

A continuing problem in trying to regulate street railways, especially by means of twenty-year franchises, was the increased complexity of their finances. By the 1880s the two principal methods of financing street railways, stocks and bonds, had become intermixed. The companies used bonds as their principal method of financing construction, and stocks were dispensed to bond buyers at no cost or deeply discounted as an inducement to invest.[28] This exchange of stock for a price well under its market value gave rise to the controversy over watered stock..

Adding fuel to the fire was the practice of transit company organizers to use the proceeds from stock subscriptions to take up-front profits out of the ventures before issuing bonds to finance construction. That practice made it necessary for the traction companies to maintain high profit margins to pay out dividends amounting from one-fifth to one-quarter of revenues to satisfy shareholders whose stock had been watered—numbers that are exceedingly high by the current rule of thumb in which corporations pay as dividends about half of profits, not revenues.[29] Stock watering gave rise to a public controversy over excess profits and put pressure on both the state and local governments to maintain the cap on fares at five cents, a measure that worked well during the nineteenth century but proved disastrous when inflation became a factor in the twentieth century.

The street railways quite simply had become cash cows that everyone was trying to milk—investors, syndicates, politicians, traction barons, property owners, and government. Although there were many street railway failures, especially in the sparsely populated suburbs, surviving financial data from Chicago traction companies indicate they were highly profitable ventures from the onset. Parmelee's original 1.5-mile horsecar line, which probably was built and equipped for less than $20,000 in 1859, generated $124,625 in revenue in its first full year of operation in 1860 and was able to pay a dividend of $25,000, or 18 percent of its receipts (revenues) of $136,079, in 1861.[30] By 1865, the system had been extended to twelve miles and produced $342,702 in revenue.[31] City Railway paid dividends continuously from 1860, and after 1890 they consistently exceeded 20 percent of revenues.[32] Indeed, over a thirteen-year period from 1886 to 1898 the company paid out $14.6 million in dividends, or 28.8 percent of its revenues of nearly $50.7 million. At that rate, a shareholder could recover his investment in dividends alone (excluding any capital gains from the sale of the stock) in less than four years.

Between 1887 and 1898, after Yerkes took control, the North Chicago Railway paid out cumulative dividends of $7.6 million, or 26.4 percent of its revenues of $28.8 million. The West Division Railway did not perform as well as the other two but still paid dividends totaling $8.2 million, or 18.5 percent of its revenues of $44.1 million, during the 1888–1898 period.[33] The street railways were so profitable that to a large extent they financed the construction of the city's earliest elevated railway lines.

YERKES FINANCING SCHEMES

Yerkes from the beginning saw the potential profits to be made in transit and assembled a syndicate with the backing of Elkins and Widener to engineer control of the North Chicago system. Together they acquired a bare majority of stock—2,505 shares at $600 each, or a total investment of $1,503,000—and created a holding company called the North Chicago Street Railroad Co., which issued $1,500,000 in bonds, the proceeds from which were used to pay for the original stock purchase. The new corporation then leased all the assets and property of the old system with an agreement to pay the underlying company interest on existing debt and a fixed dividend.[34] Thus the Yerkes syndicate in 1886 acquired a street railway system that was producing approximately $250,000 per year in dividends on about

$1.2 million in revenues without investing a dime of its own money. The tactic worked so well that the syndicate repeated the procedure in 1888 by paying $4,063,150 to get control of the West Division system, then creating a holding company that issued $4,100,000 in bonds to finance the transaction.

Once in control, Yerkes proceeded quickly to modernize the systems by converting many of them to more economical cable operations, a move that drew praise even from his arch enemy, Chicago Mayor Carter Harrison Jr.[35] Yerkes also began to attack the problem of downtown congestion, which was acute on the North Chicago system because its three horsecar lines had to cross bridges spanning the Chicago River. At times as many as six horsecars were backed up for as long as fifteen minutes because a bridge had opened for a passing ship.[36]

Since the North Chicago Railway already was carrying a high debt load as a result of its leveraged acquisition, building a downtown subway was not feasible. Yerkes reached a compromise solution in 1886 by acquiring access to the city's then little-used LaSalle Street vehicle tunnel under the river and converting it for use by cable cars—possibly the first mass-transit subway of any kind in the United States. The tunnel had been completed in 1871 for pedestrian and wagon traffic at a cost of $566,276, but it proved to have access grades that were too steep for many horse-drawn wagons and horsecars, and the structures were too dank for pedestrians.[37] Yerkes also converted the Washington Street tunnel for cable car use shortly thereafter and formed yet another company to issue $1.5 million in bonds to build a 1,517-foot cable car tunnel near Van Buren Street.[38] By the time it opened in 1894, however, electric traction had developed to the point that streetcars were more efficient and economical than cable systems, and Yerkes electrified the tunnels once the city re-

lented and allowed overhead wires in the downtown area.

THE END OF THE YERKES ERA

Despite its modernization and expansion, Chicago's street railway system—which grew from 390 miles of track in 1890 to more than 1,100 miles when it was consolidated in 1914 as the largest street railway operation in the world—was never quite able to overcome its vulnerability to traffic congestion.[39] Horsecars and cable cars had to share the streets with growing numbers of wagons, buggies, and, later, automobiles. There also were at least two external factors that prevented the street railways from attaining the economies of scale that their sheer size implied—the increased concentration of the central business district and the simultaneous decentralization of industrial and residential areas following the great fire of 1871. The railway companies themselves were operated as independent systems suffering from "patchwork fragmentation," and their riders were forced to pay double fares to transfer between lines. Samuel W. Norton in his 1906 study argues, however, that many of the seemingly independent companies were linked through cross-ownership and the syndicates.[40]

Toward the end of the nineteenth century Chicago simply outgrew the ability of a street railway system to effectively serve it. The city by then had been largely rebuilt from its disastrous fire and had been transformed from a walking city to one in which the middle-class population was largely dependent upon mass transportation to get around. The conflagration had begun the centralization-decentralization process that would continue through the twentieth century, and street railways made it possible for workers to move out of the increasingly denser, congested, and more expensive downtown area to residential subdivisions sprouting up on the outskirts of town. The owners of the street railways and a number

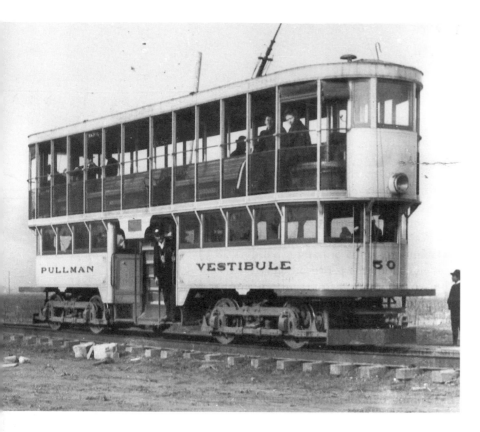

Double-deck trolley cars were tried in Chicago but had limited use because they were too high to clear the ubiquitous railroad viaducts. (Krambles Archive)

of politicians encouraged residential decentralization by speculating on fringe development. The street railway system increasingly had became a tool of private enterprise to encourage development of outlying areas and to reward land speculation, a practice dating back to Stephen A. Douglas and William B. Ogden in the 1850s. Charles Walker, superintendent of the Chicago City Railway, as early as 1866 laid out a subdivision at the end of an extension to his company's State Street line, and Yerkes did the same for his streetcar lines on the northwest side in the 1880s.[41] John Peter Altgeld, the progressive governor who pardoned the Haymarket conspirators and unsuccessfully vetoed the scandalous Ogden Gas Act, was an investor both in a street railway and in real estate in suburban Lake View.[42] Loop property owners and merchants Marshall Field and Levi Leiter were also substantial investors in the Chicago City Railway Co.[43]

The lack of any sort of organized transit planning also contributed to the problem. In the rough and tumble political atmosphere of late-nineteenth-century Chicago,

city planning was something done in the back room at Hinky Dink's saloon or in the board room of some company with a vested interest in development. The first systematic attempt at any sort of transit planning by a professional did not occur until 1902, when engineer Bion J. Arnold approached the traction problem for the City Council Committee on Local Transportation.[44]

Chicago rebuilt from the fire at a time when land values in the downtown area were rising dramatically. Simultaneously it became feasible both economically and technologically to build increasingly taller buildings, especially given the development of such advancements as elevators and steel framing.[45] The early skyscrapers greatly increased the daytime population density in downtown Chicago and also provided the street railways with a larger commutation market and increased congestion.[46] The development of the skyscraper had added to the traffic jam even before the first automobile sputtered down a Chicago street. The resulting congestion and deterioration of street railway service contributed to the growing public and political discontent with the system and its owners that Yerkes had faced in the 1880s.[47]

The introduction of cable power and electrification a few years later permitted substantial operating efficiencies that quickly translated to the bottom line of the street railway companies but did not solve the congestion problem. The Cottage Grove cable line on the outskirts of the city had a scheduled speed of about nine miles per hour over its 8.7-mile route,[48] but in the downtown area cable cars crept along at three to four miles per hour and suffered innumerable delays due to traffic congestion. By 1890 it was becoming apparent that the solution to traffic jams was to get the railways off the streets of downtown Chicago and into subways or onto elevated railways.

This transition did not take place quickly enough to save Yerkes, who by the late 1890s was receiving the brunt of the public discontent over the street railways, although his role in the building of Chicago's elevated railways was less controversial. Yerkes left Chicago in 1900 for New York, sold the bulk of his transit holdings, which were worth approximately $5 million, and invested in development and electrification of the London Tubes, a project that rehabilitated his reputation.[49] Possibly the most interesting observation about Yerkes was made in 1935, thirty years after his death in New York, by his longtime foe, Carter Harrison Jr.: "He was really a gallant though perverted soul that looked danger in the face unflinchingly. He was the stuff great war heroes are made of; with the right moral fiber he would have been a truly superb character."[50] Toward the end of the twentieth century, as the city prepared to celebrate the 100th anniversary of its Loop elevated structure, the tarnish on Yerkes's reputation started to fade as Chicagoans began to appreciate the role he had played in creating that remarkable structure.

Gridlock was already a problem in the Loop in 1909 when this photograph was taken at Dearborn and Randolph Streets. Fourteen streetcars are visible in a one-block stretch. (Krambles Archives)

6

THE ELEVATED TRAINS

◆ Chicago's elevated railway, a fretwork of steel stringers and girders that wanders the city, has become as much of a municipal landmark as any structure in existence. The deep rolling thunder from its passing trains has reassured generations of Chicagoans that they are nowhere else on earth. Downtown Chicago, the Loop, is named after the elevated railway, and many major public attractions were purposely built close to the L, as it is known locally. Less well known in this auto age is that the L was an attempt to solve the problem of traffic congestion long before the first automobile chugged down the city's streets. The Loop section of the L was built as a giant junction to consolidate the urban railway system of an entire city in such a way that it encircled the central business district. The L also represents the turning point of mass transit as a private enterprise in Chicago: it was a technological marvel that was simply too expensive for its builders to get a sufficient return on their investment to pay off the cost of its construction.

Chicago's street railways were still in their infancy when the first proposal to build an elevated railway was floated in the Illinois General Assembly in 1869. The bill to charter the Chicago Elevated Railway to build a number of single-track lines above various Chicago streets was probably prompted by the opening in New York City in 1867 of a cable-powered elevated railway. The General Assembly never considered the bill, possibly because, as Thomas R. Bullard suggested, the legislature concluded Chicago was not quite ready for an elevated railroad like the one that had just commenced service in New York. It is also possible that the General Assembly disregarded the bill because the controversy between the city and state over charters and franchises was then at a peak and a constitutional convention was impending.[1]

In any event, the city in 1869 was probably relatively well served by its street railway system, although that did not stop promoters from proposing no less than seventy elevated railroads between 1872 and 1900.[2] By the 1880s, however, downtown street traffic congestion had become such a problem that the city and state began to take some of the L proposals seriously.[3] Although the first electric elevated railway in Chicago was a freight line that had been built in 1892 to serve the Armour & Company packing plant,[4] the event that seemed to precipitate action on Ls was the Columbian Exposition. In addition to honoring Columbus, the exposition also served notice that both the industrialization of Chicago begun in 1848 and the rebuilding of the city after the fire of 1871 had been completed.

The idea of handling fair crowds provided the city an impetus for the construction of its first two elevated railways, although only one was considered permanent. The city began planning for the fair in 1885, and the Chicago & South Side Rapid Transit Railroad was incorporated in 1888 to operate a permanent elevated line between downtown Chicago and the fair site, even though Chicago was not selected by Congress as the host city until April 24, 1890.[5]

The Columbian Intramural Railway was proposed in early 1892 by the fair's management, which issued a prospectus for an electrically powered railroad with twenty-four stops to gird the 1.5-mile long fairgrounds, for the dual purpose of transportation and sightseeing. The details were left up to the bidders, who submitted proposals for everything from an elevated streetcar line to moving sidewalks to a steam-powered, narrow-gauge railroad. The winner was a group (formed by the head of a local electric company) with a proposal for a system that, somewhat surprisingly, in view of the lack of experience of everyone involved, closely resembled the modern-day L.[6]

Viewed from above, the Columbian Intramural Railway resembled a giant, three-mile C with serifs, actually loops, at either end for turning trains. Because of the expected operating environment of the six-month fair—warm weather and large crowds—the eighteen motor cars and fifty-four unpowered trailers were open and compartmentalized with seven doors along each side for quick loading and unloading. The motor cars, which looked like the trailers except for the electrical equipment slung beneath them, could pull as many as seven loaded cars, although four-car trains were standard operating practice. Possibly because of its relatively high ten-cent fare, ridership was disappointing for the first month; passenger load picked up during the Independence Day weekend, however, and the Intramural Railway for the 184 days of the fair between May 1 and October 31, 1893, carried 5,803,895 riders, or about 27 percent of the paid attendance of the fair.[7]

The trains, powered by electric traction motors slung beneath the cars, drew power from a third rail mounted on one side of the running tracks. Up to that point, trains on elevated railways had been operated by steam locomotives, as in the case of the South Side L, or trolley cars drawing their power from overhead wires.[8] Despite its demolition immediately after the exposition closed, the Intramural was a substantial influence on the fledgling elevated railway industry. Promoters of the Metropolitan West Side Elevated Railway, which was planned as a steam line, decided prior to its 1895 opening to convert it to electric traction, and all Ls designed thereafter followed that lead.[9] The Lake L was

(*facing page*) The city's first elevated railway carried passengers between downtown Chicago and the 1893 Columbian Exposition. The elevated railway has since developed to become a distinctive Chicago hallmark. Here locomotives for the Lake line in 1893 are pushed up onto the elevated structure by the engine and boxcars backing up on the right. Other new engines below the elevated structure await delivery. (Krambles Archive)

Workers raise the steel superstructure of the L at Montana Street. (Krambles Archive)

converted from steam to third rail in 1896, and the South Side L was converted two years after that.

Transporting people from downtown to the fair was another great concern. Nearly one year before the fair opened, Chicago's first standard elevated line, the Chicago & South Side Rapid Transit Co., began running trains between Congress Street just south of the central business district and 39th Street.[10] Its extension to Jackson Park began service twelve days after the opening of the fair and the start of its Intramural Railway.[11]

The line, which cost $5.7 million to build, had financial problems almost from its conception—a warning later L developers failed to heed.[12] The South Side L's promoters had incorporated five years before the fair opened, but they had so little success raising money that in 1889 they approached the prosperous Chicago City Railway Co. for financing. Chicago City Railway initially bought $500,000 in bonds; the construction company formed to build the line agreed to dispose of another $313,000 in bonds. When the new elevated company still had problems raising money, Chicago City Railway agreed to buy another $3 million in bonds in return for majority interest in the L company.[13] That meant the street railway or its stockholders owned 38,850 of the 75,000 shares of elevated company stock and held $3.9 million of its $7.5 million bonded indebtedness. By the standards of the contemporary political debate over stock watering, the building of the South Side Rapid Transit had cost half of its paper value, or capitalization, but in reality the controlling interest in its stock had been given away.

Contributing to the high cost of construction was the state's property-owner consent law. Street railways ran on public rights-of-way, but the Ls for the most part had to buy their own, a factor that drove up costs. In 1883, when proposals for elevated railways began appearing, State Senator George E. Adams, a reformer, secured

The completed structure of the L sits on concrete footings. (Krambles Archive)

passage of an act that required elevated companies to secure the consent of two-thirds of the property owners along each mile of line—essentially the same consent requirement that forced the street railways to bribe property owners along their routes. As it turned out, it was less expensive for Ls to acquire separate rights-of-way. The Chicago & South Side Rapid Transit Co., for example, became known as "Alley L," since it was cheaper for an elevated company to buy its own alley, even though it increased initial costs by as much as 50 percent, than to bribe property owners to use the street.[14] The exceptions were the Loop, where no land was available; the leg of the South Side elevated above 63rd Street west of Jackson Park; and Michael McDonald's Lake Street elevated line, for which he managed to secure a street franchise from his friends on the City Council in 1888 without first obtaining consent of property owners.

Heavy traffic to and from the Columbian fair made the new railway an instant, but illusory, success despite the depression of 1893.[15] That year, the Alley L carried 30,055,747 riders and collected $1,535,427 in fares; however, traffic collapsed after the fair closed. In 1894, ridership dropped to 14.2 million and produced only $744,167 in revenue, and the new company was unable to meet its debt service.[16] It defaulted on its bonds on April 1, 1895, and the creditors foreclosed, forcing the company into bankruptcy. In a bankruptcy reorganization of a transportation corporation—a situation in which liquidation was not an acceptable alternative—it was typical for stockholders to be wiped out and the secured creditors, the bondholders, to receive stock in the reorganized company as their settlement. In the case of the South Side Rapid Transit, however, a majority of the stockholders and bondholders were the same people, and they elected to cut their losses and to bail out of the project with a loss that amounted to 60 cents on the dollar. The receiver sold the company to the highest bidder on September 16, 1896, for $4 million, which was applied to the outstanding $10.5 million in bonds.[17] As a result, the new owners acquired for $4 million an elevated railway that cost $5.7 million to build.

The reorganized South Side Elevated Railway, unencumbered with the original debt, became marginally profitable even though as late as 1898 it still carried only 18.9 million passengers and collected less than one million dollars in revenue. Despite its faster service, the L did not have the impact on street railway ridership that Chicago City Railway's managers had expected when they invested in the project as a hedge. Chicago City Railway recorded traffic gains of nearly 5 percent in 1895 and more than 7 percent in 1896. In 1895, probably because it offered service into the central business district and because the elevated line terminated one-half mile south at Congress Street, Chicago City Railway held an 86.3 percent market share of the more than 103 million riders in the corridor.[18]

After 1896, the street railway's growth slowed, likely reflecting a stabilization of ridership and the fact that the Alley L obtained access to the Loop in late 1897.

South Side street ridership grew by only one-fifteenth of a percent that year and only one-third of a percent in 1898. By that time, Chicago City Railway's market share of the 115 million riders to and from the South Side of the city had declined to 83.5 percent, still a dominant position that enabled it to earn sufficient profits to pay its shareholders dividends equal to almost 30 percent of revenues.[19]

The three other elevated railways extending from the Loop also had financial troubles from the beginning. Michael McDonald's Lake Street Elevated Railroad, chartered a few months after the South Side line, did not sort out the problems associated with the technicalities in its charter until 1890. Even then, McDonald, whose contacts were in Chicago's political community, not on LaSalle Street, had difficulty raising the necessary capital, and he often skimmed what funds he did raise.[20] Construction that started in 1891 proceeded at a snail's pace, and abruptly in early 1892 McDonald sold the project to a group of New York investors for $2 million. They reorganized the company with another $6.5 million in bonds and $10 million in stock, the latter of which was used mainly as an inducement for purchasing bonds. While construction continued, the line finally began operating for four miles west to Homan Avenue on February 6, 1893. But the company lost $146,000 on operations in 1894, and the stock price plummeted from $28 per share when service began in November 1893 to $18 per share by July 1894. The New York investors were ready to quit. They had accumulated $17,660,697 in liabilities—stock, bonds, and accounts payable—on a project that cost an estimated $3,317,500 to build.

The line would have joined the South Side elevated in bankruptcy were it not that Charles Tyson Yerkes, concerned about its impact on ridership on his West Division street railway, formed a new syndicate in 1894, bought up controlling interest in the depressed stock for less than

$1 million, and persuaded the bondholders to renegotiate their notes. A new issue of debentures (bonds with a repayment based on the income of a company, not at a fixed rate) at seventy-five cents on the dollar was accepted by the bondholders in order to avoid the larger losses they most certainly would have incurred had the company been forced into foreclosure and bankruptcy.[21]

The Metropolitan West Side Elevated Railway, chartered in 1892 by promoters of the South Side L to build lines northwest to Logan Square and west to the suburb of Cicero, did not have trouble raising the necessary capital because of the early success of their Alley L. The stock was highly watered, however, and the company ran into difficulty soon after it began operation, even though it was designed as the nation's first permanent electrified rapid-transit system.[22] The first section opened as far northwest as Damen Avenue on May 6, 1895, and by the end of that year the line had been extended to Logan Square and Humboldt Park on the northwest and to Cicero on the west. By 1898, however, when the company generated only $1,179,363 million in revenue from 23.9 million riders on both lines, the creditors foreclosed, forcing another L into bankruptcy.[23]

Yerkes was less successful with his Northwestern Elevated Railroad, chartered in 1893 to protect his street railway interests on the North Side, than he was with the distressed Lake line. Construction started in 1894 but was delayed by strikes, material shortages, and funding problems. Construction was halted for a year in 1896 when the project ran out of money, probably because of the reluctance of the bond market to invest in another new L when the South Side and Metropolitan elevated railways were in bankruptcy.[24] The Philadelphia Widener-Elkins syndicate, Yerkes's backers in his street railway ventures, originally subscribed $1.3 million in Northwestern elevated stock but later reneged.[25] Yerkes was finally reduced to offering prospective Northwestern bond buyers a two-for-one bonus in stock (free stock worth $200 for each $100 invested in bonds) and, as an added incentive, a 40 percent bonus (free stock worth forty cents for each $1 invested in bonds) in Union Loop stock.

To keep costs down, Yerkes was also forced to snake his line through different North Side neighborhoods willing to give him the most favorable terms on land acquisition. Rushing to meet the deadline in the original charter, which required the line to be running by January 1, 1900 (or face a $100,000 default penalty), Yerkes began service on the Northwestern on December 31, 1899, with only four of its fourteen stations completed. The city shut him down the next day after an inspection discovered shoddy workmanship, including an insufficient number of rivets in the steel elevated structure. The line finally opened for good on May 31, 1900.[26]

THE LOOP

Long before construction started on the Northwestern Elevated line, Yerkes had concluded that to a great extent the financial problems of the new elevated railways resulted from their failure to get access to downtown Chicago, where their street railway competitors had a monopoly on service.[27] The South Side L came only as far north as Congress Street, the Lake Street line ended west of the river at Clinton Street, and the Metropolitan franchise was built to 5th Avenue (now Wells Street).[28] Yerkes's solution—to build a one-mile square elevated Loop over which all the L companies could operate through downtown Chicago—was simultaneously one of the most brilliant and the darkest chapters in transit history. The obstacles were many and difficult: public opinion and that of the downtown merchants was badly divided on the issue, corruption on the City Council dominated by the Gray Wolves was rampant, the elevated companies that would have to use the line if it were to be successful were independently owned, and state law and city ordinances not only imposed onerous restrictions on the project but also encouraged corruption.[29]

Despite the risks, Yerkes decided to proceed but to use subterfuge to conceal his goal until it was too late to stop the project. Hiding the objective was to help prevent the opposition from coalescing. The entire system had to be built over streets, and to comply with the Adams Law he was confronted with prohibitively expensive bribery. Acquiring downtown buildings and demolishing them for a right-of-way was out of the question. He hoped that obtaining piecemeal consent for the system, one segment at a time, would prevent property owners from organizing and driving up the cost of the requisite bribe.

Yerkes's initial move was to obtain the franchise to extend the Lake Street L across the Chicago River as far east as Wabash Avenue in downtown Chicago. This would be the first and northernmost leg of the Loop. The City Council granted him the franchise on October 1, 1894. He quickly began securing the concurrence of the property-owning merchants along Lake Street, who immediately saw the potential for increased business that riders would provide. The merchants signed the consent forms after Yerkes promised that the stairways for the entrances and exits to the elevated structure would be on the sidewalks in front of their buildings, not on side streets.

Yerkes continued to make steady progress toward his goal. He used a proposal to build a downtown terminal for his Northwestern Elevated Railroad, then under construction north of the Chicago River, as the excuse for the second, or western, leg of the Loop above 5th Avenue. Although business owners along 5th Avenue objected, he was able to obtain sufficient consent from factory and warehouse owners near the river at the south end of the line to offset the dissidents. The east and south legs of the Loop posed a problem for Yerkes's project, since he did not own the South Side and Metropolitan elevated com-

panies that were the logical users of those segments upon which the entire Loop elevated scheme depended for financial success. Therefore he incorporated the Union Elevated Railroad Co., issued $5 million in stock and a like amount in bonds, and offered contracts to those two companies. In financial distress, both companies agreed to the deal to gain access to the downtown area. By this time, property owners, especially those along Wabash Avenue, were better organized than their counterparts along 5th Avenue had been, and they formed a protective association, probably to enable them to keep tabs on the going rate for consent bribes. Yerkes apparently had to pay a rate of $25 to $100 per front foot for consent signatures. Calculated at the rate of $80 per front foot, the elevated railway project would have cost Yerkes $332,000 in bribes for a 4,150-foot section that probably cost about half that amount to build, based on the known costs of the similar Lake Street leg.[30]

Yerkes encountered the most concerted opposition to the final, or southern, leg of the elevated railway. Gaining the consent of the property owners required Yerkes's most Machiavellian skills. By this time it was obvious to everyone that Yerkes was building a loop, so his opposition was formidable. Those opposed to the project included Levi Z. Leiter, a major downtown property owner and investor in Yerkes's venture. Leiter had supported the other three legs of the Loop, but he wanted the final leg to be built over Harrison Street, where he owned buildings, instead of Van Buren Street, where Yerkes had planned the route. To get around this problem, Yerkes created still another company, the Union Consolidated Elevated Railway Co., which applied for a franchise not simply to complete the Loop between Wabash and 5th Avenue but also to extend it a mile farther west across the Chicago River. The purpose of the added mile, which Yerkes had no intention of building, was to gain the consent of enough property owners along the western section so as to offset the opposition along the eastern segment. The ploy worked. Yerkes got his franchise on July 6, 1896.[31]

The Loop, which opened for service on October 3, 1897, with trains from the Lake Street line, was probably the single most important mass-transit project ever built in Chicago. In addition to providing the city's financially shaky elevated companies with a downtown terminal and endowing Chicago with a downtown distributor almost one century before they became popular in other U.S. cities, Yerkes's project gave its name to the downtown area it girded. *A History of the Yerkes System of Street Railways,* published within a month or two of the opening of the line, refers to the elevated company and structure as the Loop and the area it enclosed as the "downtown district" or "central district," and Yerkes himself used the term "loop" to describe the cable car routes in a July 1, 1891, letter to another street railway president.[32] The common term "loop" had been used by people in the transportation business in the 1880s in reference to the complex system of downtown cable car loops in use then, but it did not become a proper noun, as in "the Loop," until after the elevated structure girding downtown Chicago was built. Sometime later the term became a synonym for downtown Chicago.

The new Loop was an immediate success—so much so, in fact, that congestion was a problem and trains crept around the structure with only a few feet of headway between them. Train traffic on the structure became so heavy that a 1908 study commissioned by the Loop Protective Association estimated that rush hour trains were delayed an aggregate fifteen minutes per trip.[33] The Loop, which boarded as many as 200,000 passengers each weekday at its peak in the 1920s, lost passengers because of the construction of Chicago's two subways in 1943 and 1951 and because of the demise of two interurban railroads between 1955 and 1963. By 1978, it boarded only 46,800 weekday passengers.[34]

The Loop may have been Yerkes's finest project, but reformers in Chicago were clamoring for his scalp before he completed it. As the nineteenth century drew to a close, Chicago's mass-transit system, much of it less than ten years old, was under a great deal of stress. The new elevated system had proved to be a technological success but a financial fiasco, raising the question of whether the system of private enterprise that had built Chicago's mainline and street railroads had reached its financial limits. That the twenty-year street railway franchises negotiated in 1883 were about to expire only fueled the criticism. While the public, press, and politicians of

Replacing bridges on the L without disrupting traffic posed a complex engineering problem. In the case of the Wells Street bridge in 1921, it involved building a new bascule bridge before the old one was demolished. (Krambles Archive)

the Gay Nineties in Chicago were dissatisfied with the privately owned transit system, no one would consider using public funds to help alleviate street congestion—a transportation problem that was getting worse. Unlike the citizens of Boston and New York, who agreed to the public financing of subways operated by private companies, Chicagoans in the nineteenth century sanctioned privately controlled mass transit and objected to subsidizing it with public funds. After 1892, Chicago required the mainline railroads to elevate their tracks to permit the free flow of traffic at street level, but Yerkes's Loop was already at capacity, and Chicago apparently did not have any plan to route its street railways through tunnels.

CHICAGO'S FIRST SUBWAYS

The year after Yerkes completed his elevated railway system, the Illinois Tunnel Co. began digging an extensive freight distribution subway system, the only one of its kind in the United States. Though it would bypass downtown congestion, it was prohibited by the city from hauling passengers.[35] The project began in 1898, apparently as an attempt by the Gray Wolves to shake down the Chicago Telephone Co. At that time Alderman Edward J. Novak, of the eighth ward, introduced an ordinance granting a fifty-year franchise to an unspecified company to provide telephone service to an area of about twenty-four square miles that included downtown Chicago. The franchise stipulated that the company bury its cables in the downtown area. Fourteen days later the state routinely incorporated the Illinois Telephone & Telegraph Co., the president of which was Albert G. Wheeler, who had been a promoter of Bathhouse John Coughlin's and Hinky Dink Kenna's General Electric Railway Co., one of their utility shakedown franchises on the South Side two years earlier.[36]

Digging for telephone conduit tunnels as wide as six feet, nine inches and as high as seven feet, six inches began in 1899

from the basement of a saloon at 165 West Madison Street run by Johnny Powers, another of the Gray Wolves.[37] By 1900, the promoters of IT&T had quietly obtained an amendment to their charter to allow them to distribute merchandise and mail, a legal change that allowed them to equip their tunnels with a freight railway. When an inspection by city officials in 1902 found that the company unilaterally had increased its tunnel dimensions to twelve feet, nine inches wide and fourteen feet high, a size that would accommodate railway passenger cars, the city ordered construction halted.[38] On April 26, 1902, a second inspection was conducted. This inspection took place partly because the city was considering building a six-track subway to carry streetcars beneath the downtown district and because the aldermen wanted to determine what effect the IT&T subway would have on it.[39] The charter for the subway system was amended again in 1903 to restrict tunnel sizes to the original dimensions and to ban passenger traffic.

When the project was completed, it operated with moderate success. IT&T's successor, the Illinois Tunnel Co., ran a sixty-mile, underground freight distribution system until it was sold for scrap by a bankruptcy court in 1959. The still-existing tunnel system in 1992 became the subject of controversy when a pile-drilling crew poked a hole in an abandoned tunnel beneath the north branch of the Chicago River and the resulting subterranean flood inundated most basements in the Loop, causing an estimated $800 million in damage.[40]

Despite various proposals in the early twentieth century to build passenger subways to reduce streetcar congestion on downtown streets and to relieve some of the pressure on the Loop elevated, Chicago was reluctant to finance from the public treasury what private enterprise was no longer capable of doing from the financial markets. Mindful of the poor fiscal performance of the elevated railway system, investors were reluctant to invest in more expensive transit schemes.

7
SUBURBAN TRANSIT

♦ The development of Chicago's suburbs was neither accidental nor evolutionary. Rather, the suburbs sprang up on the landscape with the advent of the iron horse. Antebellum railroad building connected scattered farm towns with industrial towns located along the Fox River and created more track mileage in the Chicago area than was available to any other city in the world. It was not long until real estate speculators and developers began to take advantage of this situation. It was a relatively simple matter for them to persuade the local managements of the new railroads to build new passenger stations amid farm fields, to stop a few trains there, and to offer anyone living in the newly built re-

sort hotels or summer cottages special discounted, or "commuted," fares to ride to and from work in Chicago. In some cases the railroads themselves developed the subdivisions.

These first suburbs, which developed quickly into year-round bedroom communities, typically were located in a belt four to eight miles from downtown Chicago, or the distance an average passenger train of the time could traverse in fifteen to thirty minutes.[1] As a practical matter, actual commuting time was probably double that of the train schedule, accounting for the necessity of getting to and from the depots at either end of the commute. Commuting beyond eight miles was considered too

The railroad was the principal cause of early suburban development. When the Cicero & Proviso Street Railway first began operation in the West Towns area, it served a rural population of only about forty-five hundred people. Here the train runs along Madison Street (at Oak Park Avenue) in Oak Park in the 1890s. (Krambles Archive) time-consuming, although some hardy souls endured long commutes to desirable suburban locations such as Geneva, located in the Fox Valley thirty-five miles to the west, and Glencoe, located twenty-two miles to the north.[2] Riverside was proposed for development along the Des Plaines River eleven miles west of downtown Chicago in 1868, but because it was considered too remote a site, it did not begin to grow significantly until the 1880s, by which time train speeds had increased.[3]

Within about one decade of the railroad suburbs' inception in the 1850s, suburbs were developing into year-round bedroom communities, and street railways began to creep outward from the city to the closest of the suburbs, to places such as Hyde Park, Lake View, and Ravenswood. Abetted by the great fire of 1871 that leveled much of Chicago, the railways accelerated the first migration to suburbia.[4] As the nearby railroad suburbs evolved into more densely populated streetcar suburbs, summer cottages began to give way to apartment buildings, forcing residents who wanted a place in the country to migrate farther out along the railroad lines.[5] Many of the streetcar suburbs, unable with their residential tax bases to support a growing population that demanded such urban services as paved streets, sewer, and water, were absorbed by Chicago before the end of the century.

By the time the street railways reached the suburbs, electric traction had made its appearance, resulting in the electrification of many of the suburban horsecar lines, which in turn resulted in faster and more frequent service and higher population densities as apartments began to appear alongside trolley lines.[6] Gradually the fringe of suburban development crept outward as far as ten miles from the Loop, and the mainline railroads slowly began abandoning the city market to the street railways to concentrate on the more distant suburbs. For the most part, the elevated railways were not extended to the suburbs until after the turn of the century.

By then, it was possible on the commuter trains to travel as many as twenty-five miles in less than one hour.[7] Farm towns that may have counted among their populations a handful of commuters before 1900 sprouted subdivisions and became railroad suburbs. In some cases, such as Riverside, entire new towns were platted along railroad lines. By 1913, when transportation engineer Bion J. Arnold made the first systematic survey of commuter railroad operations for a report on downtown depots, Chicago's commuter railroad traffic dwarfed its intercity passenger ridership by a considerable degree. The city's six stations on a daily basis handled 746 commuter trains pulling 3,208 cars that contained 123,188 passengers, contrasted to 591 intercity trains pulling 3,818 cars that carried 69,623 passengers.[8]

THE FIRST COMMUTER TRAINS

Neither the modern suburb nor the commuter railroad originated in Chicago. Modern suburban development can be traced to eighteenth-century London and to Brooklyn in 1816 in the United States, and while transportation historians debate whether the first commuter railroad was originally developed in Boston, Philadelphia, or New York, it is known that commuting by railroad was well established in Boston by the 1840s.[9] Despite undocumented evidence suggesting that some commuting existed on the Galena & Chicago Union Railroad after 1850, since it offered a high level of service within forty miles of Chicago, the Chicago roots of the phenomenon are traced either to July 1855, at Waukegan, located forty miles north of Chicago, or to July 1856, at Hyde Park, located about seven miles to the south.[10] At those times the Chicago & Milwaukee and Illinois Central Railroads, respectively, began operating accommodation trains, as they were known at the time, to handle local traffic. Although both services struggled in the early years, they were considered by the end of the century to be among the world's best commuter railroads. Other railroads in Chicago did not enter the commuter market until after the Civil War.

The Illinois Central probably holds the best claim on running the first commuter line in Chicago. From the inception its service was tailored solely to provide passenger travel between Chicago and an outlying area intended for development as a bedroom community of the city.[11] The I.C.'s first commuter train on July 21, 1856, inauspiciously operated empty in both directions for the nearly seven miles between the new wood-frame station located on what is today 53rd Street and I.C.'s terminal at Lake Street, the former site of Fort Dearborn.[12] Developer Paul Cornell had built his Hyde Park House resort on a three-hundred-acre site along Lake Michigan next to the Illinois Central tracks and persuaded the railroad to build a station nearby. He agreed to subsidize any deficits the service would incur. Unlike the regular passenger trains that made several scheduled stops to serve local riders, the *Hyde Park Special* made four daily round-trips between Cornell's town and the I.C.'s main terminal at Lake Street. The service had a difficult time during the Panic of 1857 and was almost abandoned, but the following year the railroad added the Woodlawn station at 63rd Street and the Kenwood station at 42nd Place.[13]

In the two months the *Special* operated in the summer of 1856, it carried almost 4,700 persons to Chicago and almost 5,600 persons to Hyde Park—figures equal to approximately 15 percent of the total ridership handled by the railroad's Chicago terminal during that period.[14] The following year, despite the financial difficulties of the railroad due to the panic, Hyde Park accounted for the greatest increase in ridership on the growing I.C. system, with 23,659 inbound passengers and 22,796 outbound passengers, or almost 43 percent of the travelers passing through the railroad's Chicago station in 1857.[15]

The Hyde Park service also established the precedent on Chicago railroads of discounted, or commuted, fares for regular riders. Commuted fares produced an average of almost five cents per boarding passenger in Hyde Park, the same fare as omnibuses in Chicago charged, versus an average of $1.31 for the railroad's five other outlying stations (Calumet, Thornton, Matteson, Richton, and Monee), which did not offer commuted fares.[16] The term "commutation" first appears in a footnote in the railroad's annual report for 1857 to designate the fare revenues from the Hyde Park station.[17] The noun "commuter" (to describe anyone who bought a ticket at a commuted fare) and the verb "commute" (to describe the act of traveling to and from work on a commuted fare) eventually came into use later in the nineteenth century.[18] Finally, in 1883 the term "suburban" entered the railroad's lexicon to describe its commutation service.[19]

Despite the financial problems of 1857, the Illinois Central set the standard for Chicago-area commuter railroads until after World War II, when the Chicago & North Western Railway finally eclipsed it. As the new suburbs grew in the second half of the nineteenth century, new stations were built and equipment was added to commuter service. Hyde Park, inhabited by about forty families in 1860, by 1880 was an incorporated village with a population of 15,724. It was no longer served by the *Special* but instead was on the route of thirty-six regular daily trains carrying 1.4 million passengers annually on suburban runs.

By the end of 1890, I.C. commuter ridership had quadrupled to 5.6 million. The height of its passenger load, however, did not occur until 1893, when, in addition to its regular suburban service that handled 11.3 million rides, the railroad carried an additional 8.8 million on special trains from Van Buren Street to the Columbian Exposition in Jackson Park.[20] (One of the engineers transferred to Chicago to drive shuttle trains during the fair was John Luther "Casey" Jones, who was killed in an accident seven years later in Vaughn, Mississippi, and was made a legend.) The

BURLINGTON NORTHERN RAILROAD

I.C.'s suburban division in 1893 extended all the way to Homewood, located twenty-seven miles south of the Loop, and included branches to South Chicago, opened in 1883; Blue Island, opened in 1893; and Addison, opened in 1893. With 133 coaches and 31 locomotives, the division was almost a railroad unto itself.[21]

The Chicago & North Western Railway, an amalgamation of three railroads (Galena & Chicago Union; Chicago, St. Paul & Fond du Lac; and Chicago & Milwaukee), in the nineteenth century operated the second largest commuter system in the Chicago area in terms of ridership but the largest in terms of trackage. The Galena, the oldest of the three predecessors, possibly carried occasional commuters before 1850.

The Chicago, Burlington & Quincy Railroad, which originally operated as the Aurora Branch Railroad over Galena Railroad tracks to Chicago beginning in 1850, built its own line to Chicago in 1864 and commenced commuter service in 1869.[22] The influence of the Burlington suburb of Riverside, however, was substantial, and in many ways it set the rules for suburban development for the next century. Landscape architect Frederick Law Olmsted, the creator of New York's Central Park, designed the community around the Des Plaines River, which provided Riverside's parklike setting, and the new Burlington depot, which became the community's nucleus. He also laid out generous lots, making them 100 feet wide and 225 feet long, and set homes back thirty feet from the streets.[23]

The Chicago, Rock Island & Pacific Railroad ran its first train on October 10, 1852, between Chicago and Joliet, located forty miles to the southwest. It did not get into the commuter business to any extent until 1869, when its subsidiary Blue Island Land and Building Co. acquired 1,500 acres southwest of Chicago and built a branch line specifically for anticipated commuter traffic between 99th Street and Blue Island. This line provided service to the developing suburbs of Washington Heights (now Beverly) and Morgan Park in the process.[24] The houses there sold for $3,000, and commutation fares were $60 per year or $15 to $17 for 100-ride tickets, an amount equal to 15 cents per ride.

The last of the major commuter railroads was the Chicago, Milwaukee, St. Paul & Pacific. It was originally a line to link Milwaukee with the Mississippi River, but it found it could not compete with other western lines that connected to the eastern railroads in Chicago. The line finally arrived in Chicago in 1872 and began commuter service to the northern suburbs within a few years.

THE ADVENTURES OF COMMUTING

Commuting could be an adventure in the early days of railroading. Service on the I.C., which entered downtown Chicago on a trestle built on land that was mounded above the water of the lake, was occasionally interrupted when storms battered the structure. Derailments were common, and wooden trains proved vulnerable to prairie fires and windstorms. A locomotive breakdown could result in delays of hours before the railroad could get a replacement to the scene. Winter snows were possibly the worst hazard to early commuters. A storm in 1855 stalled several trains for as many as sixteen days on the Aurora Branch, and the Chicago & Milwaukee was shut down for a week by snow the following year despite the efforts of a crew of two hundred men to dig out the trains along the line.[25] Later the same year another train became bogged in a drift near Rosehill, and the crew was forced to walk to downtown Chicago to telegraph for help for the passengers left back on the line.[26] As late as 1906, a weekend ice storm that coated the third rail shut down the Aurora, Elgin & Chicago (later Chicago, Aurora & Elgin), forcing passengers and crews to sleep overnight in the stalled cars.[27]

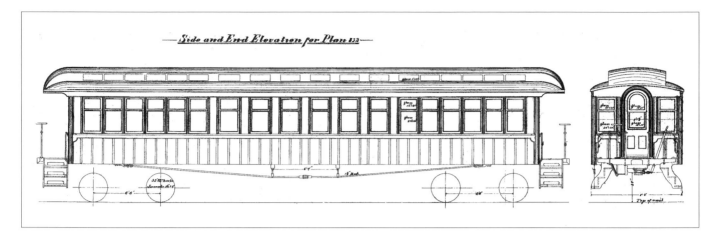

Side and End Elevation for Plan 132

The equipment on early commuter trains was usually rather spartan, far below the standards George Pullman maintained for his "Palace Car" fleet for intercity service. Indeed, until the end of the century cars and locomotives assigned to suburban service were often hand-me-downs from long-distance trains. By the time the Columbian Exposition was held in 1893, the Illinois Central had departed from that practice and was using rolling stock specifically designed for suburban service. Its suburban locomotives, typically smaller and somewhat slower than mainline engines, were known in the industry as "tank" type engines because they lacked tenders but carried coal bins and water tanks on the same frame as the engine.[28] Suburban coaches had fewer amenities but more seats than intercity coaches. For the Columbian Exposition shuttle service, the I.C. even had designed and built special high-utilization coaches with a row of doors on each side for quick loading and unloading. After the fair, the boxy cars were converted to freight operation.[29]

The typical I.C. suburban coach by the 1890s had evolved into a lightweight wooden car weighing fifteen tons (mainline day coaches weighed twenty-two tons). Lavatories were not considered necessary on short suburban runs on the I.C.; however, by 1893 a steam heating system had replaced the old coal or wood-fired stoves that roasted passengers sitting next to them but allowed people at the other end of the car to freeze. In summer, riders had to open windows to get a breeze, but

that made them vulnerable to smoke, sparks, and ash from the locomotive. Air cooling did not become a fixture on any railroad's suburban trains until the railroads converted to diesel power and modernized their suburban car fleets. The Burlington began modernizing their trains in 1950, but the I.C. did not begin this type of modernization until 1971. By the 1890s smoky kerosene lamps were replaced by petroleum-gas–fueled lamps that produced enough light for riders to read newspapers, and electric lights appeared in the 1920s. The I.C. cars of 1893 seated forty-eight passengers on standard rattan-covered coach seats in mid-car, with seats facing the aisle at either end to provide more room for people entering and leaving. Steel-frame, wooden coaches with side doors built for the I.C. suburban operation in 1903 seated one hundred people.[30]

Living along a railway could also be an adventure. The noise from steam locomotives was a transient problem, but the smoke and soot fallout from their stacks was omnipresent. The early street railways of suburbia ran on tracks laid for the most part on top of dirt thoroughfares. Although their electrification eliminated fly-ash emissions, the suburbs resorted to coating streets with oil to keep down the dust. Housewives along the lines complained that the oily residue somehow ended up in their homes, which then required frequent cleaning.[31]

Probably because of the substantial distances and low population densities of the areas they served, street railways had a

By 1890, the commuter railroads were buying coaches designed exclusively for suburban service, with few of the amenities found on intercity cars. This Pullman day coach was designed for the Illinois Central Railroad. (Pullman Inc.)

The streetcar line transformed Madison Street (shown above at Austin Avenue in 1947) into a commercial strip. (Krambles Archive)

(right) The trolleys were long gone by 1997, but their influence lingered in the form of commercial development lining Madison Street (at Oak Park Avenue). (Michael Brown)

mixed record of success in suburbia. They proved to be most successful in areas within a radius of about eight miles from downtown Chicago and least successful in outlying areas, despite the willingness of their operators to experiment with various types of mechanical traction equipment, including battery, steam, and electrically powered streetcars. Those suburban lines in areas annexed to Chicago ultimately became part of the Chicago system. Of the rest of the street railways, some failed before or shortly after commencing operations, although a few, principally the systems in Joliet, in the Fox River valley between Aurora and Elgin, and in the immediate western suburbs around Oak Park, survived by converting to bus operations beginning in the 1920s. A couple of suburban street railways prolonged their existence by transforming themselves into high-speed interurban railroads. Of the eight independent street railway systems founded in the suburbs, only one, the Chicago & West Towns Railway, which was centered in the near western suburbs around Oak Park, survived in its original form as late as the 1940s.[32]

The West Towns and Joliet systems are typical of the suburban street railways. The predecessors of West Towns were built as speculative ventures in a sparsely populated west suburban area that was already served by two commuter railroads and that would soon be served by two elevated railways as well. The Joliet Street Railway was built beginning in 1873 as an isolated mulecar line in that industrial satellite city and eventually became connected to a larger electric railway system.

The West Towns area (essentially Austin, Oak Park, Cicero, Berwyn, and Maywood) had a population of only about forty-five hundred people spread over approximately ten square miles when the Chicago & Western Dummy Railroad commenced service in late 1879. It failed in 1885 for lack of ridership, and the Chicago, Harlem & Batavia Railway, which by then was operating horsecars through the area, bought the dummy line in the resulting fire sale. It in turn was absorbed by the Wisconsin Central, a steam railroad, in 1887, and two rivals quickly appeared—the Cicero & Proviso Street Railway in 1891 and the Suburban Railroad in 1895.[33]

The operation of three street railways a few blocks apart through Oak Park, which had not yet even incorporated, was a little more than the market could bear. The Cicero & Proviso became part of Charles T. Yerkes's traction empire in 1894, probably to protect his Lake Street elevated line, and the Suburban Railroad followed in 1897, although it wound up in receivership in 1902 after Yerkes left town.[34] By 1913 it was obvious that the three railways, which by then had been through another round of reorganizations, had to share a marginal market. They consolidated into the Chicago & West Towns Railway, a 73.4-mile system.[35]

The transit situation in Joliet, which in 1900 had a population approaching thirty thousand people, was more akin to transit in cities such as Peoria, Bloomington, or Rockford than to that in the Chicago suburbs. The first two miles of mulecar service of the Joliet Street Car and Manufacturing Co. opened in 1874, and despite persistent red ink, the system was expanded to 12.5 miles by 1896. By then a rival had appeared in the form of the Joliet Electric Street Railway, which downstate traction magnate William McKinley acquired in 1896 and tried to convert into an interurban railroad as part of a network of such lines he was developing.[36] The Joliet system became part of the Chicago & Joliet interurban railway in 1901, operating trains on city streets in Chicago and Joliet and separate rights-of-way in the country. In 1915, it wound up in the hands of the Central Illinois Public Service Co., a principal creditor.[37]

THE GREAT CHICAGO ANNEXATION OF SUBURBIA

Although a handful of suburbs had incorporated prior to 1870 by special acts of

the legislature, the state's new constitution adopted that year provided the legal framework for the modern suburb. Two sections of the new constitution produced a substantial effect on local government in Illinois, one immediately and the other some years later. The first of these sections granted Chicago its own separate clause governing its municipal government and prohibiting the state legislature from chartering any new local government within its city limits. The clause also allowed Chicago to absorb any existing local government within its borders.[38]

Although it would not become obvious for years, another section of the constitution laid the groundwork for suburban government. By 1870, the state's rapid population growth had made it necessary to adopt a municipal code establishing an administrative process by which local communities could incorporate without going to the state legislature for a charter.[39] Until then, most of the rapidly growing suburbs were forced to incorporate as townships to gain the necessary powers to provide even minimal municipal services. Acting on the mandate of the new constitution, the legislature in 1872 approved a general incorporation law that not only made incorporation of cities easier but also created a whole new form of municipal government, the village.[40] By the end of 1872 there were five incorporated townships and five incorporated municipalities in Cook County outside Chicago's city limits. Of the municipalities, only Evanston could be considered a suburb: the rest were farm towns. The new form proved so popular that sixteen new suburbs were incorporated as villages by 1880 and an additional eleven were incorporated by 1890.

Soon after 1872 there were two types of suburbs—the transitional incorporated townships that for the most part were swallowed up by Chicago before the end of the century and the incorporated cities and villages that resisted Chicago's expansion in the next century. Prior to 1850, the township was responsible primarily for

bridges and roads, but after changes in state law it assumed many county functions and was allowed to incorporate. Townships quickly ran into financial difficulty trying to finance the necessary suburban development and often found annexation to Chicago the least expensive alternative. Hyde Park is a case in point. Beginning as a summer resort stop on the Illinois Central, Hyde Park by 1867 had grown to the point that it incorporated as a township. A dramatic growth spurt occurred, however, after the Chicago Fire of 1871—the population of 3,644 in 1870 jumped to 15,724 by 1880—and the township found that providing the infrastructure to support all that growth exceeded its taxing authority. A proposal to incorporate as a city was defeated in a referendum, and in 1889 Hyde Park annexed to Chicago.[41]

An amendment to state law in 1887 resolving some of the legal impediments to municipal mergers, including the method of dividing existing debt, was the cause of Hyde Park's annexation and the explosive growth of Chicago over the next few years. Chicago had added only twenty-five square miles of territory between 1837 and 1869, and by 1870 it had stopped growing in size despite the population explosion. In 1889, almost overnight the city annexed the townships of Hyde Park, Lake, Jefferson, and Lake View, and portions of Cicero. That represented an increase from 43 square miles to 168 square miles and the addition of 225,000 residents, pushing the city's population to over one million. The annexation of Washington Heights and West Roseland followed in 1890; Fernwood was annexed in 1891; West Ridge, Rogers Park, and Norwood Park were annexed in 1893; and Austin Township was annexed in 1899.

The annexations were widely perceived as a land grab, especially in surviving suburbs. The acquisition of so much underdeveloped territory, however, strained the financial resources of the city, causing it to lose interest in further expansion.[42] The mere perception of land grabbing by the

city, however, was sufficient to cause a rash of incorporations of other suburban communities hoping to avoid annexation: there were in total twenty-five incorporations between 1889 and the end of the century. By 1900, Cook County had sixty-nine incorporated suburbs, and the five outlying counties (Lake, McHenry, Kane, Du Page, and Will) had fifty-two.[43] Most were railroad communities. An additional eight new suburbs were incorporated in the first six years of the new century.

The principal suburban areas bordering the territory newly annexed to Chicago—Oak Park and Cicero on the west and Evanston on the north—illustrate what happened. Between 1889 and 1901 Oak Park assured its own independence by agreeing to allow the annexation to Chicago of Austin, its neighbor to the east, and by disannexing from Cicero Township to the south. By forming its own township and later incorporating as a village it effectively precluded annexation to Chicago.[44]

Evanston's campaign to remain independent, which lasted from 1874 to 1914, involved the annexation of two smaller neighbors, North Evanston in 1874 and South Evanston in 1892, and the ceding of a third community called Germania to Chicago in 1914. Residents believed that the construction of apartment buildings in Germania would result in a large constituency favoring a merger with Chicago. The issue of such annexation had been posed to voters in Evanston in an 1894 referendum but was rejected by a 2,155 to 642 vote.

Although statistical comparisons of the growth of Chicago and its suburbs probably are not valid before the turn of the century because of the city's annexations of 1889 and 1893, it is safe to say that Chicago's growth generally exceeded that of its suburbs until 1920. Afterward, the suburbs grew faster (see Table A2). Between 1890 and 1920 the city added an average of more than 70,000 residents per year and the portions of the six metropolitan counties

Chicago area commuter railroads relied on the Pacific class 4-6-2 until the introduction of diesels after World War II.

outside the city limits grew by an average of just under 16,000 persons annually. In the 1920s, the suburbs grew by an average of about 31,000 persons per year and the city by only 15,500 annually. The bulk of that suburban growth was in the corridors served by steam, street, or interurban railways. For the three decades after 1900, suburban municipalities collectively grew at an average of more than 23,200 residents per year—almost 19,000 of whom settled in the towns that lined the railroad tracks.[45]

Because so much of the suburban transit system, principally the commuter railroads, was regulated early in its existence by the state, most of the transit companies there were not involved in the type of political shenanigans that were imposed on the Chicago transit. Because most of the railroads were large interstate corporations, they were capable of defending themselves against activist politicians from individual suburbs. The state beginning in 1871 had imposed some economic regulation on the railroads by means of its Board of Railroad and Warehouse Commissioners, although oversight by the Interstate Commerce Commission created by Congress in 1887 eventually superseded much of the state regulation.[46] The suburban street railways were subject to some local political pressures, especially in the industrial satellite cities; however, the delicate financial condition of the transit systems precluded the kind of shakedowns that were rampant in Chicago.[47]

Excluding Chicago and the areas it eventually annexed, in 1860 there were nine incorporated municipalities—in reality, satellite industrial towns and a few farm communities—with a combined population of 21,642. These municipalities collected along the steam railroad lines radiating across the sparsely populated prairies of the six Illinois counties that eventually became suburbia. By 1900, those rail lines served 56 suburbs, with a combined population of 198,108, or 51.3 percent of the total population of the six suburban counties.[48] By 1930, the railroad suburbs had increased in number to 87, with a population of 761,751, or 70.4 percent of the total suburban population.[49]

Nonrailroad suburbs did not fare as well. The Illinois-Michigan Canal town of Lockport, which was also served by the Chicago & Alton Railroad, though not with any significant commuter service, declined in population from 2,822 to 2,659 between 1860 and 1900. In 1930, it reported a population of only 3,382. An exception was the city of St. Charles in Kane County, which was served circuitously by an electric interurban line after 1909 and for a time had limited commuter service on the Chicago Great Western Railroad early in the century. The population there increased from 2,675 to 5,377 between 1900 and 1930.

Population growth was relatively consistent along all the steam railroads in the nineteenth century. Much of the residential development within the city of Chicago occurred along the Illinois Central and Chicago, Rock Island & Pacific Railroads. The rather late arrival of the Milwaukee Road in 1872 may have contributed to the slow residential growth along its northwest suburban lines, and the construction of two electric interurban railways in the western and northern suburbs gave the people living there substantially better transportation service than other areas, resulting in a spurt in development after 1900 (see Table A3). Suburban growth followed the railroads whether they arrived late or early.

Part Two

THE TWENTIETH CENTURY

The automobile has been blamed for the deterioration of the Chicago transit system, which was considered at the turn of the century to be one of the most comprehensive in the nation. No Chicagoan, transit managers boasted, lived more than one-quarter of a mile from an L or a streetcar line. Moreover, the city's famous Loop was a model of urban transportation planning. Ridership on all systems was climbing; the major complaint about transit in Chicago was that it was too crowded.

Abruptly, at the onset of the Great Depression, the system collapsed into bankruptcy. The public and politicians of the time were stunned. It was widely believed that the arrival of the automobile had doomed transit. This is an assumption that has persisted. The evidence in Chicago, however, suggests that the city's transit system was in financial trouble long before the automobile became a competitor in the 1920s: the street railways were effectively strangled by regulations that compounded their own fiscal sins; the elevated railways did not provide a sufficient return on their substantial capital investment; and each independently owned system strongly competed for riders. The automobile, when it finally appeared, made the reorganization of the mass-transit system as a private enterprise impossible.

A collateral theory advanced in Congress a few years ago led one to believe that General Motors had directed a conspiracy in the 1930s to destroy the interurban and suburban street railway systems across the country so it could sell motor buses. In-

stead, evidence in Chicago suggests those systems were in financial trouble because they were built in thinly populated markets incapable of supporting them. The conversion to buses began as a cost-cutting measure long before General Motors was a factor, and buses never made much of an impact in suburban transit because of the increasingly dominant automobile.

Just as horses were relegated to the glue factory with the advent of the steam engine and mechanical traction, the steam engine in turn was replaced by the more efficient internal combustion engine that made powered road vehicles possible. The new vehicles abetted America's growing appetite for personal mobility. The automobile, criticized as the vehicle that destroyed mass transit in America, in reality itself became a vehicle of mass transit, replacing common carriers with a system of personal mobility. The twentieth century is therefore rightfully called the Auto Age.

The transit systems eventually adapted the internal combustion engine to their own needs. The motor bus replaced the electric streetcar, but buses became the wheels of last resort and never made much of an impact on transportation markets. The railroads replaced their steam locomotives with diesels and, with the modernization of the commuter railroad after World War II and bilevel commuter cars, were able to survive the onslaught from the automobile and in some cases even to prosper. The electric interurban railways that sprang up around the turn of the century were not so fortunate: all but one

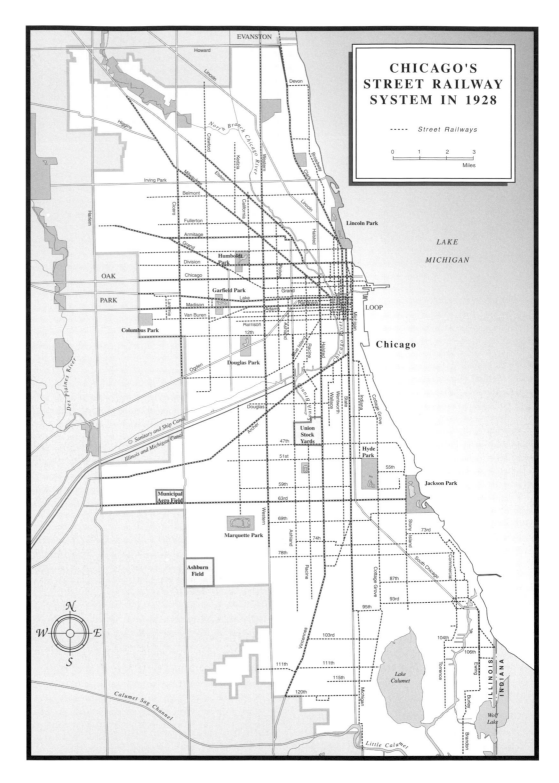

CHICAGO'S
STREET RAILWAY
SYSTEM IN 1928

- - - - Street Railways

0 1 2 3
Miles

succumbed to competition from both the auto and commuter railroads.

The defining phenomenon of twentieth-century transportation was decentralization, which superseded the suburbanization that had occurred in the nineteenth century along rail lines. Automobility made decentralization possible by freeing the developer from the railways, allowing the evolution of regional malls, office campuses, and residential subdivisions far removed from transit routes. Decentralization was also responsible for introducing to the vernacular such terms as "bumper-to-bumper" and "gridlock." The new suburban sprawl was impossible for mass transit to serve effectively, so the metropolitan transit systems concentrated on the single market they could serve successfully—the Loop commute.

8

REGULATION AND COMPETITION

♦ Private enterprise in the half century prior to 1900 had given Chicago a mass-transit system that for the standards of the time was among the best in the world. The street railway network claimed to be the largest on the planet, and the elevated system with its central Loop may well have been the most efficient. Both systems, which were still growing at the end of the century, continued to do so for another three decades, although at a gradually decreasing pace. There was no competition on the horizon: the automobile and the motor bus did not become significant factors in commuting until the 1920s, yet there were indications that Chicago's mass-transit system even before 1900 was under increasing financial stress. Over the next three decades the fiscal situation for the street and elevated railways deteriorated until both collapsed into bankruptcy. Because they were private enterprises, they could not recover.

Managers of steam railroads over most of the world were aware before 1900 that the intercity transportation of passengers was a dubious business venture justifiable only because of the substantial cross subsidy from freight operations. Urban traction systems were saddled with high capital

A highly competitive industry, Chicago's mass-transit system early on suffered financially under heavy regulation. In 1893, however, the Chicago City Railway set records serving the Columbian Exposition. (Krambles Archives)

expenses but little or no freight revenues with which to amortize at least part of the cost of such things as rights-of-way, track, and structures. Officials of the bond markets, on which urban transit systems relied for capital after the public soured on transit stocks, questioned the tenure of the nickel fare long before the public, politicians, and regulators did. Of the $62.7 million in revenues reported by the Chicago City Railway Co. in 1930, $61.95 million came from the fare box.[1] The elevated railway system, which had some minimal transfer freight service, in 1930 got $18.4 million from the fare box and $1.26 million from other sources, including freight.[2]

The elevated railways had been struggling financially since their inception, but after 1900 the theretofore continuously profitable street railway system began to have problems as well. Yerkes's streetcar network that served about 60 percent of the city wound up in receivership and reorganization shortly after he sold it.[3] As their financial situation continued to deteriorate, the street railways responded, as did most companies in similar straits, by deferring capital programs, especially by delaying the purchase of new cars and the extension of lines. Even as street railway ridership tripled, the car acquisition program deteriorated from an average of 207.6 cars per year in the period between 1900 and 1909, to about half that level in the subsequent 10 years, to only 66.4 cars per year in the 1920s.[4] Annual street railway ridership peaked at almost 900 million in 1929, up from 373.9 million in 1906.[5]

The financial practices common in the nineteenth century, especially overcapitalization, high-profit taking, and failure to amortize debt, certainly contributed to the fiscal troubles of traction companies in the early twentieth century, but their deterioration also coincided with the system of economic regulation imposed on them by state and city government. Such regulatory mechanisms as twenty-year franchises and capped fares made it impossible for street railways to cope with inflation, which doubled costs within the span of a few years, or competition. The only way the companies could cope with shrinking profit margins was to increase ridership. The post–World War I highway-building programs that made free roads available to everyone, however, brought forth new competitors—the automobile and the motor bus. Although the mass-transit system, including street and elevated railways and buses, more than doubled ridership to 1,165,654,546 rides per annum between 1900 and 1929, the number of cars registered in Chicago increased from less than 10,000 in 1910 (one car for each 219.3 residents) to 401,669 at the onset of the Great Depression (one vehicle for each 8.4 residents). Bus ridership, which was almost nonexistent even as late as 1915, by 1929 accounted for almost 6 percent of the total mass-transit ridership.[6]

Regulation became a problem for the street railways long before buses appeared. As their franchises neared expiration in 1903, the City Council's agenda in the impending negotiations was to continue the long-standing, five-cent cap on fares for another twenty years as well as to impose new taxes and service conditions. In an effort to avert the bitter controversy he assumed would inevitably accompany renegotiation of the franchises in 1903, Yerkes tried to get the state to regulate traction. A Yerkes-backed bill introduced in the state legislature in 1897 by Senator John Humphrey, a Republican from southwest suburban Orland Township, would have had the state establish a street and elevated railway commission.[7] The proposed commission, made up of three members appointed by the governor, would have required annual financial reports; regulated operations, safety, and fares, except where established by local ordinance; determined the validity of property-owner consent petitions; and controlled the issuance of franchises for new lines and extensions.[8]

The idea was not novel. In 1871 Illinois had been the first state to impose economic regulation on steam railroads. Although the powers of the Illinois Railroad and Warehouse Commission had been largely superseded in 1887 by the Interstate Commerce Commission, it remained in existence, and there had been several proposals over the years to expand its authority to traction systems.[9] The Humphrey Bill, however, evoked immediate outrage among the reformers and newspapers. The provisions for the state commission were dropped in the legislative process, and the compromise that ultimately emerged from the General Assembly as the Allen Bill would have granted fifty-year franchises. The public outcry was loud enough that the legislature repealed the Allen Bill at its first opportunity.

Chicago took up the cause of regulation by attempting to incorporate more controls in its franchise extensions of 1903. The City Council in 1899 had created a seven-member Street Railway Commission to study the situation. The following year it reported that any regulation of street railways should be controlled by a special committee of the City Council, not a special agency.[10] The following year, the City Council created its Committee on Local Transportation, which, though it could not actually regulate the traction companies, could make recommendations to do so to the full council. As a practical matter, the council's regulatory powers, as they had been from the beginning, were confined to what could be negotiated into agreements with the traction companies every twenty years when their franchises expired.

The exercise of even those limited powers was delayed for four years after the franchises expired in 1903. While the city wrestled with the issue of whether it would buy the systems outright, the old Yerkes system went through a bankruptcy reorganization, and the Chicago City Railway Co. sought a court ruling favorable to its position that it did not need a franchise extension because the controversial ninety-nine-year law passed in 1865 already extended its franchise for that duration. The case went to the U.S. Supreme Court,

which ruled on February 16, 1906, that the twenty-year franchises were valid.[11] Six months later the Illinois Appellate Court complicated the matter by ruling that the city's plan to sell $75 million in certificates to buy the street railway system was unconstitutional.[12] Both sides were finally willing to negotiate a compromise.

THE TRACTION SETTLEMENT ORDINANCES

The result of the court ruling was another set of twenty-year franchise extensions, known collectively as the Traction Settlement Ordinances, which were the most comprehensive in the city's history and for a time were considered a model for the nation.[13] They were approved by the City Council on February 11, 1907, and ratified by the voters two months later in a referendum.[14] Not surprising, the extensions continued fare caps for an additional twenty years, but they also established a Board of Supervising Engineers (one member appointed by the city, another by the traction companies) to review transit projects. For the first time in the city's history, at least some regulation of the transit system was placed in the hands of professional municipal administrators.

Financial matters, however, were left to the franchise contracts, not to the board. The Settlement Ordinances imposed an early form of income tax when the companies agreed to give Chicago 55 percent of their annual "net receipts," or profits.[15] The ordinances also mandated that the street railways contribute $5 million to a fund to finance proposed subways, stipulated that the traction companies set aside 6 percent of their revenues each year for maintenance and 8 percent for renewal and depreciation, and required that the streetcar companies build up to four miles of line extensions (eight miles, if the line was a single track) every year.[16]

One of the most important provisions in the compromise between the city and the companies was the creation of a curious financial instrument, an escrow account called the "Traction Fund." The street railways agreed to contribute 5 percent of their capital accounts to the fund so that a financial reserve might accumulate to enable the city eventually to buy them out. This innovative pay-in-advance mechanism to finance traction acquisitions eventually became a victim of the deteriorating financial condition of the street railways. The $40 million it yielded was diverted in 1939 as the city's share of the construction costs of the subways beneath State and Dearborn Streets. The Settlement Ordinances also established the base purchase prices at $21 million for the Chicago City Railway Co., which served the South Side, and $29 million for the Chicago Railways Co., which served most of the remainder of the city.[17] Finally, they stipulated a number of service changes aimed at making life easier for the commuting public, including the through-routing of cars between railways to eliminate the necessity of transfers on certain routes, free transfers to riders within a five-square-mile area around the central business district, and the addition of night service.

The financial effect of all the regulations in the Settlement Ordinances was substantial. Between 1907 and 1930 (by which time Chicago's entire street railway system was in bankruptcy), the traction companies paid more than $129.1 million in various taxes and services to the city, including $42.5 million in general taxes, $46.8 million as the city's 55 percent share of operating profits, $17.8 million for street paving, $12.8 million for right-of-way cleaning, $7.5 million for paving maintainance, and $1.9 million for track removal to allow installation of sewers.[18] The street railways under the 1883 franchise extensions were able to produce profits averaging 28.8 percent of revenues on the South Side, 26.4 percent on the North Side, and 18.5 percent on the West Side.[19] Under the Settlement Ordinances, those profit margins were cut to about 15 percent, a sum that was split between the city (55 percent) and the companies (45 percent). After World War I,

when the state Public Utilities Commission began to regulate fares and inflation became a factor in costs, the profit margins were reduced to just over 7 percent, of which sum the city still kept 55 percent.[20]

The next regulatory effort by the city culminated in 1913 with the passage of the Unification Ordinances. Since the Street Railway Commission report in 1900, Chicago had been attempting to finish the work Yerkes had begun and to consolidate its four remaining streetcar companies and four elevated companies into a single transit company. Negotiations began in earnest in 1911, but they immediately broke down when the elevated companies, which already had fifty-year franchises, understandably refused to accept the twenty-year franchise the city offered.[21]

City officials continued to apply pressure, especially to the street railways, and on May 7, 1913, they submitted their own plan for unification to the Committee on Local Transportation. The plan proposed that instead of merging the separate traction corporations, which had substantially differing debt loads, a new company be established to consolidate their operations. The City Council agreed with the concept and on November 13, 1913, approved an ordinance allowing just such a synoecism.[22] This consolidation enabled the corporate boards of the street railways together to create the Chicago Surface Lines (CSL). Although the operating consolidation made some substantial improvements possible—wider transfer privileges to the public and savings to the companies, which now jointly ordered equipment—it had one major drawback. The relative health of the City Railway on the South Side frequently masked the continuing financial problems of the Chicago Railways Co., the successor to the old Yerkes systems on the North and West Sides that accounted for about 60 percent of Chicago's street railway system.[23]

Another problem the Unification Ordinances failed to resolve was the five-cent fare cap. Within four years of its creation,

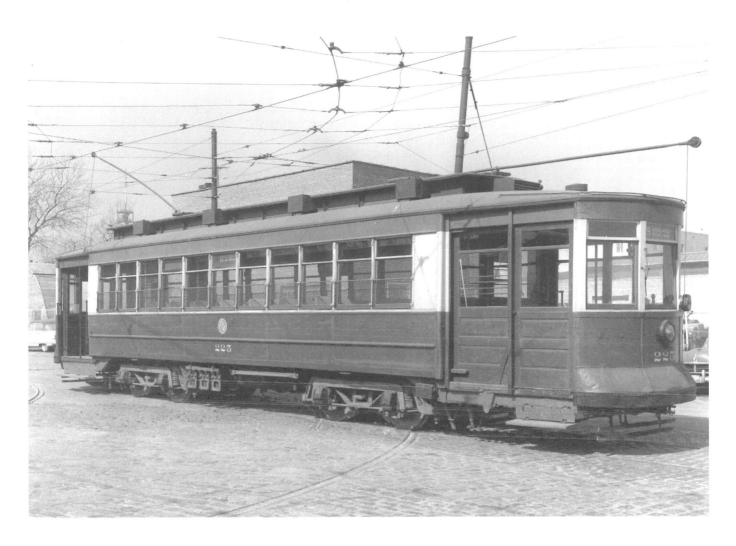

the CSL was being bled white by wartime inflation that drove up costs. "Inflation" was a word that began to creep into the transportation lexicon even before the turn of the century; it was also a relatively new phenomenon that neither the populace nor the government fully understood.[24] The consumer price index in Chicago increased substantially in the period from 1914 to 1920, from 42.7 to 85.0.[25] Although the CSL's constituent companies collectively remained profitable until just before the depression, after World War I their profit margins were insufficient to support the service expansion and line extensions mandated by the Settlement Ordinances of 1907.

Consolidated operating profits for the CSL in 1915, its first full year of operation, were $12.1 million on revenues of $31.7 million, a healthy railroad operating ratio (expenses to revenue) of 62.2 percent.

Within six years, however, that ratio had climbed to 75.6 percent, with an operating profit of only $10.7 million on revenues of $43.96 million.[26] By 1926, the year the CSL incurred the first of its constituent companies' bankruptcies, the company reported consolidated operating profits of only $12.2 million—about the same as 1915—on revenues of $58.8 million. That gave the system an operating ratio of 79.3 percent, exceedingly high considering the bonded indebtedness of the subsumed companies.[27]

The annual financial reports of both the CSL and Board of Supervising Engineers, however, failed to show the heavy debt service load that was dragging down the underlying four traction companies. The high-debt Chicago Railways Co. was especially vulnerable. In 1925, for example, it ostensibly got $6.9 million as its share of

The use of swiveling trucks mounting four wheels each in standard railroad practice enabled a 49-foot-long streetcar, such as this car built by Pullman in 1908, to negotiate sharp turns at intersections. This 26.7-ton car seated 40 riders.

(Chicago Transit Authority)

the CSL's $11.5 million operating profit. From that amount, however, the Chicago Railways Co. paid the city $1,097,195 as its 55 percent share of operating profits; $2,784,700 as interest on its first mortgage bonds; and $1,711,221 as interest on consolidated bonds. Assorted other interest payments, taxes, and corporate expenses left the company with a net income, or actual profit, of only $777,173.[28]

THE STATE STEPS IN

Economic regulation was strangling Chicago's street railway system. Despite the fact that the financial problems of the U.S. traction industry were serious enough in 1919 to cause the appointment of the Federal Electric Railways Commission to study the situation,[29] the governments of both Chicago and Illinois resisted fare increases. After Yerkes's abortive 1897 attempt to induce the General Assembly to create a street and elevated railway commission, the General Assembly did not revisit the subject until 1913. By then, Samuel Insull, the head of Commonwealth Edison Company, who as early as 1898 advocated the public regulation of electric utilities and after 1911 had a substantial financial stake in the Chicago elevated lines, induced the legislature to create the Illinois Public Utilities Commission.[30] The law gave the new agency the power to regulate fares, superseding the municipal franchise extensions of 1907 that had held fares at five cents. Much of the impetus for the bill came from various utilities concerned about similar treatment in the event they failed to get some sort of mechanism to regulate rates. They preferred regulation by an independent state agency over control by the Chicago City Council.

The Illinois Public Utilities Commission in the first six years of its existence made no attempt to meddle with the fare cap, though it did so later, when the Chicago Railways Co. in 1919 got a favorable ruling from the Illinois Supreme Court that the commission's enacting legislation took precedence over the Settlement Ordinances.[31] With fares capped, the effect of wage inflation was devastating to the CSL system, where 80 percent of operating costs were attributable to manpower. Although ridership in the five-year period between 1915 and 1919 increased 17.7 percent, the additional $5.6 million per year in revenue that it generated was insufficient to offset the 103 percent increase in wages that over the same time span added $14.6 million to annual operating expenses. The maximum wage rate for a Chicago motorman in 1914 was thirty-two cents per hour, but by the end of 1918 it was forty-eight cents per hour—an increase of 50 percent during the war. It continued to climb to sixty-five cents per hour in 1919 following a strike by transit workers, and to 80 cents in 1920 before decreasing somewhat during the 1920s.[32]

The seven-and-a-half-year struggle by the traction companies to obtain a fare increase following World War I was a classic conflict between the rights of regulated utilities to earn a fair return on investment and the pressures that the political system placed on the independent regulatory agency. The streetcar lines first filed a petition for a fare increase to seven cents on November 21, 1918, but the Public Utilities Commission denied it the following April 25. Four months later the traction companies filed for an immediate fare increase to seven cents to meet increased wage costs. The commission granted the request on August 6, 1919—four days after the petition was filed—but did not make it effective until February 1, 1920.[33] That precipitated the inevitable court fight with the City of Chicago, which first unsuccessfully challenged the increase in the Sangamon County (Springfield) Circuit Court, later in the Cook County Circuit Court, and finally in the Illinois Supreme Court.[34]

The state commission, meanwhile, held public hearings on the traction company petitions and afterward reduced fares to six cents. Then on June 19, 1920, it ordered the fares temporarily raised to eight cents;

on November 5, 1920—almost two years after the fare increases were first requested—it made them permanent. The ensuing furor caused the state legislature in 1921 to abolish the Public Utilities Commission, replacing it with the Illinois Commerce Commission (ICC), a regulatory body with essentially the same powers. Samuel Insull, by then the owner of the elevated railway system as well as the electric company, claimed to have engineered the switch in a private meeting with Mayor William Hale Thompson, state democratic chairman Roger Sullivan, one of the City Council boodlers, and various political and legislative leaders in an effort to defuse the public pressure on politicians by creating the illusion that the regulatory system was being reformed.[35]

Thompson, who adopted a public stance in opposition to the fare increases, petitioned the new commerce commission to reopen the fare case. Finally, on November 23, 1921, after hearing 3,700 pages of testimony, the commission ordered the Chicago Surface Lines to reduce fares to five cents. In response, the traction company resorted to the federal courts. There a three-judge panel on January 9, 1922, reversed the ICC decision and reinstated the eight-cent fare. When the ICC re-opened the case and set the fare at six cents, the Chicago Surface Lines successfully went back to federal court for a temporary restraining order. The court then appointed a master at chancery to examine the voluminous record of the case. He reported back four years later that the ICC's six-cent fare was confiscatory, and on May 19, 1926—seven and a half years after the case was commenced—the court concurred in the master's recommendation, and fares were set at seven cents.[36]

Unfortunately, the court's final decision occurred only seven months before the Chicago Railways Co. was forced to file for bankruptcy. Despite the fact that it had twice before been in the hands of receivers, its bankruptcy on December 15, 1926, came as a surprise to the political community, the press, and the public.[37] While a suit by Westinghouse Electric and Manufacturing Co. for a bill involving only $67,075 precipitated the bankruptcy, the real issue was a payment of $103.2 million in bonds and interest that was due on February 1, 1927, the same day the Chicago Railways Co. franchise with the city expired. Yerkes's legacy was still being felt a quarter of a century after he sold out and left Chicago and more than two decades after his death.

The earliest rapid-transit cars were wooden and required bracing underneath the car to keep the floor from sagging. Pullman designed this car for Yerkes's Northwestern L in 1898. (Pullman Inc.)

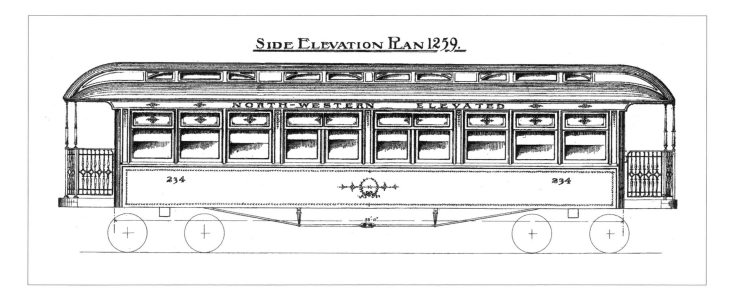

SIDE ELEVATION PLAN 1259.

NORTH-WESTERN ELEVATED

234   234

In 1899 Yerkes's Chicago Union Traction Co. was incorporated to absorb the West and North Sides streetcar systems. Capitalized at $32 million, its only assets consisted of the $5.2 million of Yerkes's already watered stock, which represented a minority interest in the North Chicago and West Division street railways that were then leased to the new company. The Union Traction Co. quickly issued $12 million in preferred stock and $20 million in common stock to various investors, including the Widener-Elkins syndicate in Philadelphia, and then used some of the proceeds to buy out Yerkes's stock interest in the two subsidiaries. A study showed that the West Division was in a precarious condition with assets of $20.7 million and liabilities of nearly $41.7 million and that the North Chicago system had assets of $17.3 million and liabilities of $23.7 million as of December 31, 1897.[38]

The Union Traction Co. suspended dividends after its first year of existence and filed for receivership on April 22, 1903, just before its franchise expired. Reorganized in 1907 as the Chicago Railways Co., it was forced into receivership again in 1910 when holders of the bonds in one of the predecessor companies won $1.3 million in judgements against it. The effect of that liability was to delay the Chicago Railways Co. from issuing new bonds to complete the improvements and extensions required by the Settlement Ordinances of 1907. Once that dispute was settled by transferring some suburban lines to the creditors, the company was finally able to sell $80.7 million in bonds to comply with the Settlement Ordinances.[39] That debt load, however, coupled with wartime inflation and the cap on fares, proved to be a crushing burden that after 1918 forced the Chicago Railways Co. to stop paying dividends on its common stock.[40]

The inevitable bankruptcy of the Chicago Railways Co. came three years before the stock market crash of 1929. The ensuing depression ultimately claimed the rest of Chicago's transit system. The deepening depression finally took its toll on the South Side's Chicago City Railway Co. on July 7, 1930, when creditors forced it and two smaller streetcar lines into bankruptcy. At the time, Chicago was still trying to negotiate yet another franchise extension with its street railways.

THE BATTLE FOR THE STREETS

One decade before the bankruptcies, a new competitor appeared on the streets of Chicago to challenge the traction monopoly—the motor bus. The elevated railways in the 1890s had cut into some street railway markets, and buses began to do the same on a limited scale in the 1920s. The earliest buses appeared principally on park boulevards, since the various local park districts granted franchises to bus lines but not to street railways. Chicago Motor Bus Co. began operating on a 9.5-mile route on Sheridan Road in 1917 with double-deck buses. The Chicago Stage Co. offered similar service beginning the next year on the South Side. In 1920, Depot Motor Bus Lines began a shuttle service between Union Station and State Street in the Loop.[41] In the next two years the bus companies merged into Chicago Motor Coach Company, which specialized in routes along the lakeshore.[42] The merger made it the second-largest urban bus company in the nation. Executives of the Chicago Surface Lines, the dominant public transit company in the city in 1917 with an annual ridership of 700 million (contrasted to only 3 million passengers on the buses), did not consider the parks' early arrangement with the bus companies as a threat to their ridership.[43] When the bus companies consolidated, Chicago Motor Coach tried to expand into traditional streetcar territory, and the CSL decided to defend its turf.

The street railway had a formidable opponent in the motor coach. The founder of the Chicago Motor Coach Company was John D. Hertz, the man whose name became synonymous with the car rental busi-

ness though he also owned companies that operated and built taxicabs and buses. Hertz (1879–1961), a native of Austria, was brought to Chicago at an early age, ran away from home after completing only the fifth grade, drifted to a waif's home, and supported himself with a $2.50-per-week job as a newspaper copyboy. He then tried driving a truck and, surprisingly, for someone who had a reputation for being frail, took up boxing, which led to a sports writer's job at the *Chicago Record*. When he lost his job because that paper merged with another in 1904, he began selling cars. He was twenty-six years old and had never been in an auto, but he was successful enough as a salesman that a few years later he had sufficient resources to buy a quarter interest for $2,000 in Walden W. Shaw's financially troubled auto agency.

Hertz effectively took control of the company and turned it around within a year. He began to look for a way to get rid of all the used cars he was taking as trade-ins, which led to the formation of a taxicab company that eventually dwarfed the auto dealership. He discovered from a study that yellow was the most visible color at a great

distance, so he painted his taxis that color and named his firm Yellow Cab Co. to match. In 1915 Hertz began manufacturing his own vehicles for taxicab service to eliminate problems encountered in commercially available autos.[44] During this time he also developed a telephone dispatch system for drivers by placing pole-mounted telephones at cab stands around the city.

In 1922 Hertz branched into bus manufacture, which led to the acquisition of Chicago Motor Coach as an outlet for his new buses. In 1924 he not only began the car rental business as an outlet for cars he was manufacturing but he also formed the Omnibus Corporation with a substantial capitalization of $25 million as an amalgamation of Chicago Motor Coach and New York's Fifth Avenue Motor Coach Corporation. His stated intention was to expand those systems by providing bus service as extensions of trolley car routes,[45] a policy that caused him to run afoul of the CSL. The following year Hertz abruptly sold off everything except the Omnibus Corporation and aggressively began a campaign to expand his transit bus system by adding new bus routes in territory where the

By 1925, the Parmelee Company had replaced its omnibuses that served Union Station with motor buses. The old Union Station is in the center and the new one is on the right. (Krambles Archive)

CSL's underlying companies held franchises but had not yet laid tracks.[46]

On the other side of the battle for Chicago's streets was a member of Chicago's establishment, CSL chairman Henry A. Blair (1852–1932). Blair's Merchants National Bank (later known as the Corn Exchange National Bank) and Blair & Company investment firm were major creditors of Yerkes's traction empire when it filed for bankruptcy in 1903. As a result, Blair ended up as the court-appointed receiver. While he had spent about ten years running the family cattle ranch in Wyoming after ill health forced him to quit his father's bank, he was back in Chicago as a vice president of Merchants National Bank in 1898 when Yerkes talked him into lending him $4.5 million from his Blair & Company investment firm so that the faltering Northwestern Elevated could complete its construction. Two years later, the investment company bought out Yerkes's remaining interest in the Loop, the Northwestern, and the Lake Ls for $5 million.[47]

Blair spent years sorting out the mess left by Yerkes. In the process he negotiated his traction empire deeper into a regulatory bind by agreeing to conditions sought by the city in the Settlement Ordinances of 1907 and in the Unification Ordinances of 1914. In an attempt to obtain financing for a consolidation of the city's elevated companies, Blair lost control of them in 1914 to Samuel Insull, on whose Commonwealth Edison Company board he also served. As a result of the Unification Ordinances, in 1914 Blair became chairman of the newly consolidated Chicago Surface Lines, as well as president of Chicago Railways Co., the former Yerkes street railway system.

By 1925, when Hertz attempted to invade Blair's streetcar territory, the Chicago Railways Co. was once again slipping toward bankruptcy. The Chicago Surface Lines, however, had sufficient resources to put up a fight. Chicago Motor Coach from its inception conducted a well-financed and aggressive, albeit unsuccessful, campaign. The complex legal battle that ensued in 1925 over whether Hertz's bus company could operate in CSL territory on the Northwest Side, even in areas where the CSL held exclusive franchises but offered no streetcar service, eventually involved the city, the Illinois Commerce Commission, and the courts. After three hearings before the Illinois Supreme Court, the ICC in 1930 finally awarded the bulk of the routes to the CSL, which had to buy buses to operate them.[48] By then, the Chicago Railways Co. was already in bankruptcy, and the CSL's resources were so stretched that it had only been able to add thirteen miles of track between 1920 and 1929.[49]

The city's independently owned elevated railway system by this time was also again in serious financial trouble, although the relative financial might of its controlling utilities empire concealed the extent of the problem. When Samuel Insull's overextended holding company collapsed during the Great Depression, there was nothing left to save a railroad that had never been more than marginally profitable.

9

THE LIMITATIONS OF PRIVATE ENTERPRISE

◆ Chicago's elevated railway system proved to be beyond the capacity of private enterprise to finance it. The yield from hauling masses of passengers twice per day on relatively short trips in a market diluted by competition simply did not generate the necessary money to operate the system. Despite huge gains in ridership—from 131,958,605 passengers carried in 1906 to 228,812,766 in 1926, when ridership peaked—Chicago's Ls never captured more than one-quarter of the mass-transit market. Moreover, they cost ten times as much as street railways to build, and they were required to purchase their own rights-of-way. By 1896 construction of an electric street railway line cost an estimated $65,040 per mile, while construction of the South Side L cost $700,000 per mile and construction of the Metropolitan line cost almost $970,000 per mile, about one third of which went toward land acquisition.[1]

The rash of bankruptcies of elevated railways in their first twenty years of existence caused investors to shift their money to unregulated industries with a better return on investment.[2] As a result, the L's managers found themselves starved for capital to expand and to modernize the line just as the automobile appeared on the scene as a competitor. Chicago spent more than $288 million between 1915 and 1930 on street construction, widening, and paving,[3] but the elevated railway sys-

tem over the same span was able to finance through private borrowing only $36.9 million in improvements and extensions. Not even the L's association with Samuel Insull's Middle West Utilities conglomerate enabled it to generate the kind of capital needed to keep the system competitive, although the sheer size of Insull's utilities empire protected the L's balance sheets until the Great Depression hit.

Samuel Insull (1859–1938) is one of those titans of American business whose rags-to-riches-to-rags story has been told many times, often with considerable embellishment. He came from a rather modest

Competition for riders diluted the market for Chicago's privately owned mass transit but especially affected the elevated and street railways. Here street-cars and buses run beneath the Lake Street L, shown at Desplaines Avenue in 1949. (Krambles Archive)

English background, the son of a Congregationalist who held a minor post at Oxford, and was forced at age fourteen to get a job as an office boy. His capacity for organization, numbers, and work enabled him to rise to the post of clerk at an auction firm. In 1879 he found a job as secretary to George A. Gouraud, a London-based banker who served as inventor Thomas Alva Edison's European representative.[4] Edison happened to be young Insull's idol, and within a few years Insull had so ingratiated himself to the inventor's staff with his zeal for organization that he was brought to New York as Edison's personal secretary. There he learned the business of electric generation so well that when financier J. P. Morgan took over Edison's dynamo business in 1892 and formed the General Electric Company, Insull headed west to take over a struggling electric firm called Chicago Edison, one of eighteen small utilities in operation there.

Under his direction, Chicago Edison gobbled up many competitors after the Panic of 1893, then built a large central power plant along the Chicago River at Harrison Street. Insull also became acutely aware of the rampant political corruption and Yerkes's use of it to consolidate his traction empire. Insull anticipated that the growing electric utility, which also operated under city franchises that would expire in 1906, might eventually become the target of a shakedown and began acquiring the exclusive rights to all the electricity-generating technology available in the United States. The Gray Wolves as well as the Roger Sullivan and John P. Hopkins faction on the City Council, sometimes known as the "Ogden Gas Crowd," finally approached Insull in 1897 to see how much he was willing to pay to prevent them from franchising a competitor. When he refused to deal, they franchised the Commonwealth Electric Company but sold the company to him four months later for $50,000 after discovering that he owned all the rights to the equipment Commonwealth would need to compete

against him. The incident surprisingly earned Insull the respect of Sullivan, who went on to become Insull's mentor, close personal friend, and political ally, which was especially useful after Sullivan was selected as state Democratic chairman.[5]

While Yerkes was unable to break the practice of bribing politicians to get what he wanted, Insull instead cultivated politicians and made allies not only of Sullivan but also later of Chicago Mayor William Hale Thompson. Insull apparently had a strong belief in his personal ability to solve problems in the business world and had limited success in ingratiating himself to Chicago high society.[6] Yerkes curtly bribed politicians to get what he wanted, while Insull used his considerable influence, or clout, as it is known in Chicago, as a captain of industry. Yerkes abandoned ship when it became necessary, but Insull went down with it.

Insull's entry into the traction business was fortuitous. Shortly after the turn of the century and Yerkes's departure from Chicago, he was approached by executives of the Lake Street Elevated about the possibility of their buying power from him. At the time, while homes were lighted primarily by manufactured coal gas, factories with large power demands, including some traction companies, had their own electric and steam generating plants. Insull, who had an expensive central station coming on line, was intrigued by the possibility of finding a customer with high daytime demands to keep the machinery running during daylight hours when other power demands were normally low.[7]

Chicago Edison Co. at the turn of the century was producing only one hundred million kilowatt hours of electricity per year—less than one-thirtieth of the power used in factories and one-twentieth of that used in homes and shops. Insull reasoned that huge customers such as the traction companies would provide him with a large enough customer base to mass produce power in central generating plants, reducing the cost enough that it would be avail-

able to everyone.[8] He signed a contract to provide power to the Lake Street line in 1902; in 1905 he added Yerkes's old streetcar lines, by then known as the Chicago Union Traction Co.; and by the end of the decade he had signed up the rest of Chicago's traction companies.

At that point much of the city's transit system was under the control of Blair's syndicate. Although the Loop was consistently profitable, the Northwestern Elevated was only marginally so, and the Lake Street L was a drain on the system. Blair had been forced to reorganize the Lake Street L shortly after acquiring it, and by 1909 he was looking for a way to consolidate the entire elevated system without having to resort to bankruptcy court. At first his group offered to buy all the outstanding common stock of the Northwestern, the Metropolitan, and the South Side elevated railways and succeeded in acquiring 90 percent of that stock. The Lake Street L was then in bankruptcy once again and could not be part of the merger.

Blair created what amounted to a voluntary holding company called the Chicago Elevated Railways Collateral Trust, but he was unable to find the necessary financing in New York to complete the consolidation. He finally approached Insull, with whom he sat on the Commonwealth Edison Co. board, and asked him to underwrite a $6 million loan to complete the merger.[9] Insull agreed, fearing that a rival utility would loan them the money to lure them away as customers, but he insisted on stock as collateral. When Blair was unable to complete the merger or to repay the loan, Commonwealth Edison became the principal stockholder of the Northwestern, the Metropolitan, and the South Side elevated railways through the Collateral Trust.[10]

The Lake Street L came under Insull's control by a somewhat different route. By the time it emerged from a reorganization in 1904 as the Chicago & Oak Park Elevated Railway, the company already was working on its fourth set of owners in

slightly more than ten years, including Mike McDonald and Yerkes. The line reached its ultimate terminal at Harlem Avenue in Oak Park in 1901, the same year Yerkes sold out and left town.[11] After a reorganization by the Blair group in 1904, the company was able to limp along until 1909, when it was so strapped for cash it began to sign IOUs, or demand notes, as they are known, to the Northwestern Elevated Railway Co. in order to cover rental payments for use of the Loop elevated. On August 11, 1911, Insull's Commonwealth Edison loaned the Chicago & Oak Park $121,702 and signed the note over to the Chicago Elevated Railways Collateral Trust. Three months later the C&OP was unable even with an extension to make the annual interest payment of $132,974 on its mortgage with the Central Trust Co. of New York, so the bank on November 11, 1911, filed to foreclose, and Judge Christian C. Kohlsaat appointed Insull as receiver of the now bankrupt company.[12]

The condition of the company was worse than anyone suspected, and before the end of 1911 Insull was forced to ask Kohlsaat for authority to issue $2 million in receiver's certificates to pay bills that included $189,000 in equipment notes, $393,000 in bonds, and $4.4 million outstanding of the original 1893 mortgage. Ultimately between 1911 and 1924, when the Chicago & Oak Park was sold at auction, Insull plowed nearly $2.8 million in receiver's certificates into the railway to keep it afloat but still owed Northwestern Elevated $343,194 for back rent and Commonwealth Edison $711,095 for power. As Insull pointed out, although the Lake Street L since its opening had never posted a profit, by the time he took control the company was unable even to meet operating expenses.[13]

Despite a penny fare increase to six cents in 1918, the following year, after Insull reported a loss of $87,982 in the six months ending May 31, 1919—exclusive of $126,024 needed to cover interest on bonds and notes[14]—the Chicago & Oak Park filed a petition to increase fares to eleven cents in the suburbs. Reorganization of the C&OP as an independent company was clearly impossible. Its only hope for survival was merger into the consolidated elevated railway Insull was in the process of creating.

CONSOLIDATION AND REFORM

Like Blair before him, Insull had concluded that the key to the survival of the elevated system was its consolidation. Blair had hired an engineering firm that estimated a consolidation, even if it did little more than permit the through routing of trains over the Loop, could save an estimated $700,000 per year in operating expenses, half of which would result from reductions in the electric power requirements.[15] Through routing, for example, would allow a train from the North Side to avoid having to make a full circle of the Loop before returning to the North Side. Instead, it would run over only two sections of the Loop and exit on a run to the South Side, a savings of approximately one mile and fifteen minutes per train.[16]

Insull, once he took control of the Collateral Elevated Railways, moved quickly to reap some of the benefits of consolidation. He picked the able Britton I. Budd, who had risen through the ranks from a repair shop worker on the Columbian Intramural Railway in 1893 to the presidency of the Metropolitan West Side Elevated in 1910, to run the city's elevated system. In 1913 Budd reformed operating practices to allow passengers free transfers between lines, organized through routing of trains over the Loop between the North and the South sides, lengthened platforms to allow longer trains, extended lines to outlying areas, and began a fleet modernization program by buying steel cars. The railways operating through the Collateral Trust bought 184 steel powered cars and 66 steel trailers in 1914 and 1915 and 105 additional steel cars in 1922.[17] The sys-

tem's financial condition, however, would not allow the purchase of enough steel cars to replace more than one-quarter of its fleet, which at the end of 1925 consisted of 1,862 cars, only 456 of which were steel. The last wooden cars were not taken out of service until the late 1950s.[18]

The reforms relieved some congestion on the elevated system but did not entirely eliminate it. Ten years after through routing was started, the average speed of the entire elevated system still was estimated at about twenty miles per hour (though this varied considerably), or not quite double the eleven-mile-per-hour average of the street railways.[19] More than three decades after through routing commenced, the average speed on the Lake Street elevated line between terminals was only 15.4 miles per hour, contrasted to an average speed of 15.3 miles per hour on the Laramie Avenue streetcar line and 9.3 miles per hour for the slowest of the city's twenty-two trolley routes.[20]

Despite the gains in efficiency from consolidation, Insull in 1922 had become sufficiently concerned over the poor financial performance of the elevated system to offer to the City Council's Local Transportation Committee to sell it to the city. When the city failed to act, Insull incorporated the Chicago Rapid Transit Co. (CRT) in 1923 and merged the other elevated companies into it, wiping off the books almost $36 million in stock by reducing to $86.5 million the capitalization of the new company. The predecessors combined had a capitalization of $124 million. Then, on January 31, 1924, the CRT bought the Chicago & Oak Park for $2.6 million, an amount that was used as a settlement of the bankrupt company's $4.1 million in debts.

Unfortunately, the recapitalization of the CRT had no effect on its underlying problems, especially on its inability to raise funds for modernization and expansion. With the exception of the continued westward march of the Douglas L from Cicero Avenue to 56th (Central) Avenue and an extension of

The area around Belmont Avenue at the Howard Street elevated line in 1964 typified the pattern of development in Chicago prior to the existence of the expressways. The highest density uses were generally within walking distance of the L. (Krambles Archive)

the Evanston line to Wilmette, Chicago's elevated system had stopped growing by 1908. Insull in the early 1920s was sufficiently able to resuscitate the CRT's credit rating—even though it was deferring some payment on utility bills to Commonwealth Edison—to enable it to borrow on top of the inherited debt load of $28.3 million an additional $18.3 million in bonds and

$18.56 million in unsecured debentures to start a modest modernization and expansion program. A debt load of $65 million had been accrued for a system that Insull admitted never paid dividends.[21]

In the meantime Insull began adding other electric railways to his empire as captive customers. One year after taking control of the Collateral Trust, Insull set up a holding company called Middle West Utilities Corporation, which eventually acquired hundreds of traction and power companies serving five thousand communities across the nation.[22] Among them over the following fourteen years were the three principal electric interurban railways in the Chicago area—the Chicago North Shore & Milwaukee, acquired in 1916 from bankruptcy; the Chicago, South Shore & South Bend, bought in 1925; and the Chicago, Aurora & Elgin, purchased in 1926.[23] Both the Aurora & Elgin and North Shore operated to the Loop over Insull's elevated railways.

Probably because of Insull's political influence and the system's history of financial problems, the Ls had somewhat of an easier time with the regulators than did the street railways. The five-cent fare was increased to six cents by the Public Utilities Commission on November 21, 1918, to eight cents the following August 19, and to ten cents one year after that. Thus the rapid-transit system succeeded in doubling its fares over a period of less than two years in which inflation, as measured by the consumer price index, increased by just under 25 percent.[24] Despite the fare increases, a 40.5 percent increase in ridership between 1911 and 1926, and reforms of Insull's new management, the system's financial problems persisted.[25] The ridership gains were considerably less impressive than they seemed because streetcar patronage in Chicago over the same span increased by nearly 56 percent.

The elevated system after 1907 began to lose market share in all areas but the commute to and from the central business district. The L's share of the mass-transit market declined steadily from a high of 28.35 percent in 1907 to only 19.7 percent in 1926, and the number of annual per capita rides on the system increased only marginally from 64.4 in 1906 to 72.4 in 1926, contrasted to an increase from 182.5 per capita rides to 276.5 on the street railways (see Table A4).[26] The year 1926 marked the first Chicago annual cordon counts, a transportation census of vehicles and passengers entering the central business dis-

trict: the elevated system carried 256,286 people per day—a market share of 29.1 percent; the street railways accounted for another 294,958 riders—33.5 percent; and autos and taxis combined carried 166,367 persons—18.9 percent.[27]

As in the case of the street railways, the weakest part of the elevated system was on the West Side, especially the Lake Street line. The problems of that transit corridor offer some insights into the origins of Chicago's impending traction crisis. Although the Chicago Rapid Transit merger tended to conceal the problem because the individual elevated lines no longer reported financial data separately, the Lake Street line remained a drain on the system. As late as 1975, the Lake and parallel Congress lines (formerly Garfield Park) were identified in an economic study as two of the four Chicago Transit Authority (CTA) routes that were losing money.[28]

Transit on the West Side especially seems to have been adversely impacted by a number of factors that can be traced back to the design of the system and the manner in which the territory it served developed. The Lake, Garfield, and Douglas elevated lines were designed essentially as grade-separated streetcar lines with stations in close proximity in neighborhoods that never attained the residential densities of the North and South sides of Chicago. All three West Side Ls also had more substantial competition than did the Ls on the North or South sides.[29] Much of the West Side was developed as small apartment buildings and single-family homes. If overlapping rapid-transit markets are taken into consideration, the mile-wide Lake Street L corridor in 1956 had a population density—or potential market—approaching 20,126 persons per square mile, and the parallel Garfield line about a mile away had a density of 16,544. In comparison, at that time the Howard Street L corridor on the North Side had a population density of 29,506, and the Jackson Park L corridor on the South Side had a density of 33,887, both of which lacked competition.[30]

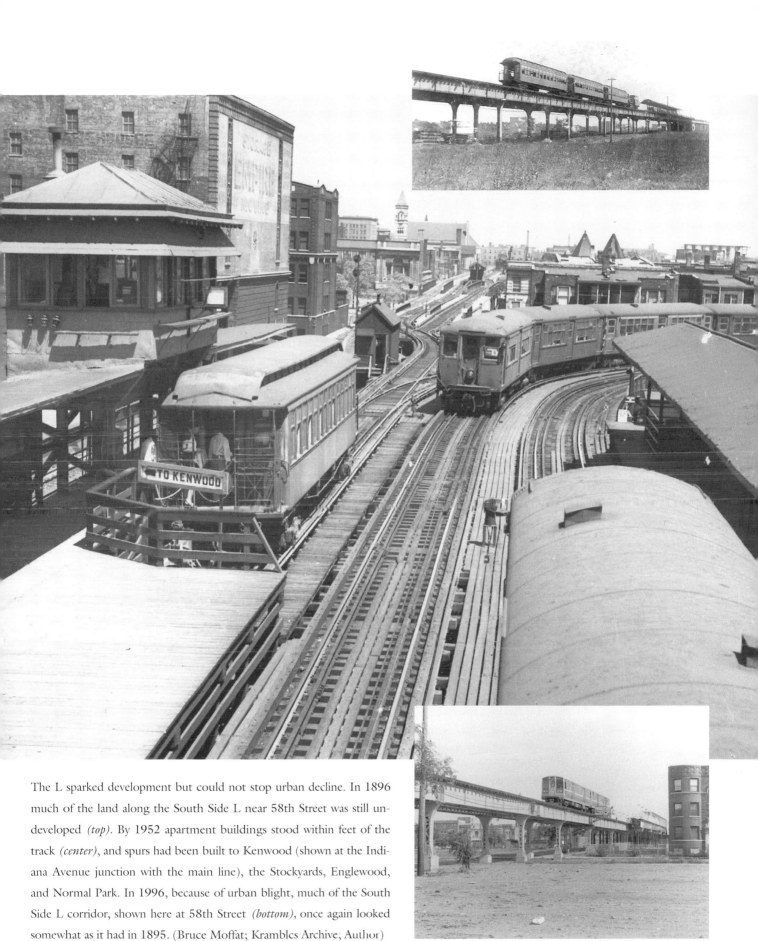

The L sparked development but could not stop urban decline. In 1896 much of the land along the South Side L near 58th Street was still undeveloped *(top)*. By 1952 apartment buildings stood within feet of the track *(center)*, and spurs had been built to Kenwood (shown at the Indiana Avenue junction with the main line), the Stockyards, Englewood, and Normal Park. In 1996, because of urban blight, much of the South Side L corridor, shown here at 58th Street *(bottom)*, once again looked somewhat as it had in 1895. (Bruce Moffat; Krambles Archive; Author)

The construction of the "elevated streetcar lines," as George Krambles once described them,[31] was typical of the thinking of nineteenth-century entrepreneurs. The three West Side lines all had closely spaced stations that averaged less than one-third of a mile apart, and more than half of them eventually were abandoned. When Chicago in the 1950s replaced the original Garfield Park (Metropolitan) elevated, which had twenty-eight stations, with the Congress rapid-transit line in the median strip of that expressway, it built only fourteen stations on the new line and subsequently closed three of them.[32] The three West Side lines had been included in the project for political reasons despite warnings from the Chicago Transit Authority staff that there was insufficient ridership to justify them.[33] The Lake Street line, originally built with twenty nine stations, or one every three-tenths of a mile, had only fourteen remaining in 1948 after the Chicago Transit Authority took over.

Ample competition for the three West Side elevated lines operating in an approximately four-mile-wide corridor was provided by no less than ten parallel street routes.[34] There were streetcar routes on both Lake and 21st Streets beneath the elevated structures, and on both Van Buren and Harrison Streets parallel to and flanking the Garfield Park L that ran above an alley between them. The Chicago & North Western Railway also provided commuter service on its main line, which ran adjacent to Lake Street, long before the elevated was built, and the Chicago, Aurora & Elgin interurban railroad operated through commuter service from the western suburbs over the Garfield Park L to downtown Chicago after 1905, though it handled only a limited amount of intermediate traffic.

Competition between the various carriers at times could be cutthroat, and the public could be quickly influenced. For example, after the Suburban Railroad, a Harrison Street railway of the early 1900s, had built a connection to the Metropolitan West Side's Garfield Park elevated at 48th (Cicero) Avenue, Yerkes abruptly bought

the Suburban and rerouted it to his Lake Street L.[35] The Federal Electric Railway Commission took note of the effects of competition when the elevated railways and streetcar lines both obtained fare increases but at different times. The elevated system got a penny fare increase to six cents in November 1918, then lost more than 5 percent of its ridership to the street railways, which were not given an identical fare increase for six months.[36]

THE FALL OF THE HOUSE OF INSULL

By 1924, the first year in which consolidated financial statements were available for the Chicago Rapid Transit Co. following its purchase of the bankrupt Chicago & Oak Park, the elevated system was still sufficiently profitable with a net income of $801,375 on revenues of $18,565,185 to sell $5 million in preferred stock and $9 million in bonds to refinance $10.5 million old debt and to finance a modest modernization program. It was also able to sell an additional $2,212,000 in bonds in 1925 for an order of new steel cars and another $3,122,000 in bonds in 1928 to roll over old debt and to finance some work on the Loop elevated required by the city.[37]

Through most of the decade the CRT benefitted from steadily increasing ridership and revenues that exceeded $21.1 million in 1929 and was able to control operating expenses to the point that operating ratios improved from 74.1 percent in 1924 to 69.9 percent in 1929. Over that span the CRT, although it did not pay dividends on anything but preferred stock, which amounted to less than one-fifth of its outstanding shares, continuously increased its cash reserves, or surplus account, from a total of $958,672 in 1924 to a balance of $3,712,014 in 1929.

The ticking bomb was the company's debt load, the service of which cost the CRT $2.3 to $2.4 million annually. Dividends on the preferred stock added nearly $500,000 per year to costs, and taxes and compensation to the city amounted to $1.8 million per year. By the eve of the

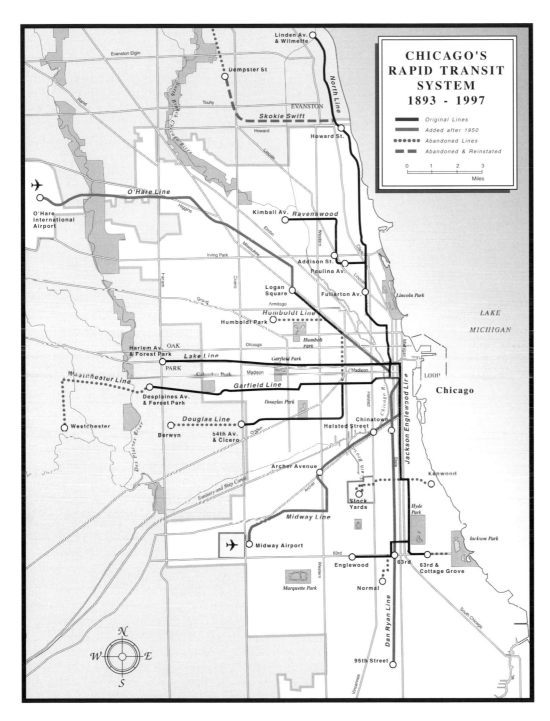

CHICAGO'S
RAPID TRANSIT
SYSTEM
1893 - 1997

Original Lines
Added after 1950
Abandoned Lines
Abandoned & Reinstated

0   1   2   3
Miles

Great Depression in 1929, those three categories consumed almost 23 percent of CRT's revenues. As it turned out, the collapse of ridership during the depression and its impact on revenue quickly drove the CRT into bankruptcy. Insull, who himself was badly extended financially, could not even save his personal fortune. Although ridership fell by more than one-third from 1929 to 1932, causing annual fare revenue to plummet by $7.4 million, the CRT was able to cut its operating budget, which accounts for roughly 70 percent of total expenses, by only $4.4 million.

Streetcars, buses, and (out of sight) an elevated line served Wrigley Field in 1935. (Krambles Archive)

The next two biggest expenses, interest on the debt and taxes (including compensation paid to the city), were sacrosanct, as were the preferred stock dividends. The only source of money available to cover the company's net losses of $1.5 million in 1931 and $2.5 million in 1932 was the surplus fund. When that was gone in 1932, the CRT's only remaining option was to defer payments to the bondholders and the city, a measure that could only be invoked by an order of the bankruptcy court.

The end came quickly for the CRT in 1932. Westinghouse Electric and Manufacturing Co. filed a creditor's suit in federal court, and the CRT, which had $65 million in debt that it could not cover, had A. A. Sprague and Britton I. Budd appointed as its receivers.[38] The total liabilities at the time exceeded $107.6 million, but that amount included more than $26 million in stock that would soon be worthless.

The collapse would have occurred sooner, but the CRT was propped up by

Insull's utilities empire, which it proceeded to drag down.[39] The collapse of the House of Insull became one of the legends of capitalism and part of the lore of the Great Depression. It was an example of how the financial overextension of a holding company could bring down its otherwise healthy subsidiaries, the power companies, and it involved the fall of one of the mighty. Insull, who in the 1920s had maintained an estate in Libertyville and a Chicago townhouse and who as a member of high society had been the prime mover behind the construction of the city's $16 million Civic Opera Building, by 1934 was a resident of the Cook County Jail with little money to his name.

Insull had weathered earlier downturns in the economy, but after the stock market crash of 1929 he was forced to borrow money to buy back Middle West Utilities stock to prop up its price. When Cleveland industrialist Cyrus Eaton, a major shareholder, the following year demanded Insull buy him out at $350 per share at a time when the principal utility subsidiaries were selling at $255 to $285 per share, Insull again had to borrow, exhausting both his credit and his ability to continue to prop up the price of the stock.[40] In 1932 he was unable either to cover or to refinance a $10 million Middle West Utilities note, and a group of New York bankers forced his resignation.[41]

Insull was indicted in October 1932 on state charges of embezzlement and larceny but fled to Greece. After the federal government charged him with mail fraud and violations of the bankruptcy act, the State Department put pressure on Athens, which ordered him to leave. He was arrested in Turkey and returned to the United States for trial. After being acquitted of the separate charges in three trials, the last in 1935, he retired to Paris, living on a pension from his utilities, since his fortune had been wiped out with the collapse of Middle West Utilities. He died of a heart attack in a Paris subway in 1938.

Public events resulted in heavy use of the mass-transit system even after the automobile began encroaching on its market. The Century of Progress fair in 1933 taxed the facilities of a streetcar line, since abandoned, serving the fair site southeast of the Loop. Lake Shore Drive appears on the right. (Krambles Archive)

10

THE CAMPAIGN FOR PUBLIC OWNERSHIP

♦ Although the concept of public ownership of Chicago's transit system was rooted in the original franchises for horsecar lines in the 1850s, the electorate was content to let it remain in private hands for almost one hundred years. The issue began to get serious consideration in the late nineteenth century during the public furor over boodle, poor service, and dubious financial schemes of the city's traction barons. The voters were quite willing to endorse public ownership of the street railways until the subject of money arose: referenda issues to appropriate money for mass transit were defeated in 1906, 1918, and 1925. Indeed, the only subsidies from the public treasury prior to 1963 consisted of a few modest federal grants. Some were authorized during World War I by Samuel Insull, then serving as chairman of the State Council for Defense Planning, to finance transit extensions to Chicago's somewhat isolated southeastern industrial district along the Calumet River. A depression-era federal grant was approved to build the State and Dearborn subways.[1]

As the debate over transit intensified in the first years of the twentieth century, political reformers came to the conclusion that the only way to clean up the mess was for the public to buy the system—so long as the transaction did not involve raising taxes. While the city was financing streets from the public treasury, virtually all financing schemes for a transit purchase by the city required the use of revenue bonds repaid from fares. Traction system owners, in contrast, favored state regulation as the remedy.

Chicago in the second half of the nineteenth century, despite the best efforts of its boosters, developed a reputation as "Gommorah of the West,"[2] a public image of sin and corruption that was sustained by Al Capone and William Hale Thompson in the 1920s, the police reaction to demonstrators at the 1968 Democratic National Convention, and political scandals into the 1990s. Young Rudyard Kipling, who visited Chicago in 1889, was particularly unimpressed:

> I have struck a city,—a real city,—and they call it Chicago. The other places do not count. San Francisco was a pleasure-resort as well as a city, and Salt Lake was a phenomenon. This place is the first American city I have encountered. It holds rather more than a million people with bodies, and stands on the same sort of soil as Calcutta. Having seen it, I urgently desire to never to see it again. It is inhabited by savages. Its water is the water of the Hugli, and its air is dirt. Also it says that it is the "boss" town of America.[3]

In that milieu, Chicago's transit system became a battleground in the war on corruption. The ultimate weapon was public ownership.

Reformers included a group of wealthy and socially prominent businessmen, academics, and professionals, as well as such populist politicians as mayors Carter Harrison Jr. and William Dever; Edward F. Dunne, who served terms as both mayor and governor; and Governor John Peter Altgeld. In general, they all came to favor public ownership of the city's traction system, especially after Yerkes was discovered to favor state regulation. The first step in any buyout was to determine the value of the system, but that proved to be complicated because two major accounting methods produced widely varying results. Because they would get the greatest return from it, the transit owners favored the capitalization method, or the cost to the city if it bought all the stock on the open market. The reformers wanted to pay replacement value, or the cost to duplicate the system, because it reduced the price considerably. The latter claimed that the system's highly watered stock, which in some instances had been given away as an inducement to buy bonds, was double its replacement value.

The first attempt at valuation was made in 1896 by George A. Schilling, at the time secretary of the Illinois Bureau of Labor Statistics and a friend of then Governor Altgeld. He calculated the replacement value of the street railway system at $31.7 million and its stock capitalization at $61.7 million.[4] Two years later a City Council special committee lowered the replacement cost to $28.6 million and raised the capitalization to $63.3 million.[5] That was not the final word, however. One year later, both Yerkes and the Chicago City Railway, by then concerned about the expiration of their franchises in 1903, allowed the Civic Federation to examine their books for yet another attempt at valuation. Edward F. Bard, the Civic Federation accountant, used somewhat different standards and determined that the liabilities of the system exceeded its assets by $39.3 million.[6]

When reformers finally got control of the Chicago City Council in 1898, the campaign for public ownership picked up steam. On April 1, 1902, the issue of municipal ownership was presented to the public in an advisory referendum and was overwhelmingly approved.[7] With that sort of public support, the reform elements then drafted the necessary state legislation, including a mechanism to finance the

(facing page) One motive for public ownership was the desire to rationalize transit routes. The motorman in this 1935 scene on Grand Avenue near Dearborn Street notes the number of an obstructing taxicab, apparently to report it to city authorities. (Krambles Archive)

The construction of subway
stations along State Street
caused some disruption of
traffic in 1940. (Krambles
Archive)

purchase—the authorization for $75 mil-
lion in certificates that were, in effect, revenue bonds. The Mueller Certificates, as
they were known from the 1903 law authorizing them, which would act as a
mortgage on the street railway system and
would be repaid from future fare revenues,
required the approval by two-thirds of the
voting electorate in a referendum.[8] The
certificates won approval quickly in an
April 5, 1904, referendum by an even
greater margin than the 1902 vote.[9] At
that point, municipal ownership of the
streetcar system seemed a certainty, except
that the courts had not yet spoken.

Chicago Union Traction, the former
Yerkes system, went into receivership in
1903 just before its franchise expired, and
Chicago City Railway, the other major system, decided to take the issue of its franchise extension to court. On May 28,
1904, Chicago City Railway got a ruling
from Federal District Court Judge Peter S.
Grosscup that the controversial ninety-

nine-year charter it got from the state back
in 1865 was constitutional and that its operating rights had not expired with its city
franchise in 1903. While the appeal of that
ruling was in progress in 1905, the City
Council let the voters have their say in yet
another referendum, this one deciding
whether Chicago City Railway's franchise
should be extended another twenty years.
It lost convincingly.[10]

With Yerkes no longer present as a
lightning rod for the opposition and with
the specter of a $75 million price tag for
streetcar lines, public enthusiasm for municipal ownership began to wane.[11] By
then Edward F. Dunne, a strong proponent of public ownership, had succeeded
Carter Harrison Jr. as mayor and induced
the City Council to proceed with buying
the street railways. In yet another referendum less than one month after the U.S.
Supreme Court reversed Grosscup and
ruled the ninety-nine-year charter in-
valid,[12] a majority of the electorate once

again voted in favor of municipal ownership, though not by the extraordinary majority required by state law. All three issues on the April 3, 1906, ballot received a majority of the votes cast, but the proposal authorizing the city to operate the street railways once it bought them failed to receive a three-fifths majority required by the Mueller law.[13]

Both sides, not to mention the public, were nearing exhaustion, and some sort of compromise seemed to be the only reasonable alternative. Dunne had the corporation counsel Walter Fischer draw up the Traction Settlement Ordinances to extend the expired 1903 street franchises for twenty years with many conditions, but he was dissatisfied with the final agreement negotiated between the city and the street railways and vetoed it. The council overrode his veto, and the voters on April 2, 1907, ratified its action in still another referendum.[14]

The issue of public ownership was settled for about ten years, at which time the city began to press for the construction of subways to relieve traffic congestion on downtown streets. Gridlock had replaced boodle as the city's principal transit problem, and the rather enlightened traction administrations of Blair and Insull caused the public to forget Yerkes's abuses. Furthermore, there was general agreement that the financing of subways was beyond the capability of the traction companies and could only be built with public funds. Civic organizations; downtown special interest groups; reformers; the emerging autoist lobby, including the Chicago Motor Club; and the street railways united in advocating public spending for solutions. Only the public balked.

The underlying cause of downtown traffic congestion was the pattern of Chicago's waterways, which resulted in the overconcentration of development in an area bounded by the lake, the Chicago River, and its south branch. The arrival of the railroads and their extensive yards closed that box on the south side, and the building of the Loop in the late 1890s resulted in an extremely compact downtown district. The "iron ring," as Carl Condit called the Loop elevated, "had a strangling effect, producing so high a density of building that the mixture of pedestrian, streetcar, truck, automobile, and wagon traffic eventually made certain Loop streets impassable during rush hours and on popular shopping days."[15] It was an expensive problem to fix.

Theoretically, such a high concentration of jobs in a relatively small area would have been ideal for mass transit, but Chicago's heavy reliance on street railways meant the system was vulnerable to downtown traffic jams. By the 1890s, three decades before the automobile was a major contributor to congestion, downtown streets were suffering from gridlock. Accurate data were not always available to the early planners and engineers, so the first documentation of the extent of the congestion problem was a partial traffic count by the city in 1907 on bridges, which showed that 57,000 vehicles per day entered downtown from the North and West Sides.[16] The number of motor vehicles registered in Chicago in 1908, the first year for which data is available, was only 5,475.[17] On a single 7 A.M. to 7 P.M. business day in May 1926, a total of 132,913 vehicles entered the downtown streets of Chicago—including 8,432 streetcars, 92,425 automobiles, and 30,224 trucks and wagons. By then the city's registered motor vehicle population had grown to 317,433.[18]

Engineer Bion J. Arnold (1861–1942) as early as 1902 suggested building a streetcar subway as well as a shuttle subway linking the commuter train stations with the central business district.[19] Similar proposals to bury downtown streetcar lines, as had been done in Boston in 1897, were important parts of every other study of urban transportation thereafter, including the influential Chicago Plan of Daniel Burnham and Edward Bennett that gave birth to the city's arterial street system. By 1916, the Traction and Subway Commission

By the Great Depression, trolley cars had driven horses from State Street. They were in turn making their last stand against autos and motorbuses. (Chicago Transit Authority)

recommended putting the Loop elevated as well as some streetcar lines underground.

Arnold, the city's most influential and probably its first transit professional, was a college-educated professional engineer who helped build the Chicago Great Western railroad. After he finished that project, he went to work for an engineering firm and became one of the nation's leading consultants on electric railways as well as

on mass transit. He produced a number of studies for Chicago and other cities and chaired the Board of Supervising Engineers, set up to keep an eye on the street railways, from its inception in 1907 until his death in 1942. He was a "progressive engineer" who believed that technology could be used to accomplish social reform in keeping with the requirements of corporations of the day. Unfortunately, the needs of the transit systems often conflicted with the political will, leaving him in an untenable position.[20] After 1915 he slowly began withdrawing from public life and spending more time running the Elgin & Belvidere Railroad, an electric interurban railway in which he invested. He served as a director for the Elgin & Belvidere, and from 1917 until 1930, when the line failed, he was president.

Early in 1916 the City Council created a commission to address the problem of congestion and appointed Arnold as one of three members to find some solutions. The commission recommended building 53 miles of rapid-transit subways and 5.1 miles of streetcar subways, plus more than doubling in size the elevated system to 157 miles and substantially increasing the street railway system to 529 miles. It also recommended unification of all street and elevated companies into a single company under the control of the City Council, though it did not advocate public ownership.[21] The City Council over Mayor William Hale Thompson's veto in 1918 approved the commission's recommendations and authorized the city to buy the transit systems for $220.1 million, including $70.9 million for the elevated system, and to create the Chicago Local Transportation Company to operate them. The proposal was submitted to the voters on November 5, 1918, in another referendum but lost by a substantial margin, 209,682 to 243,334.

Despite the defeat, downtown traffic congestion was such a problem that the city persisted. By then almost everyone in public life, though not all of transit management, realized it was necessary for the city to own the transit system before it could commit the huge sums necessary to put it underground. Another Thompson-appointed committee recommended public ownership, and in 1920 he unsuccessfully sought in the Illinois Senate the enabling legislation to create a local transportation district. Two years later the traction systems joined the act when Henry A. Blair,

president of the Chicago Surface Lines, proposed a city board of control to oversee the transit system and construction by the city of $35.4 million in streetcar subways beneath State and Washington Streets. The project included the financing of construction with money that had been accumulating in the traction fund under terms of the 1907 Settlement Ordinances.[22]

More studies, reports, and recommendations followed, culminating in 1923 with R. K. Kelker's report to the Committee on Local Transportation, which suggested once again the unification of the transit systems and the digging of subways.[23] Later that year, Mayor William E. Dever, a Democratic reformer who had upset Thompson, proposed a plan for municipal ownership that would "impose no burden on the taxpayers."[24] Chicago still wanted a free lunch. The problem, as Dever so ably outlined in a letter to the City Council one year later, was that the $40 million in the traction fund and a potential of $30 to $40 million from special assessments on adjoining property owners were insufficient to build any more than twelve to eighteen miles of subway.[25] One mile of subway beneath the Loop would cost about forty times as much as one mile of street railway in an outlying area of the city.

The price tag on public acquisition of the street railways had increased considerably. The City Council in 1925 adopted an ordinance to issue revenue bonds, officially called 5 percent municipal railway certificates: $85 million to buy the L and $162.8 million to finance the acquisition of the streetcar system.[26] The effect, including funds for expansion of both railways, would have been to impose $389.8 million in new bonded indebtedness on a system that was struggling to cover the debt service on $175.7 million in bonds. Both the Chicago Railways Co. and the Chicago Rapid Transit Co., which combined handled in excess of 70 percent of the ridership in Chicago, had by that time stopped paying dividends to stockholders because

Digging the State Street subway was much like mining *(top)*. When the soil proved unstable, however, crews were required to bore under pressure using a shield *(facing page, top)*.

of dwindling earnings. Chicago Railways was less than two years from bankruptcy. In any event, the proposal became moot on April 7, 1925, when the voters defeated it by a wide margin in a referendum.[27]

The crushing defeat, as well as the subsequent Great Depression and World War II, ended the campaign for municipal ownership for almost twenty years. The fifteen years from the onset of the depression until the end of the war were a continuous battle in bankruptcy court between the competing interests of the local, state, and federal agencies and the holders of various

types of bonds, the principal on which totaled nearly $200 million. No less than four separate plans were filed to reorganize the streetcar lines, but all foundered.

For its part, the city in 1930 belatedly scrapped the twenty-year franchises that had expired in 1927 with "terminable permits" of unspecified duration allowing the city to purchase the street railways at any time. The ordinance also optimistically required the merger of the surface and elevated systems into a single company, $200 million in modernization and extensions, construction of $85 million in new subways, a unified

The subway tunnels that ran under the Chicago River were first built on dry land, then floated down the river on barges *(left)* and submerged into trenches. (Krambles Archive)

For safety reasons, wooden cars were banned in Chicago's subways. The first subway opened under State Street in 1943. (Chicago Transit Authority)

fare system, and a 3 percent tax on revenues. The ordinance, not surprisingly, was overwhelmingly approved by the voters in a referendum on July 1, 1930.[28] It was too late. Six days after the referendum, the other three companies of the Chicago Surface Lines joined Chicago Railways Co. in bankruptcy. CSL's four companies had been unable to pay any of the principal on their bonds since their franchises expired on February 1, 1927, and Chicago Railways could not even cover the interest.[29] Two years later the rapid-transit system met the same fate. The bankruptcies, which dragged on for fifteen years, turned into a cacophony of competing financial interests, complicated by the fact that the city, the state, the Illinois Commerce Commission, and the U.S. Securities and Exchange Commission (which was created by Congress after the bankruptcy was in progress) all had a role, or at least a say, in the final settlement. The proceedings de-

volved into a melee from which there was no hope of saving the private companies.

ATTEMPTED REORGANIZATIONS

By 1933, U.S. Judge James H. Wilkerson, who was overseeing the bankruptcies on a consolidated basis, began pressing the secured creditors of the street railways, which included fifteen groups of investors but no stockholders, for some sort of an agreement on which a reorganization could be based. On September 26, 1933, he appointed Walter L. Fisher, an attorney who represented the city on many transit matters, to act as his representative in negotiations.[30] Often in the case in bankruptcy reorganizations, the stockholders have little standing and are usually wiped out when the company is reorganized. The struggle then is among the secured creditors, holders of everything from mortgage bonds to debentures, to salvage as much of their investment as possible. Usually the settlement payout, or a substantial portion of it, comes not in the form of cash but in the form of equity, or stock, in the reorganized company. This was the nature of Fisher's compromise reorganization plan of November 1, 1933. After negotiating with the banks holding the first mortgage bonds and the groups of secured creditholders in lesser positions in the pecking order, Fisher presented Wilkerson with a plan that gave the street railways' creditors a somewhat more secure position in the reorganized company.[31] When Mayor Edward J. Kelly objected to the plan and the City Council rescinded the 1930 merger ordinance and franchise extension, however, Judge Wilkerson threatened to sell the traction companies to the highest bidder at a foreclosure auction.[32]

The following year Wilkerson tried again and appointed a committee of corporate executives chaired by Rufus W. Abbott, retired chairman of Illinois Bell Telephone Co., to draft another reorganization plan. On October 27, 1935, the group reported back with a plan to merge the four street railway companies into a new Chicago Surface Lines Inc., a maneuver similar to what had occurred with the Chicago Rapid Transit Co. more than one decade earlier. The plan's downfall was its failure to provide a capital improvement fund that the city considered adequate. The street railway mortgage holders got $72,718,350 in first mortgage bonds in the new company—the same amount they held in the old—but the junior creditors got only $47.1 million, mainly in preferred stock, for their $80 million investment in

The final attempt by the bankrupt street railway system to recapture lost traffic through modernization resulted in the PCC streetcar, which was designed during the Great Depression. This photograph was taken at the new cars' public debut. (Krambles Archive)

the old companies. The stockholders were effectively wiped out: they received common stock in the new company.[33]

After surmounting objections from everyone with a financial stake in the bankruptcy, Wilkerson approved the reorganization and merger of the four street railway companies into the Chicago Surface Lines Inc. only to have the city object late in the proceedings because the plan was concerned mainly with the protection of bondholders and did not make adequate provision for expansion. One of the most significant acts of the new publicly owned transit system fifteen years later, ironically, was not expansion but contraction—the abandonment of a number of money-losing elevated lines and virtually the entire street railway system. Wilkerson's ruling in 1935 was the ultimate compromise: he approved the reorganization plan but stipulated that the receivers must first obtain a new franchise from the city.[34] When that failed to happen, the city in 1937 proposed a compromise in which everything would be merged into the proposed Chicago Transit Co., and the City Council on June 19, 1941, adopted an ordinance granting a franchise to the nonexistent company. The ordinance was ratified in a referendum on

June 1, 1942, but the Illinois Commerce Commission on May 3, 1943, in effect vetoed the plan with a report suggesting the proposed company did not have the financial resources to survive.[35]

The City Council in 1943 decided to take another stab at public ownership of its transit system and began negotiating a price. When the parties involved failed to reach an agreement, the court on September 18, 1944, encouraged the surface and rapid-transit companies to file reorganization plans. Once again the ICC ruled that the plans were too optimistic and that the reorganized companies were unlikely to produce sufficient revenues to be able to fund a badly needed $123 million modernization program.[36] By that time, the average age of a Chicago streetcar was twenty-eight years—within two years of its design life—and more than 70 percent of the rapid-transit fleet still consisted of obsolete wooden cars built more than forty years earlier. Indeed, half of the 450 steel cars on the rapid-transit system predated World War I.[37] The city truly needed to replace at least some of its streetcar lines with buses. By the end of World War II, the Chicago Surface Lines still had 3,560 streetcars but only 152 trolley buses and 259 motor buses.[38]

This streamlined, Pullman-built PCC streetcar, which seated up to fifty-eight passengers, was delivered after World War II. (Chicago Transit Authority)

Federal Judge Michael L. Igoe, who had succeeded Wilkerson in overseeing the transit receiverships, in 1944 finally exhausted his patience at the lack of progress in settling a bankruptcy that, in the case of the Chicago Railways Co., had been before the court for eighteen years. On September 18, 1944, Igoe appointed four new trustees and new management for the Chicago Surface Lines and two months later ordered them to prepare a new reorganization plan. The plan they produced got the undivided attention of the theretofore haggling credi-tors: a company with $190 million in liabil-ities on the books would be reorganized with a mortgage of $45 million and $33 million in other bonds.[39]

Then, on January 15, 1945, Igoe appealed to Chicago Mayor Edward J. Kelly and Illinois Governor Dwight H. Green, a Republican from Chicago, for assistance. As a federal prosecutor earlier in his career, Green had gained fame by putting gangster Al Capone behind bars in a trial heard by Wilkerson; he had failed, however, to win the Insull case. Igoe emphasized to

Buses began to replace streetcars on State Street in 1941. The barricades block the construction sites for new subway stations.

(Chicago Transit Authority)

the mayor and the governor that the only viable option left was public ownership. The total debt of the elevated companies exceeded $160 million; that of the surface lines stood at $190.3 million, of which almost $58 million was unpaid interest dating as far back as 1926. Chicago Rapid Transit common stock was worth only $1 per share, following a 1938 devaluation from $100.[40] With public agencies in charge of setting fares and service and the automobile firmly established as a competitor (see Table A5), there was little prospect that the privately owned traction systems could raise fares sufficiently to generate capital for modernization.[41]

Throughout the duration of the Great Depression, the transit system's financial survival as a private enterprise had been progressively undermined by the emergence of the automobile as a competitor. During World War II, however, transit ridership revived because of wartime gasoline rationing and the unavailability of new cars. In 1926, when daily mass-transit ridership reached its peak in Chicago at more than 551,000 rides, the automobile accounted for less than 20 percent of the downtown commute (see Table A6). By 1941, when the auto's share had increased to 30 percent, the transit's market share had declined below 50 percent, and its daily ridership had fallen by more than 150,000 rides.

The city's and state's political leaders even during wartime were aware of the emerging importance of the automobile, and throughout the war Chicago and Cook County planned a massive expressway system to be built once hostilities ceased and rationing of materiel was lifted. The plan for a radial system of five expressways converging on downtown Chicago was completed in 1943, one year before Igoe made his plea for assistance.

The political settlement resulting from the judge's appeal—the Metropolitan Transit Authority Act signed by Green on April 12, 1945—was a solution typical of the political thinking in Illinois for a century: the creation of a special taxing district, but one without the ability to tax. The new agency, which was to have a board appointed by both the mayor (four members) and the governor (three members), was empowered to set its own fares and service without interference from the Illinois Commerce Commission or the City Council. The principal weaknesses of the act, as it turned out, were financial. The new Chicago Transit Authority was to rely on the fare box alone to finance its operations and to pay off the bonds floated to buy the system.[42] There was no commitment of money from the state or the city. The purchase price was left up to the federal court hearing the bankruptcy cases.

Although the creditors of the surface lines sought a price of $138 million to $170 million, which would have been the price under the terms of the formula in the 1907 Settlement Ordinances, the city offered only $75 million and the court accepted it.[43] The price for the elevated system, which was not disputed, was $12,162,500. The Securities and Exchange Commission, the ICC, and the federal appeals courts all sustained the city's offer. In the end, the private investors lost $110 million in the buyout of the surface system and $149,513,979 on the rapid-transit system.[44] The new CTA got 3,560 streetcars, 152 electric buses, 259 motor buses, 1,623 rapid-transit cars, and $91 million in bonded indebtedness, to which it quickly added $25 million in revenue bonds and equipment trust certificates for an urgent modernization program.[45]

Chicago finally realized the dream of public ownership that was first proposed ninety years earlier, but the economic realities of mass transit in the Auto Age forced the city to take the draconian measures it had prevented the private companies from implementing. In the end, the cash cow the city had bought for a bargain price turned out to be a sick horse.

STEAM TECHNOLOGY TO INTERNAL COMBUSTION

By the 1920s, buses were replacing streetcars, first in the suburbs and later in Chicago, through adaptation of modern technology. The Chicago Motor Bus Co. double-decker, built in 1916, was one of the first buses to run in Chicago. It could transport fifty-one passengers, though its open top deck effectively limited seating capacity in foul weather. (Krambles Archive)

◆　The technological development that burst onto the scene in the twentieth century, causing changes not only in the way most Chicagoans moved about but also in the way their transit systems operated, was the internal combustion engine. By the 1930s it had radiated into all the urban transportation niches that the steam engine had filled in the 1800s, except large-scale electrical power generation. The steam locomotive after sixty years of development in 1893 set a world speed record when the New York Central Railroad's No. 999 hit 112.5 miles per hour near Batavia, New York.[1] In 1919 Ralph De Palma set a world record of 149.8 miles per hour in a gasoline-powered Packard.[2] The high speed, however, was of little consequence to urban commuters on congested roads,

who were more concerned with trying to travel an average of fifteen miles per hour whether they were riding in streetcars, buses, or automobiles.

The steam engine enabled the conversion from equine to mechanical traction in the nineteenth century, greatly increasing the size and the speed of transit vehicles, but by the early twentieth century steam technology was reaching its practical limits. The transit system's operating environment became the factor limiting additional gains in efficiency. The streetcars and L trains were restricted in size and in speed by street clearances, fixed routes, and the necessity of negotiating tight turns at intersections. The internal combustion engine offered the transit systems more flexibility by enabling them to convert from streetcars to less expensive motor buses and greater efficiency because the diesel-electric locomotive was clearly superior to the steam engine in urban service. The internal combustion engine also provided the rail transit systems with their greatest challenge—the automobile.

AUTOMOBILES

Before the turn of the century there was an intense rivalry between the various types of engines, although gasoline-powered cars were generally favored in the Midwest.[3] Steamers and electrics both outsold gas cars by substantial margins in 1900, but by 1905 the superiority of the gasoline engine as well as the general availability of its fuel was winning it public acceptance. The range of both steamers and electrics was limited, only about twenty miles before early steamers exhausted their water supply and electrics' batteries were drained. Steamers also were slow to build up a head of steam.[4] The changes needed to make the motor car into a vehicle suitable for commuting were evolutionary but occurred quickly in a highly competitive environment. As many as two thousand different makes of cars were manufactured in the United States between 1893 and 1953.[5] In 1909 alone, 290 makes of car were manufactured in 145 cities in 24 states.[6] At least ten different companies in Chicago tried their hand at building autos in the first quarter of the twentieth century. For a few years, Chicago was the center of production of a type of automobile commonly called the "highwheeler"—a powered buggy developed for unimproved rural roads—but it became an early victim of Henry Ford's Model T, not only because the Model T was a superior vehicle on bad roads but also because the mass-production techniques Ford employed made it cheaper to produce.[7] Inexpensive cyclecars, developed in Chicago and built for a few years before World War I, competed in price with the Model T but did not prove to be very durable.

The development of an automobile suitable for commuting by the middle class required not only the engineering of a reliable vehicle but also mass production in sufficient quantities in order to lower the unit cost to make it affordable to the customer. Henry Ford's Model T—mechanically a rather unspectacular open vehicle of 1,200 pounds powered by a four-cylinder, twenty-horsepower engine—was the first such car. The mass production techniques that Ford's company developed enabled him to cut the Model T unit price from $850 in 1909, the first full year of production, when 17,771 were sold, to $440 in 1916, when yearly production reached 734,811.[8] The development of automobile engines with progressively more power permitted larger and heavier vehicles to be built. By the end of World War I, four-to-five-passenger cars weighing in the vicinity of one ton, propelled by six-to-eight-cylinder engines developing fifty to sixty horsepower, were common. Most important, enclosed cars began to appear in increasing numbers at that time, making it possible for an owner to use his car comfortably in inclement weather. In 1919, only about 10 percent of the autos manufactured in the United States were enclosed, but by 1924 that number had increased to 43 percent, and by 1928 it was at 83 percent.[9] Heaters appeared in 1926.

The streets of Chicago and some of its adjacent suburbs at the turn of the century were in far better condition to accommodate automobile traffic than were roads elsewhere in the state, a factor that led to the early adoption of motor vehicles for pleasure driving and for commercial use in the metropolitan area. Technologically, Chicago was at least half a century ahead of the state in the development of both highway paving and bridges. Frederick Law Olmsted and Calvert Vaux in 1869 and 1870 and Daniel Burnham and Edward Bennett in 1909 gave the city master plans for such things as parkways and thoroughfares but did not deal with the technology of road building. Chicago did that on a trial-and-error basis, experimenting with planking (1840s), pine block surfacing (1850s), macadam (1863), sheet asphalt (1882), brick (1890), and concrete (1905), before it settled on the steel bascule bridge as its standard design for river crossings.[10] The city's Board of Public Works was created in 1861 to build, among other things, a street and bridge system. The State Highway Commission was not created until 1905. By 1910, when the state began to subsidize road paving in rural areas, about half of Chicago's 2,900 miles of streets already had hard surfaces.[11] At that time there were almost 10,000 cars registered in the city.

The city's paving standards, which were by then well established, uniformly called for a 9 1/3-inch thickness for street pavement, including 6 inches of concrete base, a 1.5-inch binder, and a 2-inch asphalt surface, a specification that cost $1.88 per yard, or $40,000 per mile, in 1910.[12] Faced with a potential cost of $60 million for paving its remaining 1,450 miles of dirt streets, the city adopted differing standards for street paving based on the expected traffic density, a practice in use today. From 1910 on, the city's Department of Public Works was in continuous competition to keep pace with the huge increases in volumes of traffic and the quantum increase in vehicle weights that quickly rendered earlier paving techniques obsolete. In Chicago in 1910, there were 799 motor trucks, typically light delivery vehicles not much larger than automobiles, and 58,144 horse-drawn wagons, some of which were capable of hauling 10 tons behind 3 draft horses.[13] In less than 20 years, the number of trucks in Chicago swelled to 54,428, and by 1987 the number of trucks in use in Illinois was 1.6 million—192,000 of them in excess of 10 tons in weight and 86,000 of them in excess of 30 tons.[14]

The sheer volume of automobiles—registration in Chicago went from about 5,000 in 1908 to almost 291,000 in 1925, or one car per 10 residents[15]—was another problem that influenced highway design and ultimately forced road builders to adopt the expensive alternative of grade separation (building bridges and viaducts) to avoid gridlock. In 1925 the city undertook construction of a two-level, limited access roadway named Wacker Drive, which ran along the banks of the river through the downtown area. The first highway project in the city to require the forcible relocation of businesses, it was completed in 1958 when construction of the city's expressway system was well under way.[16] Wacker was finally extended to Lake Shore Drive, Chicago's other proto-expressway, on the east in the 1980s.

Lake Shore Drive, currently a commuter expressway, evolved in stages from the park boulevards first proposed by Olmstead and Vaux after the Civil War. Initially it was built on the South Side as a two-hundred-foot wide, macadam-surface roadway with a broad center road for through traffic and narrower access roads for local traffic. Four decades later the Burnham Plan proposed connecting the park boulevard with a similar one that had been built beginning in 1893 through Lincoln Park on the North Side. That connection created a continuous scenic drive along the lakeshore. Construction began in 1917, and the southern section was completed to Jackson Park in 1929 in plenty of time to serve the Century of Progress fair when it opened in 1933 along the lake just east of the Loop. The northern section of Lake Shore Drive, which was not completed until 1933 when federal depression-era aid was available, was built forty-five feet wide as a multilane, high speed boulevard.[17]

Except for its use of median strips for mass transit, Chicago was not necessarily an innovator in expressway design. The radiation of expressways was dictated by the same geography that determined the pattern of the Potawatomi trails—Lake Michigan was Chicago's eastern boundary. The city also followed closely the fortunes of the Pennsylvania Turnpike and the Los Angeles freeway system, incorporating features of both in its postwar highway-building program. Despite the city's huge

South Water Street in 1924 or 1925, just before its demolition (looking east, with the Northwestern Elevated over Wells Street and construction along Michigan Avenue in the distance), was the site of much of the city's wholesale food market, as it had been since the days when the Chicago River (out of sight to left) was the city's principal avenue of commerce. Warehouse buildings were typically three to four stories high, and the replacement of horses by motor trucks was well under way. (Chicago Transit Authority)

railroad plant, the political establishment had decided even before the end of the depression that the city's future would ride on rubber tires, not on steel wheels.

Planning of the city's expressway system, which took eighteen years and $1.1 billion to complete, began during World War II as a joint venture of the city's Department of Public Works and the Cook County Highway Department. To refine techniques necessary for high-speed, limited freeways, two predominantly suburban expressways, the Edens and the Calumet, were built—at a cost of about $1.6 million per mile. The city then in 1949 attempted its first expressway through developed urban areas, a endeavor that required not only substantial land acquisition costs but also the demolition of hundreds of buildings. The project required the digging of a cut through west suburban Oak Park, which objected to a roadway at grade, and the relocation of hundreds of corpses in cemeteries west of Oak Park. The 15.5-mile Congress (later

Daniel Burnham's plan called for a thoroughfare on the south bank of the river, and Wacker Drive was the result. By 1997 Wacker was lined by office buildings and hotels of 20 stories or higher. The last vestige of the scene prior to Burnham's plan was the elevated structure. (Michael Brown)

renamed the Eisenhower) Expressway, which had eight traffic lanes and a rapid-transit line in its median strip, cost $183.5 million and took eleven years to complete.[18]

The Congress project paled in comparison to the building of the Dan Ryan Expressway. The Dan Ryan, which was begun in 1957, represents the culmination of the road builders' art in Chicago. The refusal of the U.S. Defense Department to allow a bascule bridge—on grounds that it might impede future wartime traffic on the South

Branch of the Chicago River—forced the city to build a sixty-foot high, two-mile-long bridge over the river and the adjacent railroad yards. Because of the expected traffic volumes, the road was designed with an extreme width of fourteen twelve-foot traffic lanes that ran for three miles south of 28th Street to its junction with the Stevenson Expressway. The cost was $282.7 million, or $25.7 million per mile.[19]

The city's plan to build a bascule bridge on an interstate expressway had been the

Conflict between water and street traffic plagued the city from its founding. The excursion steamer *South American* brought traffic on Lake Shore Drive to a halt in the 1950s when it passed through the open bascule bridge. (Michael Brown)

logical extension of Chicago's experience with moveable bridges. That the city was trisected by the river and its branches, substantial maritime traffic arteries, resulted in considerable advances in bridge technology even before the twentieth century. Highway river crossings in much of the nineteenth century were usually handled by ferries, but the volume of both maritime and street traffic in and around downtown Chicago made ferries impractical. A drawbridge to connect the North Side with downtown at Dearborn Street built as early as 1834 proved unsuccessful. Three swinging pontoon bridges were tried in the 1840s, but they were destroyed in the flood of 1848. An iron swing bridge mounted on a pier in the center of the river was built in 1856, but it proved to be an impediment to navigation. After 1900 the city settled on the double-leaf trunnion

bascule bridge, a structure in which two halves of a deck meet in the middle of a river and can be raised to let a ship pass.[20] After completion of the Cortland Street bridge on the North Side in 1902, Chicago built an additional forty-nine bascule bridges, several of them double-decked to carry elevated trains as well as cars.

TRUCKS AND BUSES

It was not long after the development of the horseless carriage that manufacturers began to adapt the internal combustion engine to vehicles built for commercial markets, principally trucks and their derivatives, motor buses. By 1903 gasoline engines were powerful enough at twenty horsepower to run small trucks.[21] The rapid development of trucks for military purposes in World War I in turn led to more powerful engines of up to fifty horsepower and to their adaptation to motor buses, which by 1917 weighed as much as 7 1/2 tons. By 1950, bus engines commonly produced two hundred horsepower to push vehicles weighing nine tons.[22] Within forty years of its appearance, the motor bus had driven the trolley car off the streets of Chicago, although bus networks never assumed the role of the street railways in shaping development.[23]

The evolution of the bus body was a fairly continuous process, but the adaptation of propulsion systems to it was not. The earliest buses in Chicago used gasoline engines, but in 1930 the Chicago Surface Lines began buying electric trolley buses to augment its streetcar system. When the two-stroke cycle diesel engine appeared in Chicago in 1939, it did not result in a wholesale conversion of the fleet (as had occurred on the postwar railroads) because the CTA found a cheaper alternative in the form of the propane engine—at the height of its popularity in 1963 it powered as many as 1,671 of the CTA's fleet of 2,658 buses. During the period between 1945 and 1954, when the railroad conversion to diesel power took place, the Chicago transit systems collectively held 2,412 buses, which were powered by electricity (561), gasoline (770), diesel fuel (130), and propane (951).[24] By 1975, however, the CTA bus fleet was entirely diesel powered.

Primitive motor buses were developed from the horseless carriage as early as 1895 in Europe. In 1900 they showed up in the United States as a twenty-seat, stretched car built by Mack. They did not, however, appear in appreciable numbers in transit service until just before World War I, when urban jitneys, essentially Model T Ford touring cars pressed into service as common carriers, became popular.[25] Within a few years new truck technology was being employed to build progressively larger buses, and bus development went in two divergent directions in Chicago. The new bus companies that appeared to provide service in areas along the lakefront, where there were

no streetcar routes, favored high-capacity, double-deck buses. The Chicago Surface Lines and the street railway companies, which were looking for a cheaper alternative to extending trolley lines into growing areas of the city, favored single-level vehicles of more modest proportions.

The search for the perfect bus in Chicago was a microcosm of what was happening throughout the United States as the nation's street railway system went into decline. On the one hand, transit systems wanted a bus large enough to handle the rush-hour crowd; on the other hand, the bus had to be small enough to run efficiently during the other times it provided service for a considerably reduced market. By the 1920s it was becoming obvious to transit systems, first in the suburbs and later in Chicago, that the bus was going to replace the streetcar. In 1917 Chicago Motor

Trolley buses, used in Chicago in the middle of the twentieth century, were eventually phased out in favor of the more flexible diesel-powered vehicles. (Chicago Transit Authority)

In the 1930s, Chicago Motor Coach bought a series of double-deck, high-capacity buses dubbed "Queen Marys," but their use was limited by railroad viaduct clearances.

(Chicago Transit Authority)

Bus Co. began operating on a 9.5-mile route on Sheridan Road a fleet of double-deck, fifty-one-passenger vehicles built by St. Louis Car Co.[26] While these vehicles had enclosed lower decks, the top decks were open because of the low clearance of the railroad viaducts, a design that effectively limited the capacity of the vehicles in bad weather. The consolidated Chicago Motor Coach, backed by John D. Hertz's fortune, bought progressively larger buses, until in 1934 the company's search for the high-capacity bus culminated with the delivery of the first of a series of completely enclosed, seventy-two-passenger leviathans that were dubbed "Queen Marys" because of their size.

There were a number of very practical reasons why the double-decker in Chicago was doomed from the beginning. For one thing, the operation of double-deckers was limited because of inadequate clearance under the hundreds of railway viaducts built between 1890 and 1920. For another, the new Chicago Transit Authority favored standard buses because they were faster to load and to unload in heavy traffic, they did not have the liability problem of circular stairways that the double-deckers had, and they were not too large to operate on late-night runs, a necessary feature because of the city's mandate that its transit system operate on a twenty-four-hour basis.[27] The last Queen Marys were phased out in mid-1950 and never replaced, although by then the CTA was already beginning to experiment with buses.

In 1948 the CTA ordered from the Twin Coach Co. a fifty-eight-passenger, forty-seven-foot, single-level bus that was built in two sections with an articulation joint between the sections to enable the vehicle to bend in the middle to negotiate turns at intersections. The articulation joint on the "Supertwin," as the bus was called, proved unsatisfactory, however, and no more were ordered.[28] More than two decades later the federal government began prodding agencies such as the CTA to reinvestigate the technology, and the agency after 1978 bought 145 single-level, articulated German buses that were 55 feet long and seated 64.[29]

The necessity of expanding service into underdeveloped areas, where it was too expensive to extend trolley lines, caused the Chicago Surface Lines in the middle 1920s to begin the search for a good single-level bus. What became the prototype for the nation's standard transit bus—a blunt-nosed vehicle seating forty passengers and equipped with a front entry door and rear exit door and a concealed engine in the rear—was designed to the Chicago Surface Lines' specifications by the Twin Coach Co.[30] The first buses delivered were put into service in 1927 on a 1.5-mile route on the Northwest Side on Diversey Avenue, Crawford Avenue (later Pulaski Road), and Laramie Avenue. By 1930 that design had developed into a vehicle about thirty feet long, ninety inches wide, and just under nine feet high that seated a maximum of forty persons.[31] Suburban buses were somewhat smaller.

The restricted environment of operating in street traffic meant that over the next four decades the size of standard buses would grow by only one-third, so that by 1970 a typical transit bus had evolved into a vehicle that was 40 feet long, 102 inches wide, and almost 10 feet high, and that seated 50 passengers.[32] By the time the Chicago Surface Lines was absorbed into the CTA in 1947, it had more than 400 gasoline and electric buses on its roster in addition to its 3,269 streetcars. Chicago Motor Coach had 595 buses when it became part of the CTA in 1952.[33] By then the CTA had already begun to phase out streetcars in favor of buses, a task completed in 1957. The increased flexibility and efficiency of the motor bus was a factor that, when combined with postwar ur-

ban decay, declining population, and the impact of the automobile, resulted in the new CTA cutting its fleet by almost half. By 1980 the CTA's surface fleet consisted of 2,240 buses.

RAILROADS

Adoption of the oil-burning engine developed by Rudolph Diesel in 1893 occurred at a somewhat slower pace on the mainline railroads than had the gasoline engine in the horseless carriage market. The relatively conservative railroads had an enormous investment in steam technology, and despite the fact that the steam locomotive was nearing its technological limits just after the turn of the century, the diesel-electric locomotive did not come into widespread use on railroads until after World War II.[34] There was then a stampede to dieselization, and the conversion of the nation's locomotives took only about ten years to complete. Because diesels were considerably more efficient than steam engines, the conversion of the Chicago commuter railroads contributed significantly to their ability to survive postwar competition from automobiles. After dieselization, the City of Chicago quietly abandoned its plans to force an expensive electrification program on the mainline railroads, a project completed on the Illinois Central commuter line in the 1920s but deferred on the other railroads at the onset of the Great Depression.

There was a collateral benefit of dieselization to Chicago's economy. Although most steam locomotive manufacturing occurred in the East, the dominant manufacturer of diesel-electric locomotives in the nation was the Electro-Motive Division of General Motors Corp. (EMD), based in suburban McCook. Diesel locomotives had been in limited use on railroads in switching service for several years, but a 1934 collaboration between EMD, the Budd Company (a Philadelphia car builder), and the Chicago, Burlington & Quincy Railroad (CB&Q) focused the

The first U.S. transit bus designed as such was the Fageol Twin Coach *(top)*, built to Chicago Surface Lines specifications in 1927. It included an integrated body, front-entrance and rear-exit doors, and an engine beneath the floor. (Krambles Archive)

The Flxible—40 feet long and 8 1/2 feet wide—was built in the 1950s to prevailing standard specifications in Chicago *(right)*. It appears here in front of a Chicago City Railway Co. streetcar barn converted by the CTA to a bus garage. (Chicago Transit Authority)

attention of the public and the railroad industry on the advantages of the new motive power. EMD was attempting to create a market for its new diesels at the same time Budd was trying to crack the railroad passenger-car market dominated by Chicago's Pullman Inc., and the CB&Q was looking for ways to reverse the decline in intercity travel as a result of the depression and competition from the auto.

The collaborators on May 26, 1934, staged a publicity run of the diesel-powered *Pioneer Zephyr* nonstop between Denver and the Century of Progress world's fair in Chicago in an elapsed time of fourteen hours—an astounding average speed of more than seventy miles per hour for a trip of more than one thousand miles.[35] Pullman had somewhat earlier developed for the Union Pacific Railroad a similar streamlined motor train called

M10000.[36] The demonstration of diesel power that was probably most influential on railroad management, however, occurred in 1941 when the Atchison, Topeka & Santa Fe Railway sent a 5,400-horsepower set of EMD diesel locomotives from Chicago to Los Angeles pulling a freight train; it made only five stops, contrasted to the thirty-five stops for water and fuel and nine changes of locomotive that steam power required.[37]

The U.S. railroads were ready to dieselize, but the war intervened before they could acquire any more than 1,517 diesel locomotives (a total of 41,911 steam locomotives were in service in 1941).[38] Once wartime production restrictions were lifted, dieselization occurred quickly. The Burlington, for example, converted first its intercity streamliners to diesel power, then its commuter division, and finally, between

1943 and 1958, its freight service. The North Western's dieselization, which happened even more abruptly, emphasized freight rather than passenger service. The gross ton miles of freight hauled by the railroad's diesel locomotives increased from only 5.1 percent in 1946 to almost 83 percent by 1952, by which time only about two-thirds of the passenger car miles were behind diesel power. The commuter division as late as 1954 still operated half its trains with steam power, although it completed its diesel conversion within a few years.[39] By 1961 the U.S. railroads had 30,123 diesels and only 210 steam engines in service.[40]

The efficiencies from dieselization coincided with the development of the high-

capacity, bilevel coach shortly after World War II. By the time it appeared, the commuter railroad was well established as a conveyance of the upper middle class—well caricatured in innumerable *New Yorker* cartoons featuring men decked out in pin-striped suits and holding briefcases while waiting for the 7:03. The trains were well lighted, heated in winter, cooled in summer, and for the most part punctual, even during heavy snowstorms. The cars on all but the I.C. were equipped with lavatories.

With the introduction of steel cars after 1900 the railroad passenger coach reached its practical limits—a box approximately eighty-five feet long and ten feet wide in which eighty to ninety people could be

Under pressure from the federal government in the 1970s, the CTA acquired a series of German-design articulated buses for high-volume routes. The buses were built in two sections with an articulation joint in the middle to enable them to negotiate tight turns at intersections. (Chicago Transit Authority) seated in comfort. Wooden cars had increased in length from thirty feet (fifty passengers) in 1835 to seventy-two feet (eighty-six passengers) in 1905, but steel construction could only add another ten to twelve feet—a modest increase in passenger capacity.[41] The only way for trains to grow was up, so as World War II drew to a close, Ralph Budd (1879–1962), president of the CB&Q, began casting around for additional innovations to make his intercity passenger trains more competitive. He settled on the idea of a dome car, in effect a glass-enclosed lounge sitting atop a coach to permit riders a grander view of the passing scenery. As a practical matter, this required building a bilevel car in which the standard roof height of thirteen feet, six inches (above the top of the rail) was raised more than two feet.[42] Crews at the Burlington's shops in west suburban Aurora went to work on the problem and in mid-1945 rolled out a dome car rebuilt from a coach.[43]

It occurred to Ralph Budd and his staff that the technological solutions to problems encountered by the Burlington in building a higher car for intercity service could be applied to increasing the capacity of cars used in commuter service.[44] The commuter divisions on American railways often were equipped with hand-me-down coaches and locomotives that had completed their useful life in intercity service, although many coaches were built exclusively for suburban operation.[45] In the 1920s both the Illinois Central and North Western acquired commuter coaches containing a considerable amount of aluminum to lighten them by three to four tons.[46]

The compelling factor in the Burlington's decision to develop a bilevel, high-capacity suburban coach was economic. Lengthening trains to accommodate the growing postwar commuter traffic as suburbs developed along the CB&Q meant lengthening suburban platforms as well. The Chicago Union Station, however, posed a principal problem—platforms could be lengthened only at considerable

cost and the capacity was insufficient to add many rush hour trains. Since Union Station also levied on its tenants a "wheel charge" for each car and locomotive using the station, the bilevel car offered the railroads some relief because it increased car capacity by 50 percent, without increasing wheel charges.[47] Edward G. Budd's engineers in Philadelphia, using what the Burlington had learned in building the dome car, went to work on the problem in 1948 and 1949 and produced the gallery car, known by that name because seating in the upper deck is suspended from the ceiling in a gallery on either side of the aisle. The 61-ton cars were 15-feet, 8-inches high and seated up to 148.[48]

The gallery cars proved so successful after their September 6, 1950, introduction on the Burlington that the North Western, Rock Island, and Milwaukee all ordered new fleets to be built on the same configuration, and the Illinois Central later ordered a self-propelled electric version for its commuter line. The earliest North Western cars seated 169—the highest capacity car in the nation. The North Western, then in the process of modernizing its commuter division, added a new twist. Using train control technology developed earlier for the electric railroads, the railroad equipped some of its new coaches as cab cars so that an engineer sitting in a small compartment in the gallery level could control the train in reverse. This meant substantial savings because the railroads could avoid having to switch engines to the front at every terminal. On a push-pull train the locomotive always stayed at the same end, pulling the train from Chicago and pushing it on the way back.[49]

The diesel locomotive and gallery car probably saved Chicago's commuter railroads. They appeared in the 1950s and gave the railroads a boost just as the automobile became a formidable competitor in suburbia. The story in the city itself was different: the newly public transit system was forced to shrink to survive, a move that meant the abandonment of its street railways.

12

PUBLIC OWNERSHIP

Many hoped that public ownership would permit modernization of Chicago's transit system. For example, Steel L cars were introduced just before World War I, but the private elevated railways lacked sufficient funds to replace more than one-quarter of their wooden fleet with them. These 1924 cars are preserved at the Illinois Railway Museum in Union, Illinois.

♦ The transfer of Chicago's mass-transit system from private ownership to public ownership was neither climactic nor auspicious. Fortunately, the Chicago Transit Authority was born in a relatively quiet period politically, when Chicago's Democratic machine ruled the city unchallenged and without much meddling from the state. When Judge Michael L. Igoe forced the transit issue in 1943, Mayor Edward Kelly, a machine Democrat, and Republican Governor Dwight Green, also of Chicago, simply ne-

gotiated a compromise satisfactory to the two political coalitions in Illinois, with Chicago on one side and the rest of Illinois on the other. The suburbs were not yet a significant factor in state politics. At the time, the ninety-six counties outside the Chicago metropolitan area, known collectively as "downstate," were still the dominant factor in the legislature. Despite the fact that Cook County contained slightly more than half of the state's population, it had only nineteen of the fifty-one legislative

districts, and most of Chicago's suburbs were in one gargantuan district.[1] The legislature was not required to be apportioned on a one-man, one-vote basis until a state constitutional amendment of 1954.

The reapportionment process was, however, slow enough that the suburbs—which in 1960 accounted for more than one-quarter of the population of the state and by 1970 collectively exceeded Chicago in population (see Table A2)—did not become a major factor in state politics until the 1970s. Prior to that time, any progress in the governance of Illinois usually resulted from political compromises between the Chicago Democratic machine and the downstate coalition in the legislature.[2] The relative stability of the new CTA meant that the legislature, which was preoccupied with a massive road building program, had little incentive to meddle in the Chicago transit question.

The Democratic machine, supplying a succession of mayors, from Anton Cermak to Edward Kelly to Martin H. Kennelly to Richard J. Daley, ensured a relatively stable political base that enabled the new CTA to reform the transit system without interference in the 1940s and 1950s. It was only when the CTA had exhausted the financial benefits of those reforms and had to ask for subsidies that the Chicago politicians began to give it closer scrutiny.[3]

It took the new Chicago Transit Authority, which came into existence in 1945, nearly two years to persuade a skeptical investing public to buy its revenue bonds so it could acquire the city's bankrupt traction lines.[4] It then took more than twenty years for the city and the CTA to begin to mobilize the transit system to cope with the realities of postwar population migrations, including the middle-class flight to suburbia. The transit system, comfortable in its dominance of the downtown market and despite warnings as early as 1954, was equally slow to adjust to competition from the automobile.[5] Its biggest problem, however, was something over which it had no control: the legislation that created the

CTA had made it dependent solely on the fare box. A transit system that was unable to survive on fares as a private enterprise was somehow expected to do so as a public entity in a declining market.

The public buyout and modernization of Chicago's street and elevated railways in 1947 and its principal motor bus system in 1952 were financed almost entirely by revenue bonds backed only by the future fare box revenues. Furthermore, by creating an independent municipal corporation in the form of a special taxing district and by giving its lenders extraordinary veto powers over the financial affairs of the new agency, Illinois avoided having to pledge the full faith and credit of either the state or the city to guarantee repayment of the bonds. Indeed, the enabling act specifically excluded any financial liability on the part of those two governments.[6]

Ostensibly, the only role government would have in the new agency would be to appoint its board of directors; but in reality the mayor, by virtue of his powers of appointment of four of the seven members, was in control. In practice, Chicago's mayor designated the board chairmen and frequently used the agency as a haven for patronage. The Chicago Department of Public Works retained control over construction projects, but the new Chicago Transit Authority operated the transit system and was responsible for its maintenance.

In its first twenty-five years of existence, the CTA was really governed by two documents—the Metropolitan Transit Authority Act that had created it and the trust agreements the CTA had signed with the banks to get its revenue bond financing. The agreements imposed some strict financial constraints on the new agency, stipulating the exact priority that various funds were to have on revenues. Operating and maintenance expenses had the highest priority, followed by interest on bonds, then the principal on them, and, finally, depreciation. The depreciation fund was intended for capital projects, but the CTA's annual contributions to it were limited to 8 percent of revenues. That effectively limited the CTA to spending about $10 million per year in capital expansion, but by 1960 the agency was unable to cover even the full 8 percent.[7]

At the start, the CTA had been able to cover the mandates of its trust agreement by reducing expenses. The agency abandoned its poorest performing rapid-transit lines, including the Niles Center, Westchester, Humboldt Park, Stockyards, Kenwood, and Normal Park spurs; modernized equipment to reduce rapid transit crew sizes from eight to two; and replaced its two-man streetcars with one-man buses. Between 1947 and 1960 nearly twenty miles of rapid-transit routes, or about one quarter of its elevated system, and its entire streetcar system were abandoned. It also reduced competition between two systems by altering a substantial number of bus routes to feed traffic to the L. By 1978, about one-third of the passengers who rode CTA trains did so on transfers from surface routes.[8] The modernization enabled the CTA to cut the workforce of the three companies it acquired almost in half, to thirteen thousand in 1964 from twenty-three thousand in 1947.[9] However, as a trade-off for those labor concessions, the CTA in 1951 agreed to include automatic cost-of-living adjustments in its contracts with the Amalgamated Transit Union. The cost-of-living adjustments were easily manageable in the 1950s when employment was shrinking, but in the next decade they had the effect of increasing CTA labor costs to 76 percent of total operating expenses in 1966 from only 56 percent in 1956.[10] Actual labor costs rose more than 50 percent, from $77 million in 1958 to $116 million in 1968, despite a general inflation rate of 20 percent.[11]

In the early years of the agency, Chicago mayors appointed to the CTA board a succession of public-spirited business leaders who, with general manager Walter J. McCarter, the longest tenured chief executive in CTA history (from 1947 to 1964), affected many reforms.[12] Ralph Budd was a respected railroad executive who served as the CTA's second, and possibly its best, chairman. He was an early proponent of railroad dieselization and was responsible for the Burlington Railroad's Zephyr streamliners in the 1930s as well as its development of bilevel cars in the 1940s. After earning his civil engineering degree at age nineteen from a small Iowa college, Budd went to work for the Chicago, Rock Island & Pacific, then moved to Panama to rebuild the cross-isthmus railroad there, before joining James J. Hill's railroad empire in St. Paul. By the time he was forty years old in 1919, he was president of Hill's Great Northern Railroad; in 1931 he was sent to Chicago to steer the Burlington through the Great Depression. His relaxed, gentlemanly, judicious manner enabled him to become the industry's most influential representative to the government during the depression.[13] When Budd retired from railroading in 1949, Mayor Kennelly picked him to run the CTA. During his tenure as CTA chairman, Budd modernized the CTA's antiquated rolling stock by buying rapid transit cars and buses; he figured out a way to finance all his purchases with a single issue of equipment trust certificates.[14]

Unfortunately, the one-time gains in efficiency made in the 1950s by Budd could not be duplicated in the 1960s. As ridership declined and inflation forced up costs, the CTA was faced with the necessity of raising fares nine times between 1947 and 1970 (see Table A7). While the percentage of the increases was not unrealistic, the timing of the price increases caused trouble. The fares were raised six times between 1947 (ten cents) and 1957 (twenty-five cents) but were not increased again until the CTA board finally acted and raised them in 1967 (thirty cents). The agency, which had already exhausted the financial benefits of the modernization program, was about to embark on an expansion program that would substantially increase its operating costs. By the end of 1970 the CTA had raised the base fare to forty-five cents.

The 1950s belief that fare increases would accelerate the decline in ridership left the CTA with no option but to begin to defer maintenance and to starve the depreciation fund, which began as early as 1960.[15] By the end of the decade, the CTA was having trouble covering its bonded indebtedness despite three fare increases in as many years. Its financial problems began to get the attention of the Chicago politicians. The agency, which until that time had been managed as if it were a privately owned utility, in 1970, for the first time in its existence, ran a deficit, which on paper was $4 million out of an operating budget of $188.7 million, although the actual difference between fares and costs was almost $14 million.[16] The financial hemorrhage that was to plague it for much of the rest of the century had begun.

Despite simmering problems, the decade of the 1960s was also a time when Chicago's political leaders and transit managers began to think about expansion to cope with the realities of a migrating population. The contraction of the Ls ended in the 1950s. The impediment to expansion, of course, was money, so the timing of the penniless CTA's new projects invariably coincided with the availability of funds from one external source or another. Poverty prevented the CTA from taking over and operating the Chicago, Aurora & Elgin interurban when it abandoned passenger service in 1957. The CTA was willing to provide service, but not without being protected from any losses the service might incur.[17] An attempt by Mayor Richard J. Daley to assemble a Chicago-suburban legislative coalition and to use the CA&E's imminent demise as a ploy to divert state gasoline tax funds from highway programs to mass transit did not receive sufficient support from the city, from the suburbs, or from downstate. Daley, who was still in his first term as mayor, decided not to force the issue.[18]

The federal government began subsidizing mass transit in the early 1960s, at which time Chicago applied for a demonstration grant to restore service on its Niles Center line, abandoned in 1948.[19] The timing of the federal government's entrance into the business of subsidizing mass transit also coincided with the demise in 1963 of the Chicago, North Shore & Milwaukee interurban, whose right-of-way the CTA hoped to use. The CTA applied to the U.S. Housing and Home Finance Agency for a grant to subsidize operation of the line from the CTA's Howard Street terminal five miles to Dempster Street in the northern suburb of Skokie (formerly known as Niles Center). The shuttle, renamed *Skokie Swift* when it began service on April 20, 1964, proved to be a success, producing an operating profit of $216,717 on revenues of just under $800,000 in its first two years of operation.[20] The Skokie line was the first extension of Chicago's L since Samuel Insull's CRT in 1930 started a line to west suburban Westchester. Indeed, the rapid-transit system had shrunk from 75.3 route miles at the beginning of the depression to about 56 miles just before the Skokie line opened (see Table A8).

The city had established itself as the pioneer of expressway median transit in the 1950s when it replaced the former Garfield Park elevated line with the new Congress Expressway, a thoroughfare containing a 9.5-mile rapid-transit line in its median as far west as suburban Forest Park.[21] This arrangement enabled Chicago to finance the project largely with highway funds and to use the original right-of-way acquired by the Metropolitan West Side L in 1892. The median transit system became a model for similar lines in other cities.[22] Chicago had made accommodations for the roadway as early as 1933 when the designers of the proposed federal Post Office at Canal and Congress Streets were induced to include an open center arch on the lower levels of the building to allow a superhighway to pass through it.[23]

The success of both the Congress project and the *Skokie Swift* influenced Chicago to proceed with plans to place rapid-transit lines in the median strips of two additional expressways. The Dan Ryan and Stevenson Expressways were designed with medians sufficiently wide for rapid transit, but the southwest line intended for the Stevenson was ultimately built in another location in order to serve the Midway Airport farther south. By 1966, the city had proceeded with the Ryan project by issuing $195 million in general obligation bonds, $28 million of which were intended for the median transit line as a one-third match for federal mass-transit capital grants that by then were becoming available.[24] The Ryan line was not intended to replace the parallel, 1892 Jackson-Englewood elevated, which ran four blocks to the east; rather, its purpose was to relieve congestion on that aging system and to extend the rapid-transit system ending at 63rd Street an additional 3.5 miles south to 95th Street.[25] Almost simultaneously, Chicago began building a $50 million extension of the Milwaukee elevated line an additional 5.2 miles from its terminal at Logan Square into the median of the existing Kennedy Expressway as far northwest as Jefferson Park, with the intention of eventually extending it to O'Hare International Airport, a goal that was reached in 1984.

RED INK AND CRISIS

The combined effect of the Ryan and Milwaukee extensions, while they increased ridership by 2.5 percent, was disastrous to the bottom line of a transit system that was already under financial stress. The two extensions in 1970 increased the operating costs of the CTA's rapid-transit system by 24 percent, or $211,000 per week.[26] For the first time in the agency's history, revenue from fares (at $174.9 million) failed to cover operating costs ($179.1 million). Suddenly, the CTA was in jeopardy of being unable to cover the principal and interest on its bonded indebtedness, then totaling $9.6 million.[27]

Two events occurred in 1970 that had a substantial impact on the transit solution: the decennial census indicated that for the first time Chicago's suburbs surpassed the city in population, and a convention was held in Springfield to revise the state's century-old constitution. The census data meant that any political solution that included a cross subsidy from the suburbs to Chicago was going to have to involve the sharing of power in any new agency created for that purpose. The Chicago delegation to the constitution convention waited until the final month to raise the issue of subsidies for mass transit. On August 1, 1970, Michael J. Madigan, a delegate as well as a state representative and a future speaker of the Illinois House, proposed a clause establishing mass transit "as an essential public purpose for which public funds may be expended." The proposed constitutional clause established the principle that public funds could be used to subsidize a private carrier, an important compromise intended to attract suburban support for a regional transportation agency.[28] Although some of the suburban systems were in worse shape than the CTA system, the problems of the CTA attracted the bulk of public attention. CTA ridership had declined to one-third of what it had been in 1946, and fares had more than quadrupled to keep the system solvent. The automobile was rapidly approaching the peak of its popularity in Chicago, which occurred in 1978, when counts estimated slightly more than one car for every two residents.[29]

The mass-transit clause was approved by both the convention and the voters in a referendum later in 1970, and Governor Richard B. Ogilvie, a Republican from Chicago, moved quickly to implement it even before the constitution went into effect on July 1, 1971. As early as February 17 he created a state office in the Department of Local Government Affairs to deal with mass transit. Two days later he successfully urged the General Assembly to budget a $900 million transportation bond issue to include $200 million for capital projects for

Redundant service has always been a feature of Chicago transit. The North Western commuter line (left of construction timbers), elevated in 1907, ran side-by-side with the Lake Street L (center) and a streetcar line on Lake Street at Pine Avenue in Austin. The ramp to the Lake elevated structure appears in the background. (Krambles Archive)

mass transit. The legislature also concurred in his recommendation to convert the Highway Department into a broad-based Transportation Department and to pass an emergency transportation act to allow the state to use its transportation bonds to cover the interest and principal on any outstanding revenue bonds or equipment trust certificates the CTA had.[30]

Ogilvie in late 1971 appointed a special commission staffed largely by people with transportation backgrounds to find a long-term solution to Chicago's transit problems. He was defeated for reelection in November 1972, largely because of his role in supporting imposition of a state income tax, and the commission hurriedly completed its work in the remaining two months of his term so that the incoming governor, Democrat Dan Walker, could not dodge the transit issue.[31] That was hardly possible. The CTA, expecting additional state relief, had taken no steps to stop what had become a financial hemorrhage and was projecting an operating deficit approaching $50 million by the end of 1973.[32] Indeed, some suburban Republicans suspected the CTA's financial crisis was carefully calculated to occur in the summer of 1973, when a new governor was installed in Springfield and the legislature was balanced to the point that one vote separated the parties, an inducement to compromise.[33]

John M. Cook had prepared a long-range economic forecast for Ogilvie's task

force indicating that the Chicago area transit system, including the CTA, suburban buses, and commuter railroads, would need about $229.7 million in annual subsidies by 1980.[34] The forecast was suppressed for fear it would destroy any political compromise before it could be adopted by the state legislature. In the autumn of 1973, Walker engineered a transfer of $12 million from the state through Cook County to the CTA, but that transfer occurred simply to keep the system running until a long-term solution could be devised. The solution inevitably required a major political compromise to include the diversion of tax funds on a regular basis to mass transit, a cross subsidy from the suburbs to Chicago, and, as a result, the shar-

ing of power between the city and suburbs in some sort of regional agency.

PUBLIC TRANSIT'S LIMITS

There is some question whether the CTA and the other public transit monopolies had reached the limits of their ability to reform urban mass transportation by the end of the 1950s. Much later, Regional Transportation Authority chairman Thomas J. McCracken suggested, "The CTA's efficiencies have reached the limit of the traditional public service model."[35] The issue of limits was first raised by economist George W. Hilton in testimony before Congress in 1974.[36] The conversion from streetcars to diesel buses had been done to

By the end of the twentieth century, the Lake elevated line had been moved to the North Western causeway, the trolley line had been abandoned, and Lake Street ceded to the automobile.

(Michael Brown)

cut expenses, Hilton said, enabling the CTA to reduce its operating costs by forty-eight cents per vehicle mile. Unfortunately, buses lent themselves to a more diffused urban development, a growth with which the transit monopolies had difficulty coping. Early in the century, Hilton continued, streetcar companies had induced city councils across the country to ban jitneys in order to preserve their franchise monopolies. When it converted its streetcar system to buses, the CTA, being an overcapitalized and unionized monopoly, chose large, fifty-passenger vehicles closest in size to the abandoned trolleys. For the most part, it operated them on the same streetcar system. The large buses provided the maximum number of seats in a vehicle in which the driver accounted for 75 to 85 percent of operating costs.[37] The inability—for political reasons—of the public transit monopolies to get rid of competing routes inherited from competitive private carriers is often cited as another factor contributing to their financial crisis in the 1970s.[38] In Chicago, for example, the most cited case of such redundant service was the operation of a bus line on Lake Street beneath the elevated railway structure. In this case, CTA officials insisted that the buses handled local traffic while the L handled commuters bound for the Loop.

By the 1980s, Milton Pikarsky, who over the years had served as Chicago's public works director as well as the chairman of both the CTA and the Regional Transportation Authority, had gone so far as to suggest that the institution of the public transit system was beginning to break down. According to Pikarsky, changes in American commuting patterns after World War II were once again making the private sector the dominant player in urban mass transportation, though not in the way it had been in the nineteenth century, when it owned and operated streetcar and elevated lines. The use of private cars had increased, and companies employing large numbers of people provided free parking. In some instances companies offered vans for pool commuting; in a few cases they ran buses for specialized routes that the mass-transit agencies were unwilling or unable to provide. Ultimately these changes could transform the role of such agencies from operator of fixed bus routes to that of travel information broker, facilitator, technical adviser, and manager of service contracts.[39]

13

SUBSIDIES AND REGIONAL GOVERNMENT

The growth of the suburbs increased the need for coordinated transportation policies. Rush-hour commuter trains in the first half of the twentieth century, such as this North Western train photographed in Glen Ellyn in 1950, reached far into Chicago's hinterland. This train consisted of coaches, seating eighty persons each, pulled by a 4-6-2 Pacific locomotive. (Krambles Archive)

♦ As transit systems across the nation experienced financial deterioration, among them the Chicago Transit Authority, the dilemma faced by state and local governments of the 1960s was whether to subsidize or to abandon mass transit. Many systems had already shrunk to the point that further cutbacks would be tantamount to abandonment. Federal and state governments were preoccupied with interstate highway building, and cities for the most part did not have the necessary funds or the willingness to spend them on a utility that had been self-supporting for a century.[1]

The sheer size of the system in the Chicago metropolitan area made liquidation unlikely. Although the CTA was beginning to expand once again after its downsizing in the 1950s, all but one of the interurban railroads were scrapped, and many privately owned suburban bus systems were threatened with extinction. Even the commuter railroad system was considering some selective pruning.

Everything being equal, the CTA could probably have survived on its fare box revenues had it not become the victim of a number of forces beyond its control,

The stainless steel cars of the 1960s, such as those assigned to the *Skokie Swift* (shown here), drew current from overhead wires instead of from the third rail common on most of the CTA system.

including the outmigration of population and jobs to suburbia. Downtown Chicago prospered, as did the fringes of the city, but urban blight infected the older areas of the inner city that were served by the Ls as well as by the bus network inherited from the street railway grid. The unemployed poor who moved into the three-flats and bungalows on the West and South Sides did not ride transit as frequently as the workers who had to commute every day. Increased auto use took its toll on transit ridership in the city, but not nearly as much as in the suburbs, where financially distressed bus systems found it impossible to cope with urban sprawl.

The most obvious first step toward improvement as the financial deterioration worsened after 1960 was for the federal government to provide subsidies for cities to buy their transit systems. Money for new equipment, maintenance, and especially expansion became the next priority. The conventional wisdom in Washington and Springfield then was that shiny, new equipment and additional routes would somehow reverse the exodus of Americans from transit to their automobiles. Neither the politicians nor the public were willing at that time to use taxes to subsidize fares.[2]

Although the federal government had given sporadic capital subsidies to Chicago transit as early as World War I, and projects such as the State and Dearborn subways and the Congress Expressway line could not have been built without them, annual federal capital grants did not appear until the 1970s. The decisions by both Washington and Springfield to subsidize transit were the result of a long, slow process. The state and federal legislatures that poured billions of dollars into highway building programs considered mass transit a private enterprise, and even after the systems were publicly acquired, they considered their financial plight as strictly local problems.[3]

It took America's large cities from 1959, when representatives first met in Chicago to plot a lobbying strategy, to 1974 to persuade Congress to provide transit operating subsidies on a regular basis. A modest experimental program was begun in 1961, and because there was not a federal agency that dealt with transit, the initial $25 million in demonstration grants was included in the Omnibus Housing Act and administered by the Housing and Home Finance Agency.[4] It was that fund that the CTA used to revive the rail spur to suburban Skokie.

Although there were clear signals in the 1960s that federal subsidies were not going to be a panacea—Washington in the postwar period had spent only $375 million on mass transit, in contrast to $24 billion on roads, aviation, and waterways—the transit lobby was persistent. In 1970 it obtained passage by Congress of the Urban Mass Transportation Act, which committed the federal government to $3.1 billion in capital grants over the subsequent three years. In 1974, the transit lobby, of which the CTA was a key member, finally received federal operating subsidies with passage of the National Mass Transit Assistance Act. Those subsidies, however, were intended to cover "new" deficits from expansion, not deficits from existing service.[5]

While operating subsidies were considered a supplement to local funds, the federal and state governments assumed almost total responsibility for capital programs. From virtually nothing in 1970, by 1980 federal subsidies had increased to 80 percent of capital expenditures for Chicago and suburban transit, and the state provided most of the remaining 20 percent. Of the $169.1 million regional capital program that year, only about $100,000 came from local sources. During the six-year period between 1980 and 1985, local funds accounted for only about 4.4 percent, or $61.4 million, of the $1.4 billion capital program.[6] That was augmented by an additional $1.173 billion in diverted highway funds after the city and state in 1979 decided to cancel the proposed Crosstown Expressway on the West Side. The transfer enabled the city to build a transit line to Midway Airport and to extend another to O'Hare International Airport, although the suburbs spent most of their share on highways.[7]

State entry into the business of subsidizing mass transit was far more abrupt than federal entry had been. The entire phenomenon occurred in the three-year span between the Constitutional Convention of 1970 and the adoption by the legislature in 1973 of the act creating a regional transportation authority.[8] Governor Ogilvie persuaded the state legislature to include $200 million in capital grants for

This steel and aluminum car, based on the technology of the PCC streetcar, became the CTA's standard rapid-transit vehicle for three decades. This car was donated to the Illinois Railway Museum in Union, Illinois.

mass transit in his $900 million state transportation (highway) bond issue, adopted soon after the new state constitution legalizing transit subsidies was ratified by voters in a statewide referendum. It was assumed those state bonds would serve as the requisite 20 percent local match for the federal capital subsidies.

With a steady source of capital subsidies assured, the various governments involved turned their attention to the problem of operating deficits that had unexpectedly

become quite large. Ogilvie appointed a task force to find a solution, and as expected, the task force recommended creation of a regional transportation authority for the six-county Chicago metropolitan area.[9] The use of a special taxing district, the Regional Transportation Authority (RTA), to fund the existing CTA effectively nullified any opposition from downstate politicians, since it left the issue of transit subsidies up to the voters of each metropolitan area to provide them.

REGIONAL TRANSPORTATION AUTHORITY

Several other provisions of the compromise that emerged from the legislature in late 1973 were notable, but none more so than that of the concept of shared power. The concept was not new: the Metropolitan Sanitary District, a jurisdiction that overlapped city and suburbs dating from 1889, when it was created to dig the Sanitary and Ship Canal, and two regional planning agencies—the Chicago Area Transportation Study and the Northeastern Illinois Planning Commission—were created after World War II to include both city and suburbs, although both were advisory agencies with no real powers. The RTA Act, however, was the first time the Democratic machine that had governed Chicago since 1932 agreed to share power within its borders with suburban Republicans. The act evenly split the appointments to the board between city and suburbs, and the eight original board members were to select a ninth member to serve as chairman.[10]

To avoid having the suburbs meddle with a utility as important to Chicago's well-being as its transit system, the existing CTA was left intact. The RTA's power over the CTA was restricted to budgetary matters, and the act was written requiring the consent of six out of nine members to pass appropriations ordinances, effectively giving either side veto power. The most important compromise from the perspective of the CTA was the one giving the RTA the power of taxation to provide a cross subsidy to Chicago from the suburbs.[11] The act originally permitted gasoline and parking taxes, but when the gas tax proved inadequate and the parking tax proved infeasible a sales tax was substituted.

The March 19, 1974, referendum on creation of the RTA clearly defined the emerging Chicago-suburban political rift. The issue carried by less than 1 percent of the vote—13,000 votes out of 1.36 million cast—largely on the strength of its showing in Chicago, where it got a 71 percent plurality. In suburban Will, Kane, and McHenry Counties, the returns showed nine voters in ten were opposed to the RTA, and in the other two suburban counties the negative vote seemed directly proportional to the distance of the precinct from a commuter railroad.[12]

In many respects, the vote was the first major display of the political strength of the newly emerging suburban, principally Republican, faction in state politics. The suburban population had tripled between 1940 and 1970, and after the 1970 reapportionment, the first year in which the suburban population exceeded that of Chicago, the suburbs began attempting to flex their new political muscle. From the beginning, Chicago and downstate legislators found it difficult to deal with the new suburban faction, since the suburbs rarely had a common agenda that could be used in the normal political process of swapping votes. In the case of the RTA, the Republican leadership in the legislature favored creation of the new agency, as did a number of legislators from suburban Cook County districts with transit service, though most suburban legislators on both sides of the aisle were adamantly opposed. Indeed, support of the RTA Act cost Republican House Speaker W. Robert Blair, one of the state's most powerful Republicans, his seat in the November 1974 general election.[13]

The Chicago machine won the first fight, the referendum, but the suburbanites proceeded to turn the new RTA into a political battleground over the next decade. While the Chicago Democrats attempted to protect their control of the CTA and the necessary money to run it, the suburbanites moved to minimize the cross-subsidy and to divert more funds to suburban transit systems. The two factions immediately became mired in a dispute when Mayor Daley, in the process of selecting a chairman, advanced the name of Milton Pikarsky (1924–1989), a respected and apolitical engineer who had served the city in a number of important jobs. Although the suburban faction had no candidate of their own, they resisted

The railroads in the 1950s experimented with self-propelled cars at off-peak times. This Budd Co. railway diesel car shown at Oak Park was one of three such vehicles bought by the North Western in 1950 and sold in 1957 when they did not pan out. (Krambles Archive)

Pikarsky's appointment, and the RTA board was unable to elect a chairman for nine months.[14] Even after the suburbs finally caved in on January 31, 1975, Pikarsky became a political lightning rod in the city-suburban struggle, and he lasted only three and a half years before being forced to resign.[15]

The Pikarsky episode indicated the extent to which the metropolitan area's transit system was becoming politicized. Even the Chicago Transit Authority became infected after the Chicago machine broke down following the death of Mayor Daley in 1976. The CTA, which had only four chairmen and two chief executives in its first twenty-six years of existence, had seven chairmen and seven chief executives in its second twenty-one years.[16] Pikarsky represents the end of the influence of technocrats in transit management and the beginning of the age of generalists whose principal skills were political.[17] The son of a Polish immigrant and haberdasher in New

York, Pikarsky was a workaholic who graduated from the City College of New York, then impressed successively more important bosses with his ability to finish complex engineering projects on deadline. Mayor Daley hired him in 1960 as a public works engineer, and in 1964, at the age of forty, Pikarsky became the youngest person in Chicago history to be appointed commissioner of public works. In that job he oversaw the rapid-transit lines built in the median strips of the Ryan and Kennedy Expressways. When CTA Chairman Michael Cafferty unexpectedly died in 1973, Daley placed Pikarsky in that job, then two years later moved him to the new RTA.[18] His failing there was that the agency needed a politician, not an engineer.

The RTA was not entirely paralyzed by the political struggle that dominated its early years. Shortly after the Illinois Supreme Court ruled the new agency constitutional[19] on June 28, 1974, but seven months before it had selected a chairman,

the RTA board, governing as a committee of the whole, began dispensing subsidies. The first major crisis occurred on March 17, 1975, when the Chicago, Rock Island & Pacific Railroad filed for bankruptcy. One month later the Illinois Commerce Commission ruled it was shutting down part of the railroad's commuter line because of unsafe tracks.[20] Ultimately the RTA acquired, rehabilitated, and reequipped the Rock Island, as well as stabilized the remainder of the transit system with subsidies to cover deficits.

The agency, however, had made no progress in solving the problem that would become its undoing—the rapidly escalating costs at the CTA. These had increased from $188.7 million in 1970 to more than $446.1 million in 1979. By then the five-year-old RTA was clearly running out of money to subsidize the Chicago transit system, which accounted for 70 percent of the RTA's budget.[21] The RTA had been forced to raise fares by 11 percent in 1976 and to impose a 5 percent gasoline tax in 1977.[22] When those measures proved inadequate, the RTA in 1979 appealed to the state legislature for a sales tax.

The decision proved to be a major miscalculation. The legislation that emerged from the increasingly hostile General Assembly later that year abolished not only the gas tax but also a state operating subsidy and replaced it with a differential sales tax of 1 percent in Cook County and one-quarter of a percent in the five collar counties.[23] The compromise was largely the result of the refusal of suburban legislators to increase the cross subsidy for the CTA, and it reduced the RTA's annual revenues by $60 million.[24] Until that time, neither the RTA nor the CTA had made much of an effort to control costs, and they spiraled upward even as ridership continued to decline. Between 1976 and 1980, CTA annual revenues increased by only $20.6 million, but annual costs increased by $167 million at an agency that in 1976 was already reporting a deficit of $105.5 million. By 1980, the deficit had

grown to $281.8 million (see Table A9).

Late in 1979, Chicago began to take steps to control costs, which would have been unthinkable for a labor-oriented big-city political machine just a few years earlier. The mood of the Chicago electorate, however, was changing. Daley died in 1976, and renegade candidate Jane Byrne upset his successor, Michael Bilandic, in the Democratic primary in early 1979 largely on the campaign issue of the city's failure to plow streets adequately and to keep the CTA running during a succession of blizzards. Byrne, mindful of how transit had become a political issue in Chicago, successfully weathered a four-day strike by transit workers in December that was settled only after the strikers were unable to prevent CTA management from operating limited rush-hour service on several elevated lines. Although the settlement did not alter the CTA's cost-of-living escalation clauses with its unions—clauses that pegged automatic pay raises to increases in the consumer price index—it was the beginning of the end for that budget-busting provision.[25]

By 1981, the RTA was facing a financial crisis bordering on insolvency. When the legislature refused to increase subsidies, the transit agency doubled fares on the commuter railroads and increased them by 50 percent on the CTA. The result was public outrage and an abrupt defection by thousands of riders. The overall decline in ridership for the system was 29.1 percent between December 1980 and December 1981, but it varied in specific areas from 9 percent on the Chicago Transit Authority, to 35 percent on the suburban bus system, to 40 percent on some commuter railroads. Analysis of station-by-station ridership data indicates a substantial shift in patronage from the railroads to the CTA at outlying stations by riders taking advantage of lower CTA fares, which offset CTA losses in the inner city.[26]

Reform of the RTA did not occur until after the defeat of Jane Byrne by Harold Washington, the city's first black mayor, in

1982, and the reelection the next year of Republican Governor James Thompson, a Chicagoan. A disenchanted state legislature dismissed the RTA board, stripped the agency of its authority to operate suburban transit systems, and—as a method of imposing fiscal discipline and forcing periodic fare increases—mandated that in the future fare box revenue must account for at least half of operating costs. As a sop to varying suburban interests, the General Assembly created two new agencies to run train and bus service in the suburbs. Republican suburban county boards were empowered to appoint the directors of Metra, the commuter railroad agency, and the largely nonpartisan suburban mayors were given the authority to run Pace, the suburban bus system. The RTA was retained to maintain budgetary oversight and to dispense funds.[27]

The political compromise of 1983 brought stability to the metropolitan transit systems for more than a decade, but by the mid-1990s, the CTA was once again suffering from declining ridership. It had lost more than one-third of its patronage since 1979 (see Table A10) and again was having difficulty operating its system with the available revenues. Some of the decline was because Chicago lost more than one-fifth of its population—more than 800,000 residents—since peaking at 3.62 million in 1950. In retrospect, the 1983 compromise mandating some discipline on the fare increase process only slowed the CTA's rate of decline: deficits that grew at the rate of $26.8 million per year in the decade of the 1970s slowed to $4.6 million per year in the 1980s (see Table A9).

Migration within the metropolitan area was probably a more serious problem to the Chicago transit system than the overall decline in population, especially to the rapid-transit system, which, unlike the bus network, could not easily be rerouted to abandon declining neighborhoods and to pick up gentrifying ones. Although Chicago government made a substantial and successful effort to bring rapid-transit

rail service to all compass points of the city by the end of the century[28]—a task completed in 1993 with the opening of the 9-mile, $410 million line from the Loop to Midway Airport—the city seemed unable or politically unwilling to continue the abandonments established between 1947 and 1960 to adjust to the changes in population and land use. For example, the population density of areas along both the original South Side (later Jackson-Englewood) and the Lake Street elevated lines had declined substantially as a result of urban blight and racial unrest in the 1960s—especially after the rioting that followed civil-rights leader Martin Luther King's assassination in 1968[29]—but full service continued to run on both. The city also made no attempt to build a rapid-transit line along the densely populated and growing affluent Gold Coast, leaving that market to the CTA bus system. Daily ridership on CTA buses entering the central area of Chicago from the North Side in 1988 was 39,202, double that of buses entering from the West Side (18,534) and sufficient by standards of the day to support a rapid-transit line.[30]

DOWNTOWN AND SUBURBAN TRANSIT PLANS

Chicago had made two serious but unsuccessful attempts at expanding its downtown transit system. The principal purpose of both projects was to enable Chicago's rapid-transit system and to a lesser extent its commuter railroads to deal with growth of the downtown area from one square mile in 1950 to six square miles by 1993. Sixty percent of that downtown growth after 1979 occurred outside the old Loop.[31] For the same reasons the Loop L was originally built in the 1890s and its two subways were dug nearly a half century later—principally to get mass transit out of downtown traffic gridlock—Chicago determined by the 1960s that its bus system was hopelessly inadequate for the task of serving as a downtown circulator. Buses vulnerable to traffic congestion were simply too slow, in some cases taking twenty-nine minutes to travel two miles during rush hour.[32]

Downtown Chicago in the late twentieth century had become transit's last stand—the only market it still dominated. However, the inability of the constricted transit system to capitalize on the doubling of office space in the downtown area from 46.9 million square feet in 1970 to 107.3 million square feet in 1992 and the resulting increase in the number of downtown parking spaces everywhere but within the Loop (from 53,710 spaces in 1970 to 74,939 in 1988) were ominous signs. In the Loop the number of spaces declined by 2,000 over the same span, and in 1988 that area accounted for less than one-tenth of the available parking in downtown Chicago but one-third of the office space.[33]

The Chicago Urban Transit District (CUTD), another special taxing district, was created as a result of a referendum in 1970 for the sole purpose of building new subways to replace the Loop after a 1968 study recommended that course of action.[34] The project recommended by the Chicago Central Area Transit Planning Study called for two new subway systems—one to replace the Loop L and the other to be an east-west subway beneath the heart of the Loop to serve as a downtown circulator connecting the McCormick Place convention center on the lakeshore at 22nd Street and the growing retail and office area along Michigan Avenue north of the Chicago River. The new agency was empowered to impose a tax on downtown property in order to provide the local match for a federal grant for the project, which was originally estimated to cost $500 million, a price tag that quickly swelled to $2 billion in the high-inflation Vietnam War years.[35] The unlikelihood of obtaining a federal grant that size caused the CUTD to scale back the project, eventually to the point that the only line left was a third north-south subway under Franklin Street west of the Loop—a pro-

ject favored by the business community because it was less disruptive to the downtown area and served Sears, Roebuck & Co.'s new skyscraper tower.

The proposed Franklin subway, however, did nothing to accomplish the purpose for which the CUTD was established, and in 1979 Mayor Byrne and Governor Thompson canceled that project, along with the proposed Crosstown Expressway on the West Side, and diverted the federal grants earmarked for them to other transportation programs.[36] The legislature finally abolished the CUTD in 1984 and transferred the $12 million remaining in its coffers to the CTA.[37]

Within a few years the city was once again at work on plans for a U-shaped circulator system, in this case a less-expensive street railway to connect the commuter railroad stations south and west of the Loop with the retail area north of the Chicago River and with the museums and McCormick Place convention center along the south lakeshore. The downtown retail community quickly advanced its interests, a line serving the State Street shopping district was added, and costs once again ballooned. The project was estimated at $689.4 million when it was abruptly canceled in 1995 after the new Republican Congress failed to appropriate money for it.[38] Despite its antiquity (it reached its one hundredth anniversary in 1997) the Loop L structure has persevered surprisingly well. As recently as 1994 it handled 37,500 passengers per day, only slightly less than the 40,700 who had ridden it in 1967.[39]

Even as Chicago contemplated modernizing the core of its transit system, the new regional transit agency was looking in other directions. By 1987, both the financial and political situations had become sufficiently stable that the RTA, which had been reapportioned after the 1980 census to give suburbanites a majority on the board, began to turn its attention to strategic planning for the suburbs. The final project in the expansion of Chicago's transit system in the twentieth century, the

By 1997, commuter trains consisted of bilevel cars, seating as many as 150 persons each, powered by diesel locomotives. This photograph was shot along the Union Pacific Railroad in Glen Ellyn.

CTA's rapid-transit line to Midway Airport, was completed in 1993. The RTA succeeded in greatly expanding service on its commuter railroad line to southwest suburban Orland Park, and in 1996, the RTA's Commuter Rail Division, commonly known as Metra (for metropolitan rail), opened a line from Chicago to Antioch near the Wisconsin border over Wisconsin Central Railroad tracks, the first

new rail line in suburbia in seventy years.

As the century waned, however, the federal government's intervention forced the RTA to readjust its priorities from expansion to cost containment. In the years spanning 1975 to 1995 Washington had provided Chicago's regional transit system with $1,165,275,737 in operating subsidies.[40] As more conservative governments in the 1990s began to look for ways to reduce budgetary deficits, transit subsidies became vulnerable to cost cutting. As early as 1977, just three years after the first federal operating subsidies began to flow, the Democratic administration of President Jimmy Carter began to balk at further increases.[41] When conservative Republican Ronald Reagan arrived in the White House in 1980, he began a concerted effort to cut federal spending. In the 1990s, Congress finally cut the appropriations for operating assistance for mass transit, putting pressure on the RTA to find ways to make ends meet.[42]

In 1995, the regional agency suggested reprivatization of some of the CTA system as a way to cut costs. Despite the conversion of the mass-transit systems from the private to the public sector, there still existed in the Chicago area as late as 1990 more than fourteen thousand privately owned buses serving schools, the airports, some transit routes, and charter services, in contrast to slightly more than two thousand publicly owned buses in transit service.[43] Privatization was the topic of a series of public hearings held by the regional agency in July and August 1995 at which were discussed cost reductions resulting from earlier privatization of systems in London, Los Angeles, San Diego, and Denver.[44] Pace, the RTA's Suburban Bus Division, had contracted bus routes to private contractors since its inception in 1983, a practice that the RTA and other

suburban transit districts had adopted earlier. As late as 1995, such contracts represented 10 percent of Pace's expenditures.[45]

Political inertia aside, the principal stumbling block to privatization was the opposition of the CTA's strong unions, locals of the Amalgamated Transit Union.[46] The Civic Federation, an organization instrumental in the early attempts to reform the Chicago transit system in the robber baron era and an early proponent of public ownership of the street railways, was also opposed to reprivatization.[47] As the twentieth century drew to a close, the RTA found that if it could not convince a skeptical legislature to raise taxes, the public agency that had rescued Chicago's privately owned transit system from bankruptcy faced the possibility of either turning over portions of its system to private enterprise once again or reducing service to cut costs.

Faced with the prospect of an annual deficit in excess of $50 million by the end of the century, the CTA in late 1997 and early 1998 did some selective pruning by eliminating ten bus routes, including the one running under the L on Lake Street. The agency also reduced bus schedules on other routes and put an end to late night "owl" service between 1 A.M. and 4 A.M. on the Douglas, Evanston, Lake, and Jackson-Englewood elevated lines. The collective effort was to save the agency $25 million in annual operating expenses.[48]

14
SUBURBAN TRANSIT

♦ The suburban transit system that radiated from Chicago, with the exception of the steam railroads, was only marginally profitable in its best years. The street railways either failed, were converted to interurbans, or replaced their trolley cars with buses by the onset of the Great Depression. The nine interurban railways, which in many cases were little more than street railways adapted for high-speed running in the open areas between suburbs, began collapsing as early as 1923.[1] By 1940 only one street railway and three interurbans, together comprising 250 miles of routes, survived. The lone street railway was converted to buses within the decade, and two of the interurban railways succumbed during the postwar expressway-building binge. For the most part, the suburban system was the victim of competition from steam railroads in established markets, high inflation during World War I, regulated fares, lack of freight traffic to help share costs, absence of public subsidies, lack of easy access to

Chicago, and relatively low population density in the suburbs.

Probably the most persistent problem of the suburban mass-transit system in the first half of the twentieth century was the lack of sufficient population density to sustain it even before there was competition from the automobile. The horsecar did not appear in Chicago until the population density of the city was nearing six thousand persons per square mile just before the Civil War. The first suburban street-railway building spree occurred thirty years later, however, when the population density of the outlying counties had not yet reached one hundred persons per square mile, although denser pockets of development existed in such places as the western suburbs, where promoters chose to build their first lines.[2] By 1920, on the eve of the first contraction of the system, the overall suburban population density was only twice what it had been in 1890, and two-thirds of it was concentrated in the railroad towns, which occupied only a fraction of the thirty-four hundred square miles that comprised suburbia.

Between 1955 and 1963, when the impact of the automobile was fully evident and the financially distressed suburban transit system was contracting once again, the density of the area was still less than 1,000 residents per square mile. By 1990 it had attained a density of only 1,261.[3] By then the suburban transit system was doomed to insignificance in all but one market, the commute to downtown Chicago that the railroads dominated. The preoccupation of suburban government with highway building, land-use planning that stressed low densities, the accelerated dispersal of population and jobs, the convenience and cost effectiveness of the automobile, and the inadequacies of the motor bus all took their toll on the suburban transit system. Late in the century, the North Suburban Transit District (Nortran) and its successor, Pace, owed as much as 40 percent of their traffic to commuters to and from Chicago.[4]

The mainline railroads, with their own rights-of-way into downtown Chicago and substantial freight and intercity passenger service to help defray expenses (including those of their downtown terminals), were in considerably better financial shape than the other systems. The railroads served an established market they had created: the railroad towns accounted for 63 percent of the population of suburbia as late as 1950. But even the commuter railroads were not immune to problems, although they did not begin to pare their suburban lines until the 1970s, when much of the U.S. railroad system in the Northeast and the Midwest was under considerable financial duress and the industry was in the process of being deregulated. Two notable early abandonments were the Illinois Central Railroad's poorly patronized Addison branch (in the 1930s) and the New York Central Railroad's line to LaPorte, Indiana (in the 1950s). Minor lines, however, operated by the Wabash (later Norfolk & Western) to Orland Park and the Chicago & Alton (later Gulf, Mobile & Ohio and still later Illinois Central Gulf) southwest along the Illinois-Michigan Canal, somehow survived to become part of the Metra system.

The Chicago & North Western Railway, the largest and wealthiest of the suburban commuter carriers, in 1975 abandoned the 16.5 miles of its Lake Geneva, Wisconsin, line beyond McHenry, Illinois. The bankrupt Chicago, Milwaukee, St. Paul & Pacific Railroad in 1981 ended service on the outermost 23 miles of its Fox Lake, Illinois, line that extended to Walworth, Wisconsin. The National Rail Passenger Corp., Amtrak, in 1990 finally halted commuter service on the 43.6-mile line from Chicago to Valparaiso, Indiana, that it had inherited from the Pennsylvania Railroad via the bankrupt Penn Central Transportation Co. All three of those abandonments can be traced to the refusal of the states of Wisconsin and Indiana to provide public subsidies to commuter railroads, prohibited in the case of Wisconsin by the state constitution. Indiana finally relented in the 1980s

(facing page) Many early suburban buses, including this 1925 vehicle, consisted of little more than a box cobbled atop a truck chassis. (Krambles Archive)

and used subsidies to save the nation's last interurban, the Chicago, South Shore & South Bend Railroad.[5]

Street railways started appearing in suburbia, primarily as mule-drawn horsecar lines, as early as 1874 in Joliet. By the turn of the century there were seven major railway systems and perhaps half a dozen smaller ones collectively comprising about 250 miles.[6] For reasons that are not entirely clear but that probably relate to suburban development patterns in the nineteenth century, the two biggest systems were both west of Chicago, one centered around Oak Park, Cicero, and Maywood, eight to ten miles from the Loop, and the other in the satellite cities strung out along the Fox River about twenty-five miles farther west.

From the beginning the suburban street railways struggled to overcome problems largely foreign to their Chicago counterparts. They were isolated from each other, typically were locally owned and undercapitalized, were prone to low ridership, and produced only marginal earnings, if any. They also tended to be more innovative than the Chicago systems. Suburban street railways experimented in 1874 with steam-powered dummy cars in Oak Park, in 1896 with battery-powered vehicles in Morgan Park and Blue Island, and in 1890 with electric trolley cars in Joliet.[7] Because of their relatively low ridership, they abandoned streetcars for motor buses as many as three decades before Chicago did, in many cases before the automobile became an established competitor. Even utilities magnate Samuel Insull, who certainly had a vested interest in electric power, established Metropolitan Motor Coach in 1926 to operate various scattered suburban bus systems he acquired as subsidiaries of his traction railways.[8] One of them, the North Shore, started bus service as early as 1922 to supplement and to feed traffic to its electric lines.[9] The Aurora & Elgin in 1924 set up the Western Motor Coach Co. to run buses in the Fox Valley, principally to dis-

courage competitors, but did not actually start service until late 1927.[10]

The seven principal street railway systems in suburbia met differing fates: two were merged into other carriers, three were converted to bus systems, and two were abandoned outright, although their descendants survived as bus divisions of the RTA's Pace subsidiary. The suburban streetcar companies also tended to consolidate into larger regional systems. Thus the Chicago & Western Dummy Railway; the Chicago, Harlem & Batavia Railway; the Suburban Railroad; and the Cicero & Proviso Street Railway eventually were combined into the Chicago & West Towns Railway in 1913. This system converted to buses between 1923 and 1948 but continued to be owned privately until it was acquired by the RTA in 1981.[11]

The street railways in Aurora and Elgin and an interurban line connecting the two cities also became a single carrier that was acquired in 1906 by the Chicago, Aurora & Elgin Railroad (CA&E), a high-speed interurban serving the western suburbs. The Aurora to Elgin part of the system, which by 1935 had been converted to buses, wound up in the hands of National City Lines, a national bus syndicate with ties to General Motors Corp. It was incorporated into the local public transit districts in the late 1960s and into Pace in 1983.[12] In the south suburbs, the original battery-powered street railway evolved into the fifty-four-mile Chicago & Southern (Chicago & Interurban Traction Co.) line between 79th and Halsted Streets on Chicago's South Side and downstate Kankakee by 1907. It was unable to compete, however, with a new highway through the south suburbs to Danville built in 1921 or with greatly improved service on the parallel Illinois Central Railroad after its commuter division was electrified in 1926.[13] The Chicago & Southern was abandoned as a railroad in 1928, and its routes were taken over by the local bus company, the predecessor to South Suburban Safeway Lines, which in turn was acquired by Pace in 1983.[14] Street railways centered on Joliet and the North Shore were variations of those themes. By 1995, the RTA's Pace bus division was operating a consolidated suburban system that used 565 of its own buses plus 120 owned by private companies with contracts to serve transit routes and with 338 smaller paratransit vehicles providing dial-a-ride service. Ridership that year exceeded 37.5 million, of which about 2.3 million were dial-a-ride and vanpool patrons.[15]

THE INTERURBAN RAILWAYS

The electric interurban railways appeared around the turn of the century, initially as carriers to serve rural communities too small or too remote for mainline railroad service. Despite their rural origins, the concept quickly migrated to the big cities, where some of the resulting interurbans developed commuter traffic.[16] The interurbans for the most part used their own rights-of-way in the countryside, but in towns they ran down the middle of the street as if they were streetcars. Their stations were often located in stores on the main street. For the most part they used heavier and faster cars than the street railways: seventy-mile-per-hour runs were common, and the North Shore even advertised eighty-mile-per-hour speeds in the 1920s.[17]

The majority of the interurbans disappeared within thirty years of their inception, victim to overly optimistic projections, inadequate markets, lack of freight traffic, and competition from cars.[18] As late as 1925 the industry as a whole reported freight revenues of only $65 million, or 15 percent of its total income. In 1930, its peak year, freight accounted for 17.7 percent of the revenues of the Aurora & Elgin, and in 1933, when the carrier was in its second bankruptcy, freight revenues were only 5.5 percent of the total, contrasted to 74.3 percent on the parallel North Western in 1932.[19] The exception was the Chicago, South Shore & South Bend, which consis-

tently through the 1950s had slightly higher revenues from freight service than from passenger service.[20]

Of the nine principal electric interurban railways serving the metropolitan area that collectively operated more than 460 miles of track in the early twentieth century, only three survived the Great Depression. These endured because they were able to convert themselves into high-speed commuter railways and moreover were able to gain access over other lines to downtown Chicago.[21] That access, which the steam railroads had from the beginning, proved critical to the interurbans. The developers of the Aurora & Elgin arranged as early as 1905 for trackage rights to the Loop over the Metropolitan West Side Elevated Railroad Co.'s lines.[22] The interurban survived less than four years after its 1953 loss of that access. The Chicago, North Shore & Milwaukee and the Chicago, South Shore & Sound Bend, the other two interurban lines to make it through the depression, similarly found access to downtown Chicago to the North Shore by means of the Chicago elevated lines and to the South Shore over the Illinois Central tracks.

The Chicago & Interurban Traction was one of two interurban lines to enter Chicago city limits without making it downtown. The other was the thirty-seven-mile Chicago & Joliet Electric Railway (1901–1933), which ran from Joliet to Archer and Cicero Avenues in Chicago. The early failures also included some lines that probably never should have been built, including the twenty-mile Aurora, Plainfield & Joliet (1901–1924); the twenty-mile Joliet & Eastern (1909–1923), which operated between Chicago Heights and Joliet; the thirty-seven-mile Aurora, Elgin & Fox River Electric (1906–1935); and Bion Arnold's thirty-six-mile Elgin & Belvidere Electric (1906–1930).

Of the three Chicago-area interurbans to survive the depression, the Aurora & Elgin and the North Shore succumbed within two decades to competition from

Early interurban railroad
cars, including this
Chicago, Aurora & Elgin
car preserved at the Fox
Valley Trolley Museum in
South Elgin, were little
more than high-speed,
heavyweight streetcars.
(Michael Brown)

the automobile and from mainline railroads, primarily the Chicago & North Western, which diluted the market and profited from the interurbans' demise.[23] The South Shore survived as the nation's last interurban in the twilight of the twentieth century predominantly as a commuter carrier. It was chartered in 1901 to operate between the Illinois-Indiana state line and South Bend 68 miles to the east but actually began operation in 1903 as a 3.4-mile streetcar line. Despite the industrial growth in northern Indiana, the railroad was not particularly successful until it obtained trackage rights to downtown Chicago in 1926 after the I.C. electrified its commuter line.[24]

The South Shore's survival in the second half of the twentieth century was threatened after the Indiana Toll Road and Chicago Skyway were built parallel to its tracks and after ridership fell from 4,241,277 in 1952 to less than half of that by 1971.[25] It was acquired in 1966 by the Chesapeake & Ohio Railroad (C&O), and it prevailed because its freight service, as late as 1975, accounted for 76 percent of revenues.[26] The C&O patiently kept passenger service operating until an inspection of the South Shore's fifty-year-old

The North Shore's electroliner epitomized the interurban car in America. This one, built in 1941, has been preserved at the Illinois Railway Museum in Union, Illinois. (Michael Brown)

cars indicated structural deterioration.[27] When in 1971 the C&O was unable to raise local funds to match a federal grant for new cars, it successfully applied to the Interstate Commerce Commission to cut service in half. After ridership continued to decline, the C&O filed a petition in 1976 to abandon the interurban's passenger service. The petition finally caused some activity in Indianapolis, where the state legislature approved creation of the Northwest Indiana Commuter Transportation District and a $3.5 million capital fund to enable the new NICTD to provide the local share for a $54 million federal grant to buy forty-four new cars and to upgrade other facilities.[28]

The North Shore traced its origins to a seven-mile street railway completed in 1892 between Waukegan and North Chicago. Over the years the venture's promoters extended the Chicago & Milwaukee Electric Railroad Co., as it was then known, south to Evanston, where riders could transfer to the Milwaukee Road commuter trains for the rest of the trip to downtown Chicago. After 1904 the railroad also began an ambitious northern extension to Milwaukee, which was not completed until late 1908, when the North Shore was in bankruptcy. The lack of direct access to downtown Chicago contained ridership, but that problem was solved in 1919 when the North Shore obtained trackage rights to the Loop over the Northwestern Elevated Railroad. Insull controlled both lines.[29] To increase train speeds slowed by street traffic in some North Shore suburbs, the interurban in 1926 completed a high-speed bypass in an undeveloped area it called Skokie Valley a few miles west of its original line. It operated both routes into the 1950s.

The North Shore possibly was the most innovative of the nation's interurbans, introducing in 1926 the concept of piggyback freight service—truck trailers carried on flat cars—and in 1941 the Electroliner—a streamlined, articulated train that was considered the high-water mark of interurban railway development.[30] The Electroliner was destined for service between Chicago and Milwaukee because the North Shore, unlike the other two Chicago interurbans, attempted to operate an intercity service as well as freight and commuter operations. Its thirty-seven-mile shoreline route, however, had never made much of a dent in ridership on the North Western's parallel commuter

line through the affluent lakeshore suburbs. After suffering long strikes in 1938 and 1948, the North Shore began a concerted effort to abandon that market.[31] Regulators finally allowed the abandonment in 1955, but gains proved illusory, probably because the North Shore was not an efficient carrier even in markets where it had an advantage. Two years after jettisoning the shoreline route, the North Shore lost more than $600,000 on operations that produced only $5.6 million in revenue. The rest of the railroad was shut down in 1963.[32]

Chicago's third major interurban, because it was a venture of two national traction railway syndicates, was built from scratch as a high-speed line parallel to the North Western to connect Aurora and Elgin with Chicago.[33] This line, however, was never more than marginally profitable, and it was forced into bankruptcy receivership in 1919 and again during the depression, when Insull's empire collapsed. In 1945, a high-traffic war year, the CA&E earned only $36,000 on revenues of more than $2.9 million, which amounted to half the revenues of the South Shore and one-third those of the North Shore.

The Aurora & Elgin was destroyed by the government's expressway building programs. In 1953 the Garfield Park L, its access to the Loop, was demolished to make room for the Congress Expressway. Commuters lost their one-seat ride to the Loop—they now had to change to CTA trains at Forest Park—and began defecting to the North Western.[34] The Aurora & Elgin abandoned passenger service in 1957 after ridership dropped and operating losses mounted.[35]

COMMUTER RAILROADS

The commuter railroad network for most of the twentieth century remained an exception to the troubles of the rest of the region's mass-transit system because it was able to maintain the dominant share of its principal market—the commute from the

suburbs to downtown Chicago. Whereas railroad ridership by the middle 1960s had declined to 2.8 percent of the nation's commuting population, in Chicago the railroads held a 13.2 percent share of downtown commuters.[36]

The big gains made by automobiles in suburbia before World War II were at the expense of the street railways, bus systems, and interurbans, not the commuter railroads. In the decade and a half after 1950, the labor force in the United States increased by 21 percent, but the number of miles of municipal streets increased by 57 percent and the number of motor vehicles registered increased by 78 percent (80% in Illinois).[37] In the same span, U.S. transit ridership in both cities and suburbs, excluding commuter railroads, declined by slightly more than 50 percent.[38] The gains in commuter railroad ridership, however, were such that by the 1970s many railroad suburbs were forced to enlarge their station parking lots and to subsidize shuttle-bus routes to the stations to prevent central business-district streets from being overwhelmed by commuter parking. North Western executives advocated this solution as early as 1968, when transit elsewhere was in general decline.[39]

The post–World War II suburban migration had a mixed effect on the railroads. Ridership at their stations in Chicago declined, and many such stations were abandoned when ridership in the suburbs was increasing and new stations were being built. The Illinois Central was probably the best example of the phenomenon: its two major lines serving Chicago once provided the majority of its ridership, but they began to decline after World War II, and the gains the I.C. made in the suburbs could not overcome its losses in the city. Illinois Central ridership had steadily increased, except during the depression, from 4 million in 1890 to 47 million in 1947, but by 1966 it had fallen to only 18.2 million. The railroad somewhat belatedly followed the lead of the Burlington and North Western and began its first modernization program since it was electrified in 1926.[40]

A study by the RTA in 1981 indicated the nature of the problem. Whereas I.C. ridership in the suburbs south of 111th Street increased more than 15 percent between 1969 and 1975, it declined almost 54 percent in Chicago. As late as 1969 city ridership on the railroad exceeded suburban ridership, 16,326 daily boardings contrasted to 13,589, but by 1975 city ridership was only half that of the suburbs. A major problem was fares. Although the I.C. held its one-way fare on the South Chicago branch to 60 cents between 1961 and 1969, it was forced to raise it to $1.15 by 1976—more than double the 50-cent fare on the competing CTA.[41] Conversely, North Western ridership, little of which originated in Chicago, increased from 15.5 million in 1953, before its modernization program was started, to 24.3 million in 1967, despite a succession of modest fare increases.

The advantage the railroads had over other transit systems was their ability to distribute costs among commuter, intercity passenger, and freight traffic, although intercity passenger traffic declined precipitously after World War II and commuter traffic had to bear a relatively greater share of the burden. It was no coincidence that the two railroads with the poorest performing freight business also had the worst commuter service, although the Milwaukee Road made an exceptional effort to try to keep its two lines on a parity with the wealthier railroads. Between 1952 and 1966, the commuters' share of total railroad passenger traffic in the United States increased to 24 percent of revenue passenger miles from 14 percent and its share of passenger revenues increased to 26 percent from 9 percent.[42]

Because the commuter divisions accounted for a fraction of the operating costs and the revenues of mainline railroads, the bankruptcies of various railroads during the depression and in the 1970s resulted not from anything that happened on the commuter divisions but from a general falloff in freight traffic.[43] As late as 1966,

when the railroad system in the Northeast and Midwest was under considerable financial pressure from overregulation by the Interstate Commerce Commission and from competition from trucks, one unpublished study indicated that the commuter services of both the North Western and the Milwaukee Road were profitable, although the latter was only marginally so. The North Western, which publicly claimed a commuter division operating profit of $2,043,000 based on fully distributed costs, in fact generated an operating profit of $4,347,039 based on incremental costs. On the same accounting basis, the Milwaukee Road reported a deficit of $1,632,863 on commuter operations but in reality produced a profit of $57,534.[44]

The financial problems endemic to the transit industry finally caught up with Chicago's commuter railroads in the 1970s. The general crisis in the railroad industry brought on by overregulation, excess trackage, and truck competition caused a wave of bankruptcies that began in the northeast in 1970 with the Penn Central Transportation Co. and spread west. The Chicago, Rock Island & Pacific filed for bankruptcy in 1975, and the Milwaukee Road followed it into receivership in 1977. By then, the commuter divisions of the I.C. and the Burlington were losing money, and the North Western's commuter lines were only marginally profitable.

The public buyout of three of the commuter railroads by the RTA and its Metra subsidiary in the 1980s was precipitated by the imminent liquidation of the Rock Island, into which the RTA had already plowed $70 million in capital grants to rehabilitate the dilapidated line.[45] The subsequent piecemeal sale of the Milwaukee Road in federal bankruptcy court and the willingness of the I.C. to finance the contract sale of its commuter division resulted in the RTA's purchase of those carriers. The lines, however, run by the Burlington Northern and the North Western, which was acquired by the Union Pacific Railroad in 1995, were operated by private owners

The area around the intersection of 95th Street and Western Avenue, though largely undeveloped in 1935, was served by both buses and streetcars and was busy enough to warrant traffic signals. Note the price of gas on the sign in the foreground. (Krambles Archive)

under service contracts with Metra.

Although the rehabilitation of the Rock Island and Milwaukee Road was the RTA's first priority for suburban capital funds, by the middle 1980s the agency's Metra subsidiary was able to embark on a modest expansion program. The agencies extended the principal Illinois Central line a few miles south to Park Forest South (later University Park) and the Milwaukee Road line a few miles west of Elgin. The agencies also increased the number of daily trains on the former Wabash Railroad line to southwest suburban Orland Park, but the largest project was the 1996 opening of commuter service over the Wisconsin Cen-

tral Railroad for fifty-three miles between Chicago and Antioch, Illinois, near the Wisconsin border. In the case of the twenty-nine-mile Orland Park line, service had been minimal—one daily round-trip—on the Wabash and on its successor, the Norfolk & Western Railway, as late as the 1970s. The RTA added a round-trip train, and when it came into existence in 1984, Metra incrementally increased the service to six daily round-trips. The Wisconsin Central, a single-track freight line from the western suburbs to Wisconsin, had never before been used for commuter service.

As the twentieth century neared the end, the Chicago commuter railroad sys-

tem, despite almost seventy years of competition with the automobile, had survived and was expanding. In 1995 it operated 14 lines comprising 505 miles served by 228 stations, 130 locomotives, and 898 cars and carried 73.9 million passengers. Between the decennial censuses of 1970 and 1990, ridership on the commuter railroad system increased by slightly more than 9 percent, though the population of the Chicago metropolitan area increased by only about 3 percent.[46]

The suburban political community was too fragmented to take much of a common interest in transit systems during the first six decades of the twentieth century,

and there was little of the acrimonious debate that characterized attempts to regulate transit in Chicago. Beginning in 1871 with the Board of Railroad and Warehouse Commissioners, a succession of state agencies regulated the suburban systems. By 1900 most regulatory duties had been assumed by the Interstate Commerce Commission, and the state board was little more than an information-gathering agency with few real powers of regulation.[47] In 1913 the Illinois Public Utilities Commission took over the original state agency's responsibility to set fare and service levels on intrastate carriers, including the street, elevated, and interurban

The Evergreen Plaza mall (background) and an elaborate system of traffic signals dominate the intersection of 95th Street and Western Avenue in 1997. (Michael Brown)

Motor buses played a negligible role in guiding suburban development. Bus routes were added as an afterthought to office towers built along expressways in such places as Schaumburg, which in the 1950s was little more than a rural crossroads. (Pace)

railways. In a reorganization in 1921, that agency became the Illinois Commerce Commission.

Although such issues as fare increases and service abandonments resulted in considerable debate and lively public hearings before the ICC, the suburban community for forty years seemed relatively content with having the state regulate its transportation. The first shock wave of the postwar suburban transit crisis occurred when the ICC was unable to prevent the abandonment of the Aurora & Elgin and North Shore interurbans, and the state legislature was forced to intervene. The result was the Local Mass Transit District Act, which authorized the creation in the suburbs of special government districts similar to the Chicago Transit Authority.[48] The new law, however, was not put into use by the emerging suburbs for one decade.

The south suburbs acted first as the financial condition of the transit systems worsened and the threat of more abandonments increased. At the instigation of Park Forest Mayor Bernard Cunningham, a group of municipalities used the dormant state law to form the South Suburban Mass Transit District in 1967. The district served as a conduit for federal capital grants to buy new buses for lease to South Suburban Safeway Lines, which as a private carrier was ineligible for direct federal grants, and later to acquire new bilevel cars for the Illinois Central Gulf Railroad.[49] Joliet created its own transit district in 1969, and encouraged by railroad officials, some western suburbs along the Burlington line did the same in 1970.

The Burlington project, which originated in a railroad staff budget meeting in 1969, indicates the sort of enlightened self-interest that was at play. Since on one summer afternoon more than 40 percent of the railroad's commuter cars had air-conditioning failures, and parts to repair the nineteen-year-old propane-fueled compressor motors were getting difficult to find, the head of the railroad's mechanical department suggested a $25 million modernization program for both cars and locomotives. The railroad, however, was reluctant to budget that sort of expense when it expected a profit of only $12 million in 1969. The solution to this problem was the creation of the West Suburban Mass Transit District. As a local match for the federal grants the district received, the railroad donated its fleet to the district.[50]

As a practical matter, suburban transit districts were limited to advisory and grant conduit roles because they had no authority to levy taxes for subsidies. Such taxation was rejected by conservative electorates in several referenda, most notably in Joliet in 1969.[51] An exception was the North Suburban Mass Transit District (Nortran), chartered in 1971 by eighteen northern and northwestern suburbs with the intention of operating the failing United Motor Coach Co. system. It became an operating transit agency when United was finally acquired in 1975,[52] and one decade later it became the nucleus of the Pace system.

The auto-dominated suburbs, which had voted overwhelmingly against the RTA and its transit taxes in 1974, ultimately followed the lead of Chicago nearly thirty years earlier and acquired publicly what was left of the transit system. In doing so, the suburbs saved the commuter railroad system that had given them birth more than one century before.

15
THE AUTO AGE

♦ The Columbian Exposition of 1893 was staged to celebrate the 400th anniversary of the discovery of America and to announce Chicago's arrival as a world-class city. It also offered to the world a look at the latest technology and a preview of the twentieth century. Alongside such popular amusements as the Ferris wheel, Octave Chanute staged an international symposium on flight, something not actually achieved for another decade; the steel, whalebacked liner *Christopher Columbus* steamed up and down Lake Michigan; and the Intramural Railroad circled the fairgrounds demonstrating the application of electric traction to mass transit. The ship proved to be the only passenger vessel of its kind ever built, but aviation and electric traction both had bright futures.

Somewhat surprisingly in view of the influence it would have on transportation in the next century, little attention was paid to the automobile. The Transportation Building displayed forty-three types of bicycles and three hundred horse-drawn carriages but no horseless carriages. Though several applications had been submitted to show both steam and electric carriages at the transportation exhibit, according to the official fair historian, they were later withdrawn. The two autos demonstrated at the fair appeared in other pavilions—the German exhibit included a gasoline "road carriage" and the Electric Building held William Morrison's battery-powered car. The two vehicles were used primarily for giving rides around the grounds and seem to have been lost among the exposition splendors.[1]

Within one decade the motor car was common enough on Chicago streets that the city began to regulate both vehicles and drivers, one of the first jurisdictions in the nation to do so.[2] By 1908, 5,475 autos were registered in Chicago. By then, autoists had banded together in clubs to resist regulation and to lobby for better roads. Indeed, the National League for Good Roads had been founded by General Roy Stone at the Columbian Exposition.[3] Such organizations were a factor in establishing by 1910 the order of battle of the Auto Age: government provided the roads and rules, and the traveler was responsible for his own wheels. During the next few years, the exploding auto population forced government to favor the street over mass transit as the tool for shaping Chicago,[4] a task made more difficult because the rail transit system had established patterns of density incompatible with auto use—reflected, for example, in the parking problem that still afflicts many of Chicago's older neighborhoods.

A series of well-publicized accidents in 1899 caused Chicago to begin regulating drivers. As early as 1900, the city required an annual driver's test and a $3 driver's license, annually renewable for $1. The license could be revoked for traffic violations, which at the time were identical for horse-drawn and motor vehicles.[5] As the auto population grew, the city started using licensing fees as a source of revenue to build and to maintain roads. Shortly after it began licensing drivers, the city required each vehicle to be licensed at $3 annually and drivers to display license plates. The state eventually assumed this function, though Chicago continued to charge registration fees.

The resistance to taxation, even the imposition of tolls, was relatively minor over the years, probably because government from the beginning dedicated those funds to road building and repair programs. By 1908 the financial pressures on the city to maintain its street system solely from property taxes and from special assessments forced it to adopt the nation's first vehicle tax—$5 for horse-drawn vehicles and $20 for motor vehicles.[6] Within five years, however, the individual political agendas of the City Council had diluted that program by requiring 85 percent of the revenue to be spent in the wards in which they were raised.[7] In 1929 Illinois adopted the motor fuel tax to support road construction, a taxation program pioneered in 1919 by three western states.[8] The original state tax of three cents per gallon was incrementally increased to nineteen cents by 1990.

Early proliferation of the automobile was impossible to control. Those with the financial wherewithal could buy a vehicle, and unlike other transportation systems that required enormous capital investments, the early motor car could be built affordably with a modicum of technical knowledge by mounting a small engine on the back of a carriage. Americans were tinkering with self-propelled road carriages long before Gottlieb Daimler in 1885 completed the auto engine from which the modern automobile traces its lineage.[9] The local J. I. Case Threshing Machine Co. built a steam buggy for Dr. J. M. Carhart, of Racine, Wisconsin, as early as 1871; Edwin F. Brown, a Chicago bicycle manufacturer, built a steam-powered vehicle in 1887; and Clyde J. Coleman successfully drove through Chicago's streets in an electric surrey he built in 1892. That same year Morrison first demonstrated his electric automobile in Chicago.[10] Morrison sold his car for $3,600 to Harold Sturges, an executive of the American Battery Co. in Chicago, who then put it on display at the Columbian Exposition.

(facing page) The auto age produced beautiful machines but brought new challenges for transit planners. This one-of-a-kind horseless carriage was built in Benton Harbor, Michigan, but not in time for the Chicago *Times-Herald* race of 1895. It was restored by David Kolzow. (AACA Museum, Inc., Hershey, Penn.)

The seminal year for the automobile in America was marked by an auto race. The Chicago *Times-Herald*'s offer in 1895 of $3,500 in prizes to the first- and second-place winners drew three vehicles from Germany built by Karl Benz, a Duryea gas buggy from Massachusetts, Sturges's Morrison electric, and an electric from Philadelphia. The purse also stimulated tinkerers in the Chicago area to build at least six cars specifically for the race—among them, two powered by gasoline, one by steam, one by compressed gas, and one by electric engine. Although none of the vehicles made it into the race, it is believed the tinkerers eventually finished and tested all six.[11] The race, a novelty, received considerable national attention in the press not only because it was the first U.S. auto race but also because two cars were able to finish—the Duryea and a Benz—under less than ideal conditions: a winter storm had deposited a foot of snow on the Chicago area two days earlier and the wind had blown it into drifts.[12]

Held in conjunction with the race was the nation's first auto show. Though the race received a great deal of notoriety, the show was a modest affair staged in a small, Wabash Avenue salesroom donated by the Studebaker Co., which at the time manufactured only horse-drawn conveyances. There were twelve exhibits, including steam-, electric-, and gasoline-powered cars made by Duryea, Benz, Chicagoan George W. Lewis, and Elwood P. Haynes of Kokomo, Indiana. Despite the press coverage, the race and show elicited more interest from tinkerers willing to build their own cars than any clamor from the American public to buy them. Of course, automobiles of the time were considered toys of the inventors and the rich rather than utilitarian vehicles for the common man. There was not another such show held in Chicago until 1900. At the city's ninth annual auto show, some fifteen years later, a visitor who had been to the 1895 show observed, "The public [was] not ready. The man with money had to go to Europe and ride in those rigs over the superb roads of France before he would put up his money to buy or build."[13]

THE AUTO INDUSTRY BEGINS

Despite what the critics said, the automobile had captured the public's attention. In the last five years of the nineteenth century, at least twenty-two companies were formed in the Chicago area to build and sell horseless carriages; twelve of these companies actually got vehicles into production. The explosive growth of the auto industry continued after the turn of the century. In the decade beginning in 1901, no less than sixty-eight models of cars were produced in Chicago by twenty-eight companies formed for that purpose. Nineteen were built by manufacturers of other products as diverse as sewing machines, bicycles, and carriages venturing into the auto market, and eighteen were produced by individuals, machine shops, and garages that built prototypes but never raised sufficient capital to manufacture cars on any scale. One retail business, Sears, Roebuck & Co., built autos between 1908 and 1912 to sell through its famous catalogue. During the beginning of the century Chicago seemed to thrive as an automobile manufacturing center, producing 134 models of cars, but it never really rivaled Detroit as the nation's auto center.

Chicago's emergence as an early auto center was due to a number of factors besides simply that the city's machine shops had the technical capability to fabricate parts for cars and engines. With paved streets and a population in excess of two million, Chicago had a strong local market for cars. Because it was the nation's railroad center, people from other parts of the country could easily come to Chicago, buy their car on "Auto Row" along Michigan and Wabash Avenues south of the Loop, and ship it home on the train.[14] This was an attractive option because the deplorable condition of rural roads made intercity trips by car an adventure. Furthermore, locally man-

ufactured cars were common in the United States because Detroit in the first decade of the century had not yet developed a national system of dealers. By the 1920s, however, auto production in Chicago had dwindled to only seven models.[15]

Typical of the city's early auto pioneers was William O. Worth, who despite repeated failures doggedly pursued the business of building cars and ultimately wound up peddling them. He built his first vehicle in 1895 for a wagon company in Benton Harbor, Michigan, that intended to enter it into the *Times-Herald* race; the auto was not, however, completed in time. After a falling out with his sponsors, Worth moved back to Chicago and formed the Chicago Motor Vehicle Co., which occupied offices at 341 South Wabash Avenue and a factory in south suburban Harvey. It built both horse-drawn and horseless carriages for a few years before its managers decided to concentrate on delivery trucks and motor buses.

The change did not save the company, which declared bankruptcy in 1906. The next year Worth moved to Evansville, Indiana, to form another auto company. He moved again within a year, this time to downstate Kankakee, Illinois, and when his company there failed in 1909 he took a job in Aurora as the manager of a garage and repair shop. He was back in the manufacturing business in 1911 with the Krickworth Motor Wagon Co. in Chicago. After that venture collapsed, he drifted through a number of jobs in the industry, including auto sales. He died in relative obscurity in Oak Park in 1938.[16]

Some early Chicago auto manufacturers eventually faltered because they focused on technology that consumers failed to adopt. The Woods Motor Vehicle Co., a firm founded in 1896 by Clinton E. Woods, was the most successful of Chicago's electric car manufacturers. Before it went out of business in 1918, Woods built 13,583 vehicles, mainly electrics, although near the end the company manufactured dual-powered cars with gasoline engines, gener-

ators, and electric motors. More typical of the Chicago manufacturing failures was the Chicago Electric Vehicle Co., organized with Chicago Edison Co. president Samuel Insull, which lasted only until 1901.

Most Chicago companies closed their doors within two years after building a prototype to display at Chicago's annual automobile shows. Typical of such ventures was the Chicago Motocycle Co., organized in 1898 by Charles Dickinson, a wealthy seed company owner who later in his life became one of the city's aviation pioneers.[17] The partnership ambitiously announced a line of electric, gasoline, and steam cars but was unable to produce a two-cylinder runabout until 1902. The following year it introduced at the Chicago Automobile Show a three-cylinder runabout capable of operating on multiple fuels and sold under the Caloric name; however, the engine did not perform up to expectations, and the company was out of business before the end of the year.[18]

A number of individuals built cars for their own use or custom built them for others. Bicycle maker Ignaz Schwinn built about six personal cars in as many years, and Dr. Courtney L. Smith, of Aurora, built a steam car for his own use. Frank S. Betz & Co. for a time manufactured gasoline carriages for one of the largest groups of early auto users: physicians, who found

Woods electrics, manufactured in Chicago for twenty years, eventually succumbed to gas-powered cars. (Owls Head Transportation Museum)

The wagon-style wheels on this 1909 Staver high-wheeler enabled the vehicle to operate on inferior rural roads. (Waukesha Engine Historical Society)

them more reliable than horses and had the financial wherewithal to buy them.[19]

Undoubtedly the most successful car that originated in Chicago was the Rambler. Thomas B. Jeffrey was a Chicago manufacturer who named his gasoline-powered car after his well-known Rambler bike. He built his first single-cylinder auto in 1897, and his son, Charles, built two additional machines the next year that were displayed at the Chicago and New York auto shows in 1900. The Jeffreys sold their bicycle business in 1901 and bought a factory in Kenosha, Wisconsin, to build cars. When Thomas Jeffrey died in 1910, his son

was unable to keep the company solvent. Charles Nash bought Jeffrey's company in 1916, and he, along with the American Motors Corporation after 1954, continued to build Ramblers. The 4,204,000th and last Rambler rolled off the Kenosha production line on June 30, 1969.[20]

Detroit had already established itself as the auto center when Preston Tucker decided to enter the business of manufacturing cars with his Torpedo. Beginning in 1946 Tucker raised $26 million to launch his auto company from a leased factory on Chicago's Southwest Side. His operation, however, proved to be undercapitalized, and his managerial skills were insufficient to save it. Indicted on various charges relating to securities fraud and acquitted in a four-month trial, he produced only fifty-one cars before filing for bankruptcy in 1949.[21]

The Rambler and Tucker's ill-fated Torpedo notwithstanding, probably the last independent automobile manufacturing company of any size in the Chicago area was the Elgin Motor Car Corp., of suburban Argo, which built 16,784 conventional cars between the start of production in 1916 and its bankruptcy in 1924 after moving to Indianapolis. The company had borrowed heavily after World War I and was overextended when the postwar recession hit.[22]

Chicago vehicle manufacturers began to diversify into new areas of the market. Several Chicago manufacturers produced a farm car, the "highwheeler," essentially a motorized buggy with a high center of gravity, that negotiated muddy roads. Chicago became the center of manufacture of highwheelers, which until the introduction of the Model T Ford in late 1908 had few rivals in farm country. Holsman Automobile Co. produced at least 2,439 highwheelers, International Harvester Co. produced 4,500, Sears produced 3,500, and Staver Carriage Co. produced 7,518, in their Chicago factories between 1903 and 1914.[23]

Holsman Automobile Co. was typical of the highweeler manufacturers. Henry K. Holsman (1866–1963), an architect, decided to build his own automobile after buying a couple of horseless carriages in 1900 that did not perform well on the muddy streets in the vicinity of the family's home at 9024 South Hoyne Avenue in Chicago. He started the company in late 1901 in a South Side store-turned-factory and had a production model, a single seat, rope-drive vehicle priced at $625, ready for public scrutiny at the Chicago Automobile Show in January 1903. He built only thirteen cars that year, but by 1906–1907 the company was flush with orders. The undercapitalized company's troubles began in 1908 when orders failed to keep pace with the inventory stockpiled in anticipation of record sales. When sales continued to lag, Holsman shut down his company in 1910 and went to work for Independent Harvester Co. in Plano, Illinois, as an engineer. He eventually returned to the practice of architecture. In its best year of 1907, Holsman Automobile Co. built 748 cars, producing revenues of $602,100.[24]

Another type of vehicle, the cyclecar, made a brief splash on the scene at this time. Of the thirty-six new automobile models introduced between 1911 and 1920 by Chicago manufacturers, twelve were cyclecars, briefly popular as a cheap alternative to the Model T. Cyclecars were small, two-seat sports cars, dressed with spoked wheels, built from motorcycle components. Chicago inventor Francis A. Woods built the nation's prototype cyclecar in 1910, and between 1913 and 1916 he built production models called the Woods Mobilette in south suburban Harvey. The Puritan Motor Co.'s rival cyclecar was probably more popular, but the company only lasted for two years, from 1913 to 1914, before the fad began to fade.[25]

Two of the most successful auto manufacturers, International Harvester and Diamond T, abandoned automobiles to concentrate on truck production. Within a few years two other major manufacturers converted their production from private cars to taxicabs. Partin Manufacturing Co., which built 1,874 cars under that name in Chicago between 1913 and 1917, was reorganized as Commonwealth Motors Corp. and was moved to suburban Joliet, where it built 4,340 cars. In 1921 it merged with Markin Body Corp., changed its name to Checker Motors Corp., began production on taxicabs, and moved to Kalamazoo, Michigan.[26] The company finally abandoned vehicle production altogether in 1982. Another taxicab manufacturer was John Hertz. Beginning his career as an auto salesman, Hertz was promoted to partner in the Walden A. Shaw Livery Co. auto dealership in 1908. By 1915 he

The Woods Mobilette was a cyclecar built in Chicago to compete in price with the Model T. (AACA Museum, Inc., Hershey, Penn.)

was building taxicabs under the name of the Yellow Cab Manufacturing Co. By 1921 the enterprise had branched into the manufacture of private cars under the Shaw, Hertz, and Ambassador names. In 1925 he sold the manufacturing company to the General Motors Corp.[27]

The large sums of capital necessary to produce autos competitively was a major reason for the extinction of the industry in Chicago. The various Chicago ventures that went through formalities of incorporation during the first two decades of the industry did so with capital ranging from $10,000 to $150,000. An exception was Clinton E. Woods, who organized his electric car company in Chicago in 1899 with some wealthy backers from the utility industry, including Insull, with substantial capital of $10 million. In contrast to Woods's capitalization, in 1903 Henry Ford entered the industry in Detroit with only $28,000 and a dozen workmen.[28] Af-

ter World War I the cost of entry into the auto manufacturing business became prohibitive. By 1925, Chicago had ceased to be a producer of cars, except for Tucker's meteoric fling, and had become predominantly a consumer of them.

Though people had been relatively quick to adopt the car after the turn of the century, major limitations on the early auto market existed. First, until Henry Ford developed the mass-production techniques for his Model T, buying the average car was a prohibitively expensive venture for a man of modest means.[29] A Chicago-built runabout in 1905 cost $2,500, as did a 1906 Apollo produced by the Recording Scale Co., of Waukegan. A 1907 C-F four-seater was priced at $2,000. The 1908 Model T, in contrast, cost just $845, an amount that within a few years Ford reduced to $345. The deplorable condition of suburban and rural roads, which in some instances were little more than unmarked, rutted dirt trails, also hindered the market.

There were less than 10,000 autos registered in the city in 1910, and during the following decade the city added only about 7,674 new cars per year to its registration rolls. In 1921 alone the number of registered autos increased by more than 51,000, and throughout the decade of the 1920s the Chicago auto population increased annually by an average of almost 32,000 vehicles. By way of contrast, per capita transit ridership in Chicago also increased steadily until 1926, when it hit the record high of 366 rides per capita, before starting a long decline that lasted until just before World War II. In 1930 there were 406,619 autos in Chicago, or one per 8.3 residents, each of whom, at least statistically, also rode the streetcars, buses, or L an average of 315 times during the year.[30]

THE DESIRE FOR PERSONAL MOBILITY

The growth in popularity of the auto and its eventual use as a commuter vehicle in Chicago resulted from more than the reduction in unit price made possible by mass production and the intensive marketing effort by the industry. The nation seemed to have developed an appetite for personal mobility beginning in the nineteenth century with the horse and buggy. Indeed, James E. Vance Jr. argues that mobility has been an innate aspiration of Americans from the founding of the Republic, a liberty as dearly held as any guaranteed on paper.[31] Long before historian Frederick Jackson Turner declared at a meeting held in conjuncion with the 1893 Columbian Exposition that the American Frontier was at last closed, Americans had turned their attention from the horse to the cheaper bicycle for personal mobility.[32] By 1900 three hundred U.S. manufacturers produced more than one million bicycles annually.[33] Chicago boasted the nation's second largest manufacturer, the Thomas B. Jeffery and R. Philip Gormully enterprise, which produced the famous

Rambler; the Spalding Company, a sporting goods manufacturer; and a firm founded by Ignatius Schwinn, whose name would later become synonymous with American-built bicycles. Bicyclists, who organized in 1880 as the League of American Wheelmen, were the first nonagrarian lobby for improved roads.[34]

Buggies experienced an explosive growth after mass-production techniques greatly reduced their costs following the Civil War, although the cost and space required to keep horses limited their use in cities. By the 1890s, there were more than eight thousand buggy and wagon factories in the United States, including Henry and Clem Studebaker's substantial wagon works in South Bend, Indiana, which employed seventy-five thousand workers to manufacture two million vehicles per year.[35] Once the internal combustion engine was developed, it was a relatively easy task to mount it on the rear of a buggy, replacing the horses in front. Sears, Roebuck & Co., which in the 1890s sold its horse-drawn Acme Queen buggy for $55 plus freight, by 1909 produced a powered version with a two-cylinder, ten-horsepower engine for $395.[36]

Although statistical evidence on the boom in personal travel is scanty for the early part of the twentieth century, what is available indicates that people traveled substantially and increasingly used cars as roads improved. Intercity travel, which was only 500 miles per capita in 1920—50 miles by auto and 450 by train—within ten years had grown to 1,910 miles per person per year—219 miles by train and 1,691 by auto. By 1950, intercity travel in the United States was more than 3,300 miles per person per year; by 1990, that number had grown to 8,014 miles.[37]

Those who bought a car for personal use amortized the cost by using it to commute as well, a phenomenon that has been documented as early as 1912 in Chicago. Commuting picked up steam during the Great Depression, when it seemed prudent to forego streetcar fares in favor of the car,

The 1909 Chicago-based Sears highwheeler, sold by catalogue, was an unsuccessful rival of the Model T Ford for America's farm-vehicle market. (David Kolzow)

which otherwise would sit idle in the alley behind the commuter's house.[38] A large segment of the public quickly discovered it preferred the convenience of commuting by automobile, which in many areas of Chicago and its suburbs was clearly superior to anything mass transit could offer.[39] The car offered comfort, flexibility of scheduling, limited walking and waiting, protection from the elements, room for passengers at no extra cost, and a faster and cheaper ride than mass transit could provide.[40] Once the commuter made an initial investment in a car, it was then available for all sorts of family business and activities, including the Sunday ride in the country that bicycles had popularized years earlier. The post–World War II decline in mass-transit riding in Chicago, first obvious on Saturdays and Sundays and at nights, was attributed to the adoption of the five-day work week, the increased use of cars for errands and pleasure, and as Werner Schroeder noted, the television. People began to stay home for their entertainment instead of hopping a streetcar to go to a movie in the Loop.[41]

URBAN SPRAWL

As the twentieth century entered its final decade, the region's two principal planning agencies independently issued reports that were widely disseminated by the critics of urban sprawl. The Northeastern Illinois Planning Commission (NIPC) in 1991 reported that the six-county Chicago metropolitan area in the two decades from 1970 to 1990 grew in size (developed land area) by 46 to 65 percent but only by 4.1 percent in population.[42] The Chicago Area Transportation Study (CATS) used computer models to project that between 1980 and 2010 the metropolitan population would grow by 15 percent but transportation demand would increase by 23 percent.[43] By the time those reports were issued, a number of fiscal impact studies in such suburban communities as Crystal Lake, Naperville, and Du Page County had concluded independently that growth for the most part did not pay for itself and that existing residents and businesses had to pay increased taxes to cover the costs of the infrastructure needed for new development.[44] Such studies led to imposition of the economic impact fees on developers.

Decentralization was neither unique to Chicago nor, as some apologists for mass transit have suggested, the result of a plot by Detroit to maximize profits by eliminating competition.[45] Perhaps John R. Meyer and Jose A. Gomez said it best:

For several decades, cities in the United States and world have been suburbanizing and decentralizing because of increased urban populations, rising real incomes, and falling transportation costs. Urban overcrowding has been relieved by expanding boundaries. This tendency is discernible as far back as reliable data is available, and in all parts of the world—developed and underdeveloped, with and without widespread ownership of the automobile.[46]

Decentralization began rather modestly in the nineteenth century when railroads found that they had outgrown their freight yards and terminals and were forced to look for larger sites farther from downtown.[47] The Galena & Chicago Union built its first yard along the Chicago River at Canal and Kinzie Streets beginning in 1848, but over the following half century it was forced to build progressively larger freight classification yards farther from the city. Finally, in 1903, the successor Chicago & North Western built a gigantic classification yard in Proviso Township on the western edge of Cook County. The Illinois Central, which had its original yards along the lakefront, moved to progressively larger sites until in 1926 it built the Markham Yard in suburban Homewood, twenty miles south of the Loop.[48] The Milwaukee Road expanded to suburban Bensenville, and the Burlington expanded to Cicero.

In Chicagoland, the phenomenon of suburbanization that the populace had grown comfortable with over the years sometime in the early twentieth century mutated into urban sprawl, as detractors called decentralization. The sylvan bedroom communities described in the American Dreams of authors Catharine Beecher, Andrew Jackson Downing, and Calvert Vaux between 1840 and 1875 had become a century later what Robert Fishman describes as "technoburbs,"[49] complete communities with their own malls, industry, and residential subdivisions. They also were auto dependant. Chicago's suburbia collectively did not reach a million residents until 1930, when the automobile was just beginning to make an impact, and it grew by less than half a million over the next two decades. Between World War II and the 1990 decennial census, it gained about three million new residents while Chicago lost more than eight hundred thousand (see Table A2).

Chicago pioneered the construction of rapid-transit lines in the median strips of expressways. The Congress line, photographed here on a Saturday morning in 1996 when traffic was light, replaced the Garfield Park L in the 1950s. The line uses the Dearborn Street subway in the downtown area.

Suburbanization had been constrained by the nineteenth-century railroad network and the impracticality of living more than about a mile from the local depot, but the motor vehicle removed that shackle because it could go almost anywhere and its only limitations were fuel availability and road conditions. Fuel was left to private enterprise, but the state and federal governments after World War I began an aggressive road-building program. The state's first inventory of roads in 1905 indicated there were 7,864 miles of improved roads in Illinois, 1,900 of them in Chicago and most of the rest in northern Illinois, where limestone for surfacing was plentiful. By 1995, the six metropolitan counties had 54,119 miles of paved streets and highways, including 2,462 lane miles

of expressways, 17,142 of arterial roads, and 34,515 of municipal streets.[50]

Systematic public planning for roads began in 1910 when the Chicago Plan Commission was created by referendum to implement the Burnham Plan, which put heavy emphasis on avenues and thoroughfares. By 1923, a time when mass-transit ridership was approaching record levels, the Chicago Regional Planning Association was formed to coordinate such things as road widths and highway construction. The park boulevards that had been built as pleasure drives were forbidden to commercial traffic after the turn of the century and were taken over by motorists, who found them faster than arterial streets. In response, the city tried to create more boulevards by posting stop signs along the arterial streets to reduce the interference of cross traffic.[51]

In the 1930s the city, state, and federal governments finally turned their attention to planning a highway system for the future rather than simply trying to keep up with growing traffic, although funds for such expressways were not available until after World War II.[52] President Franklin D. Roosevelt had sketched out a diagram of a rudimentary interstate expressway system in 1937, but nothing came of it.[53] In early 1940 the chairman of the Chicago Regional Planning Association publicly advocated an urban expressway system. The following year, basing their move on the early success of the Pennsylvania Turnpike that opened on October 1, 1940, Illinois became one of five states to create an independent toll-road authority,[54] but the war intervened before any project could get under way. The master plan for a network that included both radial and circumferential freeways—the most ambitious public works project in the state's history and one that made inevitable the transformation of suburbanization into decentralization—was percolated during World War II by the Cook County Department of Highways, the Chicago Plan Commission, and the Chicago Department of Public Works.[55] Construction on the $1.1 billion system began in 1947.

To a great extent, because the expressway system in Cook County consumed all available transportation funds, the state in 1953 dusted off the idea of tollways and created the Illinois State Toll Highway Commission to extend Chicago's expressways farther into suburbia and also to build a circumferential Tri-State Tollway as a beltway around the city.[56] The Chicago transit system, although it was by then publicly owned, did not receive any subsidies on a regular basis until after the expressway system was essentially complete.

THE WESTERN SUBURBS

The western suburbs of Chicago illustrate the influence of the transportation systems, especially the highways and expressways, on decentralization. The western suburbs—comprising a wedge-shaped area of roughly 450 square miles extending from the Chicago city limits for 30 miles across portions of Cook, Du Page, Kane, and Will Counties to the Fox River—are traversed by the metropolitan area's two original railroads and three expressways at roughly five-mile intervals. By 1900, most of the west-suburban population was concentrated in fifteen towns with a combined total of 46,000 residents strung out along the two railroads, but over the next two decades a population explosion occurred. By 1920, there were twenty-four suburbs along the railroads, and their combined population had jumped almost sevenfold to 353,310. The twelve scattered farm towns in the areas had a combined population of only 32,000. Evidence suggests that the building of the electric railroads was more important to this early boom than was anything the steam railroads or highway builders did. The inner western suburbs into which the street and elevated railways were extended from Chicago gained more than one-quarter of a million inhabitants. The outer suburbs through which the Aurora & Elgin interurban railway was built parallel to the North Western after 1900 had a population spurt more than double that of the adjacent corridor in which the Burlington Railroad had a monopoly on service.[57]

Growth patterns in the western suburbs after World War II indisputably indicate the influence of the automobile. The established railroad suburbs collectively gained more than 190,000 residents in the fifteen years after World War II, but the rural areas between the rail corridors gained more than 100,000 in population and ten new incorporated municipalities, even though the expressway system was still under construction. With the expressways completed, new cornfield suburbs over the following two decades collectively gained nearly 175,000 residents, considerably outgrowing the railroad suburbs, which counted 113,000 new residents.

Census data indicated by 1980 that in suburban Du Page County, served by those five highway and commuter railroad corridors, about 85 percent of all commuters drove to work—most of them alone in their cars—and fewer than 10 percent rode mass transit.[58] The 1990 census indicated that the western railroad suburbs combined had a population of 700,000 and an average daily railroad ridership of almost 80,000.[59] The expressway suburbs at that time had a population of more than 378,000.

IMPACT OF THE AUTO ON DEVELOPMENT

The auto began to influence both architecture and land use in Chicago long before the depression, but its full impact was not felt until after World War II, when it accelerated the decentralization process and influenced communities to redesign themselves to accommodate automobility. The single-family home built on a large lot continued to dominate residential construction. New commercial and industrial parking lots required to accommodate the growing auto population did much to reduce density, as did zoning ordinances adopted after 1970 to prevent street gridlock.[60] The auto freed the suburbs from the necessity of building business districts clustered around train stations, and strip centers with big parking lots sprang up on the edge of town. Multistory parking garages arose in downtown Chicago.

Much of the later residential growth in the suburbs was the result of relocation of industry there. In the three decades following 1960, Chicago lost about 2,800 jobs and more than 25,000 residents per year, while the suburbs gained about 42,100 jobs and 56,600 residents per year. In 1960, Chicago accounted for 57 percent of the population and 68 percent of the employment of the Chicago area, but by 1990 it accounted for only 39 percent of both population and employment, which, coincidentally, was the percentage of companies

in the metropolitan area that claimed Chicago as their corporate address.[61]

Not surprisingly, the gas station was the first architectural structure designed specifically to accommodate the automobile. Although the first drive-in gas stations date from 1905, the Standard Oil Company of Indiana opened its first gas station in Chicago in 1913. By the end of 1914, Standard Oil had fourteen stations in operation. In 1917, Allan Jackson, a Standard Oil area manager in Joliet, established what became the company's prototype gas station in the Chicago area and possibly the architectural prototype for the commercial building of the Auto Age—a brick structure set on a paved lot with a canopy that projects out over some gas pumps.[62] While the first drive-in restaurant opened in Dallas in 1921, the first motel opened in California in 1925, and the first supermarket opened in Jamaica, Long Island, in 1930, it was in Chicago that Robert E. Wood, Sears vice president in charge of factories and retail stores, as early as 1925 concluded from population trends that the chain needed to locate its smaller department stores in areas where the company could provide ample free parking.[63]

Besides the oil and auto companies, Jewel Tea Co. was probably the first Chicago firm to understand automobility and to transform itself completely in response. Founded in 1899 as a home-delivery service for coffee and tea, by 1917 the firm distributed 150 products.[64] When a trend by municipalities in the early 1930s to limit door-to-door peddling began, Jewel in 1932 bought the financially distressed Loblaw Groceteria chain of seventy-seven food stores in the Chicago area that became the nucleus of Jewel's supermarket chain.[65] Accommodating its new automobility, Jewel started the office migration to suburbia in 1930 when it moved from Chicago to a 211-acre office campus in northwest suburban Barrington following the motorization of its delivery fleet.[66] Despite Jewel's pioneer campus, the outmigration of office complexes to suburbia did not begin in earnest until after World War II.[67] By 1992, fifty-four of the one hundred largest publicly held corporations in the Chicago area had relocated to the suburbs, many to sprawling office campuses that were small company towns unto themselves.[68]

Although the lure of cheap land to replace obsolescent facilities in Chicago was the main impetus for the outmigration, the demolition of industrial buildings in the way of expressway construction in Chicago also spurred a number of companies to move. The Sanford Manufacturing Co., a maker of inks and pens that had rebuilt in Chicago after the 1871 fire, moved to suburban Bellwood in 1947 after being told its factory at Congress and Peoria Streets was in the path of the Congress (later the Eisenhower) Expressway.[69] Federal Signal Corp., a safety equipment and municipal vehicle manufacturer, lost its factory and offices at 87th and State Streets to the Dan Ryan Expressway and moved to suburban Blue Island in 1958.[70] W. W. Grainger, an industrial supplies distributor, lost buildings to the construction of both the Congress and the Northwest (later the Kennedy) Expressways before moving to suburban Skokie in 1962.[71]

The regional shopping center, a collection of stores under one roof surrounded by spacious parking lots, dates from a 1922 layout in Kansas City. The concept spread to Chicago after World War II, when developer Philip M. Klutznick included a small retail town center in his planned south suburban community of Park Forest.[72] Klutznick's original Park Forest Center, with only ten stores, quickly grew to accommodate shoppers. A study by Real Estate Research Company in 1950 issued the surprising conclusion that 74 percent of shoppers at the center, the first phase of which opened in 1949, were arriving by automobile; some shoppers drove as many as thirty miles to get there.[73] It did not take Chicago's department-store chains long to

assess the situation and to move into action. In 1952 Goldblatt's announced that it would build a store in the Park Forest Center; in 1955 Marshall Field & Co. also announced its plans to build there; in 1963 Sears, Roebuck & Co. followed suit. By the time available land was exhausted in the early 1960s, the center consisted of 60 stores containing 700,000 square feet of retail space surrounded by enough parking space for 3,000 cars.[74] From that development evolved giant malls dotting the suburban landscape at intervals of 10 miles, each containing 2 million square feet of enclosed retail space and parking for 8,000 autos.[75] By 1992 the Fox Valley retail complex, with 4 million square feet, contained more retail space than did the State Street shopping area in Chicago's Loop, with 3.5 million square feet.[76]

Despite the changes to the landscape that decentralization had caused, it was still possible in 1997 to see within the urban sprawl the vestigial outline of the railroad city of 1900. The street railways, the victims of automobility, were gone, but the elevated and commuter railroads still funneled thousands of workers to downtown Chicago each day. Because of those railroads, downtown Chicago suffered somewhat less from decentralization than did other Midwest cities, such as Detroit and St. Louis, which became completely

Suburban government often ignored mass transit or subsidized its competitor. DuPage County built two multistory parking garages (background) in its new complex of offices and courts but did not include a station along the North Western commuter line adjacent to the complex.

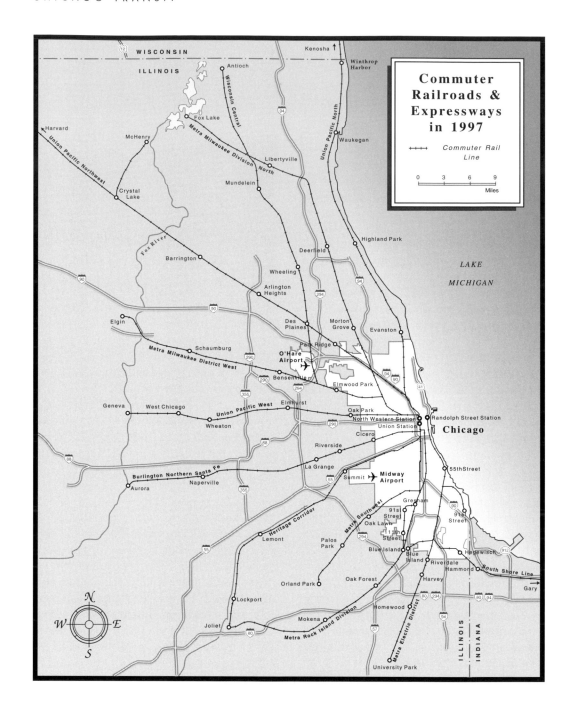

Commuter
Railroads &
Expressways
in 1997

Commuter Rail
Line

0   3   6   9
Miles

dependent on the auto and the expressways. Although the automobile has become the dominant mode for commuting in most of the metropolitan area, mass transit continues to transport the principal share of commuters to downtown Chicago, despite its 82,413 parking spaces.[77] The 1980 Chicago cordon count, tabulating how many people entered the central business district on a typical spring weekday, indicated 499,719 arrived by mass transit and 202,582 by car.[78]

EPILOGUE

♦ Chicago's transit system survived the twentieth-century onslaught of the automobile in good shape, compared to the systems of other American cities. The street railways were gone, replaced by buses, but the rapid-transit system and commuter railroads survived and grew in size during the last two decades. Local travel in the decade ending in 1990, as measured in vehicle miles, jumped by 20 percent, but population of the region increased only 2 percent. The automobile's share of the commuter market continued to grow—to 79.7 percent of the total market in 1990 from 75 percent a decade earlier—and transit's share continued to shrink, to 15 percent from 18.2 percent over the same span, primarily because of decentralization.[1]

The failure to relieve traffic congestion by inducing commuters to carpool alarmed transit planners. As the decade ended, more than two-thirds (67.5 %) of the commuters in the region drove to work alone, up from 58.2 percent in 1980. The population of Chicago declined about 7.4 percent in the period between 1980 and 1990, but auto registrations increased almost 10 percent to nearly 1.2 million. During the same time, auto registrations in the suburbs jumped nearly 32 percent, although the population increased only 7 percent. By the end of 1990 there were four cars for every ten residents of Chicago and eight cars for every ten suburbanites.[2]

The commuter railroad system continued to gain riders after it recovered from the RTA's disastrous doubling of fares in 1981, but ridership on the CTA continued its downward spiral despite new lines to O'Hare and Midway airports. The bus system was especially hard hit, losing almost 40 percent of its riders between 1980 and the end of 1994. The rapid-transit system lost 20.6 percent of its patronage in the same period (see Table A10). By the end of the century, the CTA had resumed its financial bleeding, prompting the inevitable call for greater subsidies.

The transit system has today reached a fairly stable place in the commuter market. Trains and buses dominate the Loop, while automobiles hold sway in the decentralizing sprawl everywhere else. In these final decades of the century, rush hour has increased in duration and density and has become bidirectional as more Chicagoans drive to jobs in the suburbs, a market that trains and buses are ill-equipped to serve.

The term *reverse commute* has come to describe not only Chicagoans on their way to jobs in suburbia but also, somewhat inaccurately, residents of towns in rural areas sixty to ninety miles distant who drive interstate highways to reach jobs in the suburbs. The region's tollway system, which was designed and built primarily as an interstate bypass of downtown Chicago, is now predominantly a commuter road. The railroad suburbs, however, have survived both the malling of America and the urban sprawl that has pushed the metropolitan limits thirty-five or more miles from the Loop.

As the new millennium approaches, the transit system's managers have timidly advanced theories about expansion and the

Past transportation plans have not always been a success. In the 1970s the CTA converted State Street into a transit mall for buses; the venture was abandoned twenty years later and the street returned to normal use. (Chicago Transit Authority)

possibility of constructing a circumferential rail line in the suburbs in order to adjust the radial, Loop-focused commuter railroad system to the realities of urban sprawl. The Chicago Area Transportation Study's latest recommendations, those proposed in its 1997 long-range plan, have advocated among other measures a circumferential commuter railroad line using the Elgin, Joliet & Eastern Railway right-of-way in a belt thirty miles from the Loop. This plan would capture the intra-suburban commute long ignored by the transit systems. The recommendation includes a proposal to distribute future transportation dollars to favor the highway system (57 %), about the same split proposed in the 1990 plan.[3]

The decision on what Chicagoland's transit system will look like in the next century probably will be made by economic forces, just as it was in the past. As long as oil is cheap and plentiful, the automobile will predominate and mass transit will be relegated to niche markets. In the twenty-first century, however, the automobile could be challenged by emerging communications systems—such as cellular telephones, satellite television, facsimile machines, and the Internet—that could make much of the existing commuting unnecessary.

TABLE A1

Early Chicago Area Population Density

Year	Area (square mile)	Population	Population Density (square mile)
1830	0.417	40–50 (est.)	120
1840	10.635	4,417	417
1850	9.76*	29,963	3,070
1860	17.492	109,260	6,246
1870	35.7565	298,977	8,361
1880	35.7565	503,185	14,073
1890	179.157 †	1,099,850	6,139
1900	190.638	1,698,575	8,910
1910	191.3255	2,185,283	11,422
1920	199.372	2,701,705	13,551

Sources: U.S. Bureau of Census and James D. Riley, *Map of Chicago Showing Growth of the City by Annexations,* Bureau of Maps, Chicago Department of Public Works, 1922. U.S. Bureau of Census, 1830, 1840, 1850, 1860, 1870, 1880, 1890, 1900, 1910, 1920.

* Excludes several disannexations.

† Includes both the annexation of 133 square miles and the mergers into Chicago of the townships of Hyde Park and Lake View in 1889.

TABLE A2

Population Figures for Illinois

Year	Illinois	Downstate*	Metropolitan Area	Chicago	Suburbs†
1890	3,826,352	2,434,462	1,391,890	1,099,850	292,040
1900	4,821,550	2,736,800	2,084,750	1,698,575	386,175
1910	5,638,591	2,936,126	2,702,465	2,185,283	517,182
1920	6,485,280	2,503,157	3,982,123	3,212,000	770,123
1930	7,630,654	3,181,008	4,449,646	3,367,438	1,082,208
1940	7,897,241	3,327,598	4,569,643	3,369,608	1,200,035
1950	8,712,176	3,534,576	5,177,600	3,620,962	1,556,638
1960	10,081,158	3,860,245	6,220,913	3,550,404	2,670,509
1970	11,110,285	4,133,018	6,977,267	3,369,367	3,607,900
1980	11,418,461	4,316,133	7,102,328	3,005,072	4,097,256
1990	11,349,661	4,169,426	7,180,235	2,783,726	4,396,509

Source: U.S. Bureau of Census, 1890, 1900, 1910, 1920, 1930, 1940, 1950, 1960, 1970, 1980, 1990.

* Includes all ninety-six counties outside the Chicago metropolitan area.

† Includes data for suburban Cook, Du Page, Kane, Will, Lake, and McHenry Counties.

TABLE A3

Growth of Railroad Suburbs

1860–1930

Rail Line (terminal)	1860		1900		1930	
	Suburbs	Population	Suburbs	Population	Suburbs	Population
West						
Burlington (Aurora)	2	8,610	9	54,968	12	215,704
North Western* (Geneva)	1	645	9	7,752	14	165,090
Northwest						
North Western (Harvard)	2	2,667	10	14,033	12	45,685
Milwaukee Road (Elgin)	1	2,797	6	24,231	9	53,849
North						
Milwaukee Road (Fox Lake)	0	0	4	2,358	9	15,300
North Western† (Waukegan)	2	4,264	11	42,413	14	173,174
Southwest						
Rock Island (Joliet)	1	2,659	4	36,048	7	65,485
South						
Illinois Central (Richton Park)	0	0	3	6,305	10	27,464

Sources: Data extrapolated from U.S. Bureau of Census, 1860, 1900, and 1930, and Illinois Secretary of State, *Blue Book,* 1906 and 1932.

Note: Includes areas outside those annexed to Chicago through 1900 and excludes suburbs served by minor railroad lines, such as the Chicago & Alton to Joliet, the Wabash to Orland Park, and the Illinois Central to Addison.

* The Chicago, Aurora & Elgin provided service in corridor after 1900.

† The Chicago, North Shore & Milwaukee provided service in corridor after 1900.

TABLE A4
Chicago Transit Ridership

Year	Surface	Rapid Transit	Buses*	Total	Per Capita
1906	373.9	131.9	——	505.8	247
1910	481.8	164.8	——	646.6	296
1915	619.5	164.7	——	784.2	318
1920	768.0	190.6	6.4	965.0	357
1925	840.9	216.0	57.5	1,114.4	360
1926	874.2	228.8	55.8	1,158.8	366
1927	881.9	226.3	59.3	1,167.5	362
1930	821.2	182.9	58.3	1,062.4	315
1935	664.7	127.5	40.0	832.2	246
1940	672.2	123.7	57.4	853.3	251
1945	844.8	157.3	75.1	1,077.2	305
1946	917.0	157.9	72.7	1,147.6	319
1947	888.5	145.7	85.8	1,120.0	312
1950	641.6	110.6	80.9	833.1	224
1953	501.1	111.7	73.7	686.5	187

Source: Werner Schroeder, "Metropolitan Transit Research Study," 1954.

Note: Originating rides in millions.

* Includes Chicago Motor Coach only.

TABLE A5

Mass Transit and Auto Registration

Year	Mass Transit (originating rides)		Autos	
	Total	Per Capita	Total Registered	Population per Auto Ratio
1908	546,455,339	262	5,475	381.3
1910	646,698,084	296	9,963	219.3
1915	784,221,472	318	34,441	71.5
1920	965,068,100	357	86,709	31.2
1925	1,114,510,727	360	290,956	10.6
1926	1,158,893,750	366	317,433	10.0
1927	1,167,521,289	362	337,502	9.6
1930	1,062,431,825	315	406,619	8.3
1935	832,220,952	246	396,727	8.5
1940	853,320,614	251	549,537	6.2
1945	1,077,207,431	305	427,779	8.4
1950	833,112,451	224	705,197	5.3
1953	686,560,076	187	764,942	4.8

Source: Werner Schroeder, "Metropolitan Transit Research Study," 1954.

TABLE A6

Passengers Arriving in Chicago Business District by Mass Transit and Automobiles on a Single Day

Year	Mass Transit	Share	Autos	Share
1926	551,244	62.6%	166,367	18.9%
1931	472,852	56.1%	203,961	24.2%
1941	400,778	48.6%	251,962	30.6%
1952	431,062	48.7%	244,081	27.6%

Source: Chicago Department of Streets and Sanitation, "Cordon Count of Chicago's Central Business District," 1926, 1931, 1941, and 1952.

Chicago Transit Authority Fares

Year	Surface	Rapid Transit	Transfers
1947	$ .10	$ .12	$ 0
1948	.13	.15	0
1949	.15	.17	0
1952	.20	.20	0
1957	.25	.25	0
1961	.25	.25	.05
1967	.30	.30	.05
1968	.40	.40	.05
1970	.45	.45	.10
1976	.50	.50	.10
1979	.60	.60	.10
1981	.80	.80	.10
1981	.90	.90	.10
1988	1.00	1.00	.25
1990	1.25	1.25	.25
1991	1.50	1.50	.25

Source: Chicago Transit Authority, *Basic Rates of Fare History,* 1995.

Note: Prices indicate base fares.

Expansion and Contraction of the Chicago Rapid Transit System

Years	Route Miles Added/Subtracted*	Cumulative Miles of System*
1891–1900	+42.15	42.15
1901–1910	+25.65	67.8
1911–1920	+1.25	69.05
1921–1930	+6.25	75.3
1931–1940	0.00	75.3
1941–1950	-10.5	64.8
1951–1960	-8.75	56.05
1961–1970	+17.0	73.05
1971–1980	+5.2	78.25
1981–1990	+7.5	85.75
1991–1995	+9.0	94.75

Note: Calculated from route maps of the transit system for the years 1891 to 1995 and a private document in the possession of George Krambles (1986) estimating the first track miles for the years 1900, 1910, 1920, 1931, 1940, 1960, 1975, and 1986.

* Refers to the first track miles, or the primary route miles of the system (excluding the double counting of tracks over which more than one route operated), sidings, yards, and passing and express tracks.

Chicago Transit Authority Financial Position

1970–1995

Year	Costs	Fare Revenue	Fares as % of Cost	Operating Deficit	Base Fare
1970	$188.7	$174.9	92.7%	-$13.8	$0.45
1975	$284.3	$169.7	59.7%	-$114.6	$0.45
1980	$504.8	$223.0	44.2%	-$281.8	$0.60
1985	$585.0	$295.7	50.5%	-$289.3	$0.90
1990	$717.1	$389.2	54.3%	-$327.9	$1.25
1995	$749.4	$389.1	51.9%	-$360.3	$1.50

Source: Chicago Transit Authority Budgets, 1970–1995.

Note: Dollar amounts, except for base fares, in millions.

Postwar Transit Ridership in Chicago

Year	Surface*	Rapid Transit	Total	Per Capita	Registered Autos per 1,000 Population
1950	641,597,249	110,603,719	752,200,968	230	194.8
1955	510,603,672	112,889,976	623,493,648	174	231.9
1960	421,832,145	122,924,491	544,756,636	151	240.7
1965	389,131,966	114,833,953	503,965,919	143	260
1970	296,176,300	105,598,382	401,774,682	119	299
1975	280,186,720	89,476,235	369,662,955	113	374
1980 †	298,634,642	98,629,447	397,264,089	135	316
1985 †	270,210,277	99,102,146	369,312,423	123	378
1990 †	234,442,412	93,237,373	327,679,785	117	376
1994 †	184,798,576	78,353,934	263,152,510	95	395

Note: Discrepancies between Chicago auto registration data provided by the Illinois Secretary of State's office and by the City of Chicago occur after 1973. In 1974, Chicago reported 1,090,045 registered autos and the state reported 1,506,173 in Chicago. In 1994, Chicago reported 1,090,088 and the state reported 1,264,407. The table uses Chicago auto registration data throughout.

* Includes buses and streetcars.

† Recalculated to conform to earlier data from reporting system modified by the Chicago Transit Authority in 1978.

While the widespread Chicago area was the site of a number of transportation disasters in the nineteenth century—including the nation's first railroad disaster (1853)—the city's street, elevated, and commuter railroads were free of calamity for the first half century of their existence. Given that the early elevated system operated on very tight headways (distance between trains), without signals or guardrails, and with vulnerable wooden cars, it is truly amazing that only four accidents were documented between 1895 and 1913 (all involved cars falling from the platform) and that not a single fatality was reported as a result.[1]

The following pages contain a synopsis of some of Chicago's major disasters and transit accidents. For each major accident that can be called a disaster—and the designation is subjective—hundreds of minor accidents claimed lives when pedestrians were hit by streetcars, commuters fell onto the third rail or in front of trains, and autoists were hit at crossings. For example, the Chicago area in 1990 reported that 326,346 motor-vehicle collisions resulted in 771 fatalities—only slightly less than the death toll of the *Eastland*, the state's worst transportation disaster, and nearly twice the death toll of the Chicago fire.[2]

THE NATION'S FIRST TRAIN DISASTER

April 25, 1853 A collision between the Michigan Central and the Michigan Southern intercity trains killed twenty-one people at a right-angle diamond crossing at Grand Crossing, Illinois, south of Chicago.[3]

THE GLENWOOD TRAIN WRECK

July 13, 1904 A collision at Glenwood, Illinois, between a freight train and a passenger train carrying children killed eighteen. An Illinois Central Railroad excursion train carrying Sunday school pupils from Doremus Congregational Church in Chicago, returning from an excursion to Momence, Illinois, ran into a Chicago & Eastern Illinois Railroad freight train backing down the mainline without authority and without a flagman to protect its rear.[4]

SOUTH SHORE CRASH NEAR MILLER

June 19, 1909 A head-on collision between two interurban trains on the Chicago, Lake Shore, & South Bend (later the Chicago, South Shore & South Bend) Railroad east of Miller, Indiana, resulted in the deaths of twelve persons and injuries to fifty-two. The Indiana Railroad Commission found in its investigation that the crew of an eastbound train failed to follow written orders to wait on a siding at Wilson, Indiana, for a westbound to pass and proceeded down the mainline. The accident was almost identical to one that occurred two months earlier west of Gary in which forty-seven persons were injured.[5]

THE WESTERN SPRINGS CRASH

July 14, 1912   A Chicago, Burlington & Quincy Railroad mail and baggage train slammed into the rear of a passenger train stopped for a signal at Western Springs, Illinois, killing fourteen. Survivors gave conflicting accounts, but the crash has been blamed on the failure of the brakeman of the stopped train to set out a torpedo—an explosive warning device—far enough behind his train to alert the crew of an express train following it by about nine minutes of its location.[6]

THE *EASTLAND* DISASTER

July 24, 1915   The *Eastland*, a lake excursion steamer, capsized in the Chicago River, killing 844 in what remains the worst transportation disaster in the city's history.

THE KENOSHA CROSSING WRECK

February 23, 1930   A high-speed, chain-reaction collision at a crossing near Kenosha, Wisconsin, between an automobile and two Chicago, North Shore & Milwaukee Railroad trains resulted in twelve deaths and ninety-five injuries in what still stands as the worst grade-crossing accident in Chicagoland history. A southbound passenger express traveling from Milwaukee to Chicago at seventy miles per hour and a northbound freight were approaching the Wisconsin Highway 43 grade crossing from opposite directions when the driver of a Buick sedan passed a car stopped for flashing signals and drove onto the tracks in an attempt to beat the freight train over the crossing. The car was hit by the passenger train and hurled two hundred feet. Both occupants of the car died. The passenger coaches, still on the tracks but rocking from the impact of the collision, then sideswiped the passing freight train, causing both trains to derail.[7]

THE GRANVILLE REAR-END WRECK

November 24, 1936   A rear-end collision involving a Chicago Rapid Transit elevated train and a Chicago, North Shore & Milwaukee interurban train at Granville Avenue killed ten and injured thirty-six in what for many years was the worst crash on the elevated system. A northbound elevated train of eight wooden and steel cars was stopped on an express track waiting for clearance to switch to a local track when the North Shore express, made up of three steel cars, slammed into it at an impact speed of ten miles per hour. Federal investigators attributed the number of casualties to the fact that the steel coaches on the North Shore telescoped through the wooden rear coach of the elevated train, demolishing it. Although investigators blamed the crash on the North Shore motorman for failing to see the elevated train and thus failing to apply his brakes in time, they recommended that the CRT install automatic signals to separate trains properly, phase out wooden cars as soon as practical, and stop mixing wooden and steel cars in the same trains, a practice discontinued on standard railroads long before. The CRT train had included two steel cars, three cars in which wooden superstructures were built above steel underframes, and three wooden cars.[8]

THE NAPERVILLE CRASH

April 25, 1946   A rear-end collision of two intercity passenger trains in suburban Naperville, one stopped for a safety check, killed forty-five. The accident was attributable to the failure of the engineer of the second train to heed a red signal.[9] It ranked with the 1972 Illinois Central crash as the worst train disaster in the region's history.

THE WORST CHICAGO STREETCAR ACCIDENT

May 25, 1950 A collision at 6:30 P.M. of a streetcar and a gasoline truck on State Street between 62nd and 63rd Streets in Chicago killed thirty-three in the worst streetcar accident in U.S. history. According to an expert witness, a Chicago Transit Authority Presidents' Conference Car (or PCC streetcar) carrying about sixty occupants was traveling south on State Street at an excessive speed of twenty to thirty miles per hour when it hit a switch aligned so as to redirect it around a flooded viaduct that blocked service further south. Despite the presence of a flagman in the street to warn him, the motorman did not slow down in time, and the streetcar was diverted by the switch into a northbound tractor-trailer truck carrying gasoline for delivery to service stations. The tanks of the gasoline truck ruptured in the collision, and the resulting fire killed the truck driver and thirty-two streetcar passengers, destroyed the truck and the streetcar, and damaged a number of nearby buildings. Sixteen streetcar riders were able to escape through the side door or the rear window, which was equipped with an emergency escape device. Most of those killed were trapped against the rear doors, which had no such device.[10]

THE WILSON AVENUE REAR-END COLLISION

November 5, 1956 A rear-end collision between two trains at the Wilson Avenue elevated station on Chicago's North Side killed eight and injured two hundred. The accident occurred when a Chicago Transit Authority elevated train slammed into the rear of a North Shore interurban train stopped in the station to pick up and discharge passengers. After hearing evidence, a Cook County coroner's jury concluded that the motorman of the CTA train was at fault and recommended that the agency install automatic block signals on its elevated lines. Such signals had been installed in the State and Dearborn Streets subways when they were built, but the elevated lines had never been equipped with signals. Instead, motormen were expected to watch for other trains. The CTA ultimately equipped the elevated lines with a more sophisticated cab signal and a speed control system with the capability of overriding a motorman, but the L suffered two more rear-end collisions in the 1970s despite the technology.[11]

THE LISLE AUTO CRASH

September 7, 1967 A two-car, head-on collision between west suburban Downers Grove and Lisle killed ten people in the area's deadliest traffic accident involving only automobiles. The driver of one car, a lone occupant, had been drinking and was speeding when he crossed into the opposite traffic lanes and collided with another car. Nine people, all family members, died in the other car.[12]

CHICAGO'S WORST RAILROAD CRASH

October 30, 1972 A rear-end collision of two Illinois Central Railroad commuter trains at 27th Street in Chicago killed forty-five. The accident occurred when train No. 416, a four-car northbound train of new bilevel cars, overshot the 27th Street station by six hundred feet and had to back up to board and discharge passengers. Train No. 720, which was not scheduled to stop at 27th Street, smashed into the rear of No. 416 at approximately fifty miles per hour. As in the 1946 Naperville crash, much of the death toll was attributed to the heavyweight steel cars of the second train, which telescoped into the first train's new bilevel cars of lighter construction. A third northbound train, No. 718, which passed on an adjacent track at the moment of the crash, was not damaged.[13]

THE LOOP CRASH

February 4, 1977 A slow-motion, rear-end collision involving two Chicago Transit Authority trains on the Loop elevated structure at Wabash Avenue and Lake Street killed eleven. The accident was extraordinary in that it occurred at less than ten miles per hour on a railroad line protected by the most elaborate signal system then available. Many of the deaths resulted when four of the eight cars of the second train derailed and plunged to the street below. The accident happened when a motorman ignored a red signal in his cab and drove his train around the Wabash-Lake curve into the rear of a standing train. Although the federal report did not address the issue, some CTA officials believed that derailment at such a slow speed could only have occurred because the motorman failed to apply the brakes and possibly even continued to power the train after the collision.[14]

SOUTH SHORE GAUNTLET BRIDGE

January 18, 1993 A Chicago, South Shore & South Bend Railroad commuter train passed a red signal and crashed into another train on a single-track gauntlet bridge in Gary, Indiana, killing seven. The National Transportation Safety Board ruled that the sixty-nine-year-old motorman who blew the signal was to blame.

THE FOX RIVER GROVE SCHOOL BUS COLLISION

October 25, 1995 A Union Pacific Railroad express commuter train struck a school bus carrying high-school students at a crossing in Fox River Grove, tearing the bus body from the chassis and killing seven aboard. No one on the train was hurt. The bus had been stopped at a red traffic signal at U.S. Highway 14 parallel to and adjacent to the railroad with the rear end of the bus protruding over the tracks.[15]

APPENDIX C: GLOSSARY OF CHICAGO AREA TRANSIT NAMES

The names of area transit lines have changed over the years because of line extensions, contractions, marketing programs, and changes in corporate ownership. That the old names often persist long after they have been changed officially only adds to the confusion. Listed below in descending order from oldest to most recent are the various names in public use over the years to designate existing transit lines. Although extensive, the list is not all-inclusive.

The names are listed under either their current street names or their geographical locations, and the outlying terminals are designated in parentheses.

COMMUTER RAILROADS

North Western System

Chicago & Milwaukee Railroad (to Waukegan)
Chicago & North Western North Line (to Kenosha)
Metra/Union Pacific North Line (to Kenosha)

Milwaukee Road

Chicago, Milwaukee & St. Paul Railroad (to Rondout and Janesville)
Chicago, Milwaukee & St. Paul Evanston Branch (to Wilmette)
Chicago, Milwaukee, St. Paul & Pacific North Line (to Walworth)
Metra/Milwaukee District North Line (to Fox Lake)

Wisconsin Central

Metra/Wisconsin Central Division (to Antioch)

North Western System

Illinois & Wisconsin Railroad (to Cary)
Chicago & North Western Northwest Line (to Harvard and Lake Geneva)
Metra/Union Pacific Northwest Line (to Harvard and McHenry)

Milwaukee Road

Chicago & Pacific Railroad (to Elgin)
Chicago, Milwaukee & St. Paul West Line (to Elgin)
Chicago, Milwaukee, St. Paul & Pacific West Line (to Elgin)
Metra/Milwaukee Division West Line (to Elgin)

North Western System

Galena & Chicago Union Railroad (to Junction)
Chicago & North Western Galena Division or West Line (to Geneva)
Metra/Union Pacific West Line (to Geneva)

Burlington Route
Aurora Branch Railroad (to Junction)
Chicago, Burlington & Quincy (to Aurora)
Burlington Northern (to Aurora)
Metra/Burlington Northern Santa Fe (to Aurora)

Alton
Chicago & Alton Railroad (to Joliet)
Gulf, Mobile & Ohio (to Joliet)
Illinois Central Gulf (to Joliet)
Metra/Heritage Corridor (to Joliet)

Wabash
Wabash Railroad (to Orland Park)
Norfolk & Western (to Orland Park)
Metra/Southwest Service (to Orland Park)

Rock Island Lines
Chicago & Rock Island Railroad (to Blue Island and Joliet)
Chicago Rock Island & Pacific (Suburban Division to Blue Island and
    Mainline to Joliet)
Metra/Rock Island Division (to Blue Island and Joliet)

The I.C.
Illinois Central Railroad (to Blue Island, South Chicago, Addison, and Matteson)
Illinois Central Gulf (to Blue Island, South Chicago, and University Park)
Metra Electric (to Blue Island, South Chicago, and University Park)

CHICAGO RAPID TRANSIT SYSTEM

South Side
Chicago and South Side Rapid Transit Railroad, also known popularly as the Alley L
    (to Jackson Park, Englewood, Kenwood, Normal Park, and Stock Yards)
Chicago Rapid Transit Co. Jackson Park, Englewood, Kenwood, Normal Park,
    and Stock Yards lines
Chicago Transit Authority Green Line (to 63rd Street and Englewood)

Chicago Transit Authority Dan Ryan Line (to 95th Street)
Chicago Transit Authority Red Line (to 95th Street)

West Side
Metropolitan West Side Elevated Railroad Co., popularly called the Met
    (to Berwyn, Forest Park, Logan Square, and Humboldt Park)
Chicago Rapid Transit Co. Douglas Park (Berwyn), Garfield Park (Forest Park),
    Humboldt Park, and Logan Square lines
Chicago Transit Authority Douglas (Cicero), Congress (Forest Park), and
    Milwaukee (Jefferson Park) lines
Chicago Transit Authority Blue Line (to Cicero, Forest Park, and O'Hare

International Airport)

Lake Street Elevated Railway Co.
Chicago & Oak Park Elevated Railway
Chicago Rapid Transit Co. Lake Street line (to Forest Park)
Chicago Transit Authority Green Line (to Forest Park)

North Side
Northwestern Elevated Railroad Co. (to Ravenswood and Howard Street)
Chicago Rapid Transit Co. Ravenswood, Howard, Niles Center, and Evanston
   (to Wilmette) lines
Chicago Transit Authority Red Line (Howard)

Chicago Transit Authority Purple Line (Evanston)

Chicago Transit Authority Yellow Line (Skokie)

Chicago Transit Authority Brown Line (Ravenswood)

Southwest Side
Chicago Transit Authority Orange Line (to Midway Airport)

SUBURBAN TRANSIT SYSTEMS

West
Aurora, Elgin & Wheaton Railroad
Aurora, Elgin & Chicago Railroad
Chicago, Aurora & Elgin Railroad
Aurora, Elgin & Fox River Electric Co.
National City Lines (Aurora, Elgin, and Joliet)
Aurora and Elgin municipal systems
Pace

West Chicago Dummy Railroad
Chicago, Harlem & Batavia Railroad
Cicero & Proviso Railroad
Suburban Railroad
Chicago & West Towns Railway
Bluebird Coach Lines
Leyden Motor Coach
West Suburban Transit
West Towns Bus Co.
Pace

North
Suburban Coach
White Bus Lines, Des Plaines Coach, Glenview Bus Lines, Evanston Bus Lines
United Motor Coach

North Suburban Mass Transit District (Nortran)
Pace

Milwaukee & Chicago Electric Cars Co.
Bluff City Electric Street Car Co.
Chicago, North Shore & Milwaukee Railroad
Waukegan-North Chicago Transit
Pace

South

Kankakee Electric Co. and Chicago & Interurban Traction Co.
South Suburban Motor Coach Co.
South Suburban Safeway Lines Inc.
Pace

Joliet Street Railway
Central Illinois Public Service Co.
Chicago & Joliet Electric Railway
National City Lines
Joliet Mass Transit District
Pace

NOTES

CHAPTER 1: THE CITY OF MUD

1. Bessie Louise Pierce, *A History of Chicago* (Chicago, 1937), 1:11–12; Milo M. Quaife, ed., "Property of Jean Baptiste Point Sable," *Mississippi Valley Historical Review* 15 (June 1928): 26–27.

2. Dean Snow, *The Archaeology of North America* (New York, 1976), 59–61; Brian M. Fagan, *Ancient North America* (New York, 1990), 436–41; and David M. Young, "The Secret City," *Chicago Tribune Magazine,* June 13, 1976, 18, 55–61. Cahokia, which was occupied between A.D. 900 and 1300, at its height of power covered four thousand acres and had a population estimated at between fifteen thousand and forty thousand individuals.

3. John Boatman (*An Anthology of Western Great Lakes Indian History,* ed. Donald L. Fixico [Milwaukee, 1987], 25), citing various accounts in the Wisconsin State Historical Society collections in Madison (based on the manuscripts of Nicholas Perrot describing his visit to the Winnebagos in 1667), said that sometime prior to the arrival of the French an estimated five hundred Winnebago warriors in a flotilla of canoes capsized in a storm on Lake Michigan, with a loss of several hundred lives.

4. Francis Parkman, *France and England in North America* (New York, 1983), 1:803–5.

5. Kenan Heise and Michael Edgerton, *Chicago: Center for Enterprise* (Woodland Hills, Calif., 1982), 1:26.

6. Milo Quaife, *Chicago's Highways Old and New: From Indian Trail to Motor Road* (Chicago, 1923), 122.

7. Charles Hadfield, *World Canals* (New York, 1986), 355, dates the end of America's canal-building period with completion of the Illinois-Michigan Canal and the St. Lawrence River locks.

8. Milo M. Quaife, *Lake Michigan* (Indianapolis, 1942), 141. The *Sheldon Thompson* arrived in Chicago on July 10, 1832, followed by the *Henry Clay, Superior,* and *William Penn,* also bringing troops.

9. *Chicago Daily Democrat,* September 19, 1848. Captain Robert C. Bristol opened the city's first steam-powered grain elevator in a four-story building with a capacity for storing eighty thousand bushels (the mechanical process had been invented in 1842 in Buffalo by William Dart). William Cronon, *Nature's Metropolis* (New York, 1991), 64–65, 76, 111–12.

10. James D. Riley, *Map of Chicago Showing Growth of the City by Annexations* [map] (Chicago: Bureau of Maps, Chicago Department of Public Works, 1922), indicated the area of the city at incorporation in 1830 was .4137 square miles.

11. James M. Putnam, *The Illinois and Michigan Canal* (Chicago, 1918), 10–58. G. P. Brown, *Drainage Channel and Waterway* (Chicago, 1894), 318–416, pointed out that the Metropolitan Sanitary District that financed the Sanitary and Ship Canal in 1900 as a replacement for the I-M Canal was empowered to levy taxes to raise money for construction. That project, however, was perceived primarily as a solution for the city's sewage disposal problems.

12. *Chicago Daily Democrat,* February 16, 1848.

13. Cronon, *Nature's Metropolis,* 80–82; Wyatt Winton Belcher, *The Economic Rivalry Between St. Louis and Chicago* (New York, 1947), 89–91, 167–68; James Neal Primm, *Lion of the Valley* (Boulder, Colo., 1981), 211, 215–34. Missouri committed $33.52 million to build 914.2 miles of railway; it later sold its interests for $6.13 million. The city and county of St. Louis contributed another $6.3 million.

14. Illinois Central Railroad Company, *Report and Accounts to Shareholders,* 1857, 1–2. Shareholder meetings were held that year in both Chicago and London.

15. John Lewis Peyton, *Over the Alleghenies and across the Prairies* (London: Simkin, Marshall and Co., 1869), 325–29, is a classic description of Chicago based on his 1848 visit.

16. Edwin F. Mack, *Old Monroe Street: Notes on Monroe Street of Early Chicago Days* (Chicago, 1914), 13.

17. Ibid., 13.

18. Quaife, *Chicago's Highways,* 157–61.

19. Martin O. Walker was the younger brother of Samuel B. Walker, who in partnership operated a livery stable in Chicago after 1844 and an omnibus service somewhat later. A. T. Andreas, *History of Chicago from the Earliest to the Present Time* (Chicago, 1884), 2:118; *Chicago Tribune,* May 29, 1874.

20. Quaife, *Chicago's Highways,* 159.

21. Andreas, *History of Chicago,* 1:258; *Album of Genealogy and Biography,* Cook County, Ill., Chicago, 1897, 139–40; and *Chicago Daily Democrat,* May 25, 1858.

22. Pierce, *History of Chicago,* 1:336–39.

23. Chicago Department of Public Works, *A History of Chicago Public Works* (Chicago, 1968), 48.

24. Andreas, *History of Chicago,* 2:57–59.

25. Chicago Bureau of Public Efficiency, *Street Pavement Laid in the City of Chicago* (1910), 10. In 1910 four miles of creosote-impregnated wood block was laid on residential streets. In the same year the city laid almost thirty miles of asphalt streets. Anecdotal evidence from the Chicago Department of Streets and Sanitation employees indicates that some wood block surfaces survived in alleys as late as the 1980s.

26. The data was contained in a handwritten document of uncertain origin and date, salvaged by Chicago Department of Streets and Sanitation officials from Board of Public Works documents being purged by the city in 1985–1986. The first macadam surface on Market Street dated from 1867, but Andreas, *History of Chicago,* 2:68, indicates the city had twenty-two miles of macadam streets by 1863. Another brief history, also of uncertain date and origin salvaged during the same purge of records, indicates that portions of State Street in the Loop by 1901 were paved with an eight-inch base of gravel topped by five inches of concrete, although the center of the street between the streetcar tracks remained surfaced with wood blocks.

27. Pierce, *History of Chicago,* 1:339.

28. Ibid.

29. Quaife, *Chicago's Highways,* 130–33, places the cost of the 19-mile plank road from Chicago to Doty's Tavern (modern Riverside) at $16,000 ($1,600 per mile) and the 23-mile northwest plank road to Wheeling at $51,000 ($2,217 per mile). Pierce, *History of Chicago,* 2:315.

30. Andreas, *History of Chicago,* 2:56; Pierce, *History of Chicago,* 1:336–39, 2:319.

31. Carl W. Condit, *Chicago, 1910–1929: Building, Planning, and Urban Technology* (Chicago, 1973), 32.

32. Andreas, *History of Chicago,* 1:142.

33. Alfred D. Chandler Jr., *The Visible Hand: The Managerial Revolution in American Business* (Cambridge, Mass., 1977), 15–77, gives an account of business in preindustrial America.

34. Rolf Achilles, *Made in Illinois* (Chicago, 1993), 14.

35. Ibid., 29.

36. John Moses and Joseph Kirkland, *The History of Chicago* (New York, 1895), 1:240–41.

37. Cronon, *Nature's Metropolis,* 77, map.

38. J. B. Mansfield, *History of the Great Lakes* (Chicago, 1899), 1:185. In 1833, only two of the eleven steamboats registered on the Great Lakes visited Chicago. The two round trips from Buffalo took twenty-five and twenty-two days, respectively, and apparently included intermediate stops. By 1839, when Chicago was booming, eight vessels were assigned to the Buffalo-Chicago route and the round trip was down to sixteen days.

39. James R. Vance, *Capturing the Horizon: The Historical Geography of Transportation since the Sixteenth Century* (Baltimore, 1986), 363. Horsecars had the practical effect of allowing cities to expand their built-up limits to as much as 2.5 miles from the central business district, a walk of thirty to forty minutes.

CHAPTER 2: HORSE POWER TO MACHINE TECHNOLOGY

1. Juliet Clutton-Brock, *Horse Power: A History of the Horse and the Donkey in Modern Society* (Cambridge, 1992), 156. The earliest domesticated horses were too small—typically no taller than 13 1/2 hands (54 inches from hoof to withers)—for hauling passenger vehicles much larger than chariots. Oxen were used for heavy transport until, beginning in the fifteenth century, larger horses were bred—draft horses reached 20 hands (80 inches) and more than a ton in weight.

2. Vance, *Capturing the Horizon,* 355. The omnibus, a horse-drawn coach for urban routes dating from 1662 in Paris, by 1831 had reached New York and Philadelphia. The name "omnibus" originated with the sign reading "Omnes Omnibus" above a hatter's shop adjacent to the transit terminus in Nantes.

3. Andreas, *History of Chicago,* 3:164.

4. Continental Air Transport, a service between the downtown hotels and airports, traces its lineage to Parmelee's company.

5. William D. Middleton, *The Time of the Trolley* (Milwaukee, 1967), 21.

6. Werner Schroeder, "Metropolitan Transit Research Study" (Chicago, 1954), 195. Unpublished work in CTA Library.

7. Andreas, *History of Chicago,* 2:119.

8. U.S. Department of the Interior, Census Office, *Report on the Transportation Business in the United States at the 11th Census (1890),* Washington, D.C., 1895, part 1, 683–85. The data cited does not include 41.2 miles of cable-car routes and counts double-track routes as a single mile. Therefore, Chicago had 390.33 miles of street railway trackage but only 193.11 miles of street railway routes.

9. George W. Hilton, *The Cable Car in America* (San Diego, Calif., 1982), 235.

10. Thomas R. Bullard, *Illinois Rail Transit* (manuscript, Oak Park, Ill., ca. 1987), 17, 20–21. North Chicago City Railway had 1,700 horses in 1885, Chicago West Division Railway had 3,246 in 1884, Chicago City Railways had 1,468 in 1881. Andreas, *History of Chicago,* 2:164. Parmelee's depot transfer company owned 250 horses in the 1880s. U.S. Census Office, *12th Census (1900)—Agriculture,* Washington, D.C., U.S. Department of the Interior, 1902, 498–99.

11. George H. Douglas, *Rail City: Chicago USA* (San Diego, 1981), 144; James J. Flink, *America Adopts the Automobile, 1895–1910* (Cambridge, Mass., 1970), 105.

12. Heise and Edgerton, *Chicago,* 1:103–4; Donald L. Miller, *City of the Century* (New York, 1996), 195–210; and Cronon, *Nature's Metropolis,* 218–47, all discuss the importance of Chicago's meat-packing industry.

13. Glenn Yago, *The Decline of Transit: Urban Transportation in German and U.S. Cities, 1900–1970* (Cambridge, U.K., 1984), 135–37.

14. Quaife, *Chicago's Highways,* 42–43. In 1833, when connecting stagecoach service to Chicago was first established, the 165-mile trip from Niles, Michigan, to Detroit took the better part of three days, with changes of teams every 12 to 15 miles. Pierce, *History of Chicago,* 1:103n.152, indicates that in 1834 the 157-mile stagecoach trip between Chicago and Peoria took three days of constant travel (an average trip speed of 2.18 miles per hour) and required a fare of $10. By 1841, the 160-mile Chicago-Galena trip was down to 2 days (3.33 miles per hour).

15. John H. White Jr., *The American Railroad Passenger Car* (Baltimore, 1978), xiii (chart on the evolution of a generic passenger day coach) and 12–13; and John H. White Jr., *American Locomotives: An Engineering History, 1830–1880* (Baltimore, 1968), 73.

16. Oliver Jensen, *The American Heritage History of Railroads in America* (New York, 1975), 45–53; Vance, *Capturing the Horizon,* 270–71.

17. White, *American Railroad Passenger Car,* 3–12; M. N. Forney et al., *The American Railway: Its Construction, Development, Management and Appliances* (New York, 1972), 139–40.

18. Smith Hempstone Oliver, *The First Quarter Century of Steam Locomotives in North America,* United States National Museum Bulletin 210 (Washington: Smithsonian Institution, 1956), 53–55; Charles T. Knudsen, *Chicago & North Western Railway Steam Power* (Chicago, 1965), 1–3.

19. Knudsen, *Chicago & North Western Railway,* ix (table) and 12. Samson may have gained some weight during a rebuilding by the successor Chicago & North Western Railway in 1868.

20. White, *American Railroad Passenger Car,* 581.

21. Hilton, *Cable Car in America,* 13, indicates that the term *dummy* refers to attempts to mute their exhausts, not to their disguised appearance. John H. White Jr. in "Dummy

Tech," *Invention & Technology* (Spring 1998): 34, said dummies were disguised for aesthetic reasons and to avoid spooking horses.

22. Pierce, *History of Chicago,* 2:327; Harry P. Weber, *Outline History of Chicago Traction* (Chicago, 1936), 18.

23. Robert David Weber, "Rationalizers and Reformers: Chicago Local Transportation in the Nineteenth Century" (Ph.D. diss., University of Wisconsin, Madison, 1971), 280.

24. Frank Rowsome Jr., *Trolley Car Treasury* (New York, 1956), 35–37.

25. *Chicago Daily Journal,* December 2 and 3, 1859, as cited by Weber, "Rationalizers and Reformers," 89; Hilton, *Cable Car in America,* 13; Middleton, *Time of the Trolley,* 27–34.

26. Central Electric Railfans' Association (CERA), Vol. 1, *Chicago's Rapid Transit Rolling Stock, 1892–1947,* Bulletin 113 (Chicago, 1973), 2, indicates they were unusual in that the locomotive and tender were a single unit and were equipped with two compound cylinders of different sizes to drive the pistons.

27. CERA, *Rolling Stock, 1892–1947,* 161–63.

28. Knudsen, *Chicago & North Western Railway,* 47, 84–90.

29. George Krambles and Arthur H. Peterson, *The CTA at 45* (Chicago, 1993), 56.

30. Bruce G. Moffat, *The L* (Chicago, 1995), 124.

31. Hilton, *Cable Car in America,* 149. In 1887 the Chicago City Railways, which did not convert its entire system to cable, reported costs of 23.16 cents per mile for horsecars and 10.57 cents per mile for cable cars.

32. Ibid., 48. San Francisco (at 52.8 miles) was longest, followed by Chicago (41.2 miles). Chicago, however, had more equipment (710 grip cars) and passengers (237 million in 1892).

33. Debate has risen about whether the 1882 downtown cable loop by Chicago City Railway or the loop elevated structure was responsible for downtown Chicago's nickname, the Loop.

34. Hilton, *Cable Car in America,* 31.

35. Ibid., 235–36.

36. Ibid., 133.

37. Ibid., 153.

38. An ordinance temporarily extending street railway franchises required the conversion of all horsecar and cable lines.

39. Alan R. Lind, *Limiteds Along the Lakefront: The Illinois Central in Chicago* (Park Forest, Ill., 1986), 55–65.

40. Schroeder, "Metropolitan Transit Research Study," 195–99. The initial cable-grip cars seated a maximum of twenty-four persons because there had to be room for an operator, or gripman, in the center of the car, but each grip car could tow up to three trailers, each seating thirty persons.

41. Alan R. Lind, *Chicago Surface Lines* (Park Forest, Ill., 1974), 399.

42. White, *American Railroad Passenger Car,* xiii, 103–15; James D. Johnson, *A Century of Chicago Streetcars* (Wheaton, Ill., 1964), 33–35.

43. Middleton, *Time of the Trolley,* 121.

44. CERA, *Rolling Stock, 1892–1947,* 105, and *Chicago's*

Rapid Transit Rolling Stock, 1947–1976, Bulletin 115 (Chicago, 1976), 185. Each motor car was equipped with two 125–horsepower motors.

45. CERA, *Rolling Stock, 1892–1947,* 75, 105. The Metropolitan West Side Elevated Railway on February 19, 1894, ordered one hundred electrically equipped but unpowered trailer coaches from Pullman Palace Car in Chicago, and on August 26, 1894, the line ordered fifty-five motorized coaches from Barney & Smith Co., of Dayton, Ohio.

46. Middleton, *Time of the Trolley,* 235–37.

CHAPTER 3: DEVELOPMENT OF THE RAILROADS

1. Robert P. Howard, *Illinois* (Grand Rapids, 1972), 202–7, citing George M. McConnel, "Recollections of the Northern Cross Railroad," *Transactions of the Illinois State Historical Society* 13 (1908): 145–52, indicated that the only internal improvements project completed at the time of the collapse was the Meredosia Railroad. It had cost $1 million to build and by 1842 was not producing enough revenue to cover operating expenses and was reduced to using mules to pull its trains after its single locomotive wore out. The railroad was sold at auction in 1847 for $21,000.

2. Howard, *Illinois,* 198–202.

3. William H. Stennett, *Yesterday and To-day* (Chicago, 1905), 7–8.

4. H. Roger Grant, *The North Western: A History of the Chicago & North Western Railway System* (DeKalb, Ill., 1996), 28–29.

5. Andreas, *History of Chicago,* 1:247.

6. Stennett, *Yesterday and To-Day,* 11.

7. William B. Ogden, *Galena & Chicago Union Railroad Report to Stockholders,* April 5, 1848, 8–9.

8. There does not seem to be agreement as to when the railroad officially commenced operation. Andreas, *History of Chicago,* 1:247; and Pierce, *History of Chicago,* 2:35, place the inaugural run on November 20 and the commencement of revenue service sometime thereafter. The Galena & Chicago Union Railroad Co., *Second Annual Report to Shareholders,* March 5, 1849, 10, claims that the railroad was completed to the Des Plaines River and commenced operation on December 15, 1848. The *Chicago Daily Journal,* October 26, 1848, reports that a test run had been made on October 25, 1848.

9. The term *earnings,* despite its inconsistent use in financial reporting over the years, is used throughout this text to describe a corporation's net income (profits after taxes, special charges, and administration). Galena & Chicago Union Railroad Co., *Third Annual Report to Shareholders,* June 5, 1850, 10.

10. William Edward Hayes, *Rock Island Lines News Digest,* October 1952, 3.

11. Howard, *Illinois,* 198–99. In addition to the 1827 federal land for the Illinois-Michigan and Wabash-Erie (Indiana) canal projects, the cash poor but land rich Congress established the precedent in 1802 for transportation land grants that allowed states along the route of the National Road from Washington, D.C., to St. Louis to finance its construction using a

percentage of the proceeds from the sale of federal land, on the justification that a highway would encourage settlement. U.S. Department of Transportation, *America's Highways, 1776–1976: A History of the Federal Aid Program* (Washington, D.C., 1976), 16–22.

12. Carlton J. Corliss, *Main Line of Mid-America: The Story of the Illinois Central* (New York, 1950), 24–28.

13. Heading west were the Galena & Chicago Union, the Chicago & Milwaukee, and the Illinois & Wisconsin—all three later merged, respectively, into the Chicago & North Western. Also heading west were the Chicago & Rock Island, and the Aurora Branch, later known as the Chicago, Burlington & Quincy, which obtained operating rights over the Galena Railroad to get to Chicago. Arriving from the east were the Michigan Southern & Northern Indiana, later commonly known as the Lake Shore; the Michigan Central; and the Pittsburgh, Fort Wayne & Chicago, an adjunct of the Pennsylvania Railroad. The Illinois Central was the original railroad detoured to serve the growing Chicago terminal, which was followed in later years by such lines as the Monon, Baltimore & Ohio, the Wabash, and the Milwaukee & Mississippi railroads.

14. Harold M. Mayer and Richard C. Wade, *Chicago: Growth of a Metropolis* (Chicago, 1969), 28–30.

15. Cronon, *Nature's Metropolis*, 55–91; Jensen, *American Heritage History of Railroads*, 54–56; and Mayer and Wade, *Chicago*, 35–52, among others.

16. Chandler, *Visible Hand*, 28, 79–80, 188–94.

17. Ibid., 17, 28, 41, 79–80.

18. Grant, *North Western*, 13.

19. Computed from tables of tonnage and valuation of ships on the Great Lakes in 1858, cited by J. B. Mansfield, *History of the Great Lakes*, 439 et seq.

20. Chandler, *Visible Hand*, 16.

21. Stennett, *Yesterday and To-day*, 11–17.

22. William Z. Ripley, *Railroads: Finance and Organization* (New York, 1915), 11–14; Chandler, *Visible Hand*, 92.

23. Stennett, *Yesterday and To-day*, 17, 23, 48, and 63.

24. Chandler, *Visible Hand*, 192–93.

25. Andreas, *History of Chicago*, 2:119–21, 136–37.

26. Bullard, *Illinois Rail Transit*, 15; Yago, *Decline of Transit*, 136; Ann Durkin Keating, *Building Chicago: Suburban Developers and the Creation of a Divided Metropolis* (Columbus, Ohio, 1988), 69; Weber, "Rationalizers and Reformers," 23.

27. Bullard, *Illinois Rail Transit*, 15.

28. Illinois Central Railroad Co., *Annual Report to Shareholders*, March 19, 1856, table of ridership by station.

29. John Van Nortwick, "Report of the Chief Engineer," *Galena & Chicago Union Railroad Report at Annual Meeting of Shareholders*, April 5, 1848, pp. 16–17; Richard P. Morgan, in the Galena & Chicago Union stock prospectus of August 10, 1847, as quoted by Stennett, *Yesterday and To-day*, 9–10. Prospective passenger and mail revenues were estimated at $180,000 or nearly 49 percent of projected total revenues.

30. Van Nortwick, "Report of the Chief Engineer," 17.

31. Kenneth T. Jackson, *Crabgrass Frontier: The Suburban-*

ization of the United States (Oxford, U.K., 1985), 21, 25–30; Henry C. Binford, *The First Suburbs: Residential Communities on the Boston Periphery, 1815–1860* (Chicago, 1985), 126–49.

32. Illinois Central Railroad Co., *Annual Report to Shareholders*, March 19, 1856, p. 16, table of ridership by station.

33. Charles B. George, *Forty Years on the Rail* (Chicago, 1887), 88–90.

34. Mayer and Wade, *Chicago*, 40, 42.

35. White, *American Railroad Passenger Car*, 222–66. Some very large industries were totally dependent upon the railroads. George Pullman's giant, three-thousand-employee plant on Chicago's South Side became famous for its sleeping cars but also manufactured thousands of horsecars, streetcars, and rapid transit vehicles between its founding in 1859 and its withdrawal from passenger-car building in 1979. Harold M. Mayer, "The Railway Pattern of Metropolitan Chicago" (Ph.D. diss., University of Chicago, 1943), 42.

36. *Railway Age*, July 12, 1889, 455.

37. Mayer, "Railway Pattern of Metropolitan Chicago," 89–90.

38. Mayer and Wade, *Chicago*, pp. 100–101.

39. The first convention of any note held in Chicago, The Rivers and Harbors Convention of 1847, preceded the railroads.

40. Condit, *Chicago, 1910–1929*, 50.

CHAPTER 4: EVOLUTION OF THE STREET RAILWAYS

1. International Harvester Co., *Roots in Chicago: One Hundred Years Deep* (Chicago, 1947), 12.

2. *The Morton Salt Tapestry* (Chicago, 1973), 1.

3. Andreas, *History of Chicago*, 1:255.

4. Mayer and Wade, *Chicago*, 38

5. William Edward Hayes, *Iron Road to Empire* (New York, 1953), 19.

6. Andreas, *History of Chicago*, 3:164.

7. Parmelee Transportation Co., *An Essential Link in American Transportation, 1853–1953* (Chicago, 1953), 7–14.

8. Andreas, *History of Chicago*, variously identified the first Chicago omnibus operators as Samuel B. and Martin O. Walker (2:118) and Franklin Parmelee (3:164); Pierce, *History of Chicago*, 2:323, states that the city's first line began in 1850 and ran from Lincoln Park to the business district but does not otherwise identify its operators.

9. Pierce, *History of Chicago*, 2:323–24.

10. Ibid., 2:323.

11. Vance, *Capturing the Horizon*, 354–59.

12. Anonymous, *A History of the Yerkes System of Street Railways* (Chicago, 1897), 12.

13. Weber, "Rationalizers and Reformers," 76.

14. Pierce, *History of Chicago*, 2:324–25.

15. Andreas, *History of Chicago*, 2:119; Pierce, *History of Chicago*, 2:324; *Yerkes System*, 12.

16. Weber, "Rationalizers and Reformers," 19. Antimonopoly sentiment was popular in the United States after President Andrew Jackson's fight against the Second Bank of

the United States in the 1830s. This trend continued into the 1870s in the case of the steam railroads and later in the case of mass-transit systems.

17. Ibid., 10–15, 45–47.

18. Andreas, *History of Chicago,* 2:119.

19. Ibid., 2:121.

20. Weber, "Rationalizers and Reformers," 20.

21. *Yerkes System,* 13.

22. Andreas, *History of Chicago,* 2:118–19.

23. *Yerkes System,* 17, indicates that about half the 2,200 employees were conductors and drivers.

24. Miller, *City of the Century,* 177.

25. Ross Miller, *American Apocalypse* (Chicago, 1990), 143 71.

26. *Yerkes System,* 14, 16–17.

27. Weber, "Rationalizers and Reformers," 25–26; Yago, *Decline of Transit,* 53 generally and 134–36 relating to Chicago.

28. *Chicago Tribune,* October 6 and 25; November 17, 18, 29, and 30; and December 5, 6, 8, 13, 16, 22, 23, and 24, 1874.

29. Weber, "Rationalizers and Reformers," 23–26, 60 73, provides the best narrative of this corrupt period of Chicago transit.

30. Ibid., 65.

31. Ibid., 72–73.

32. *Chicago Tribune,* February 25, 1895; August 29 and December 24, 1896.

33. Cudahy, Brian J., *Destination Loop: The Story of Rapid Transit Railroading in and Around Chicago* (Brattleboro, Vt., 1982), 15–16.

34. Forrest McDonald, *Insull* (Chicago, 1962), 83, Weber, "Rationalizers and Reformers," 70.

35. McDonald, *Insull,* 89.

36. Bruce Moffat, *Forty Feet Below* (Glendale, Calif., 1982), 7 8.

37. Weber, "Rationalizers and Reformers," 88–89.

38. *Chicago Tribune,* November 30, 1875, and January 2, 1876. The ordinance was effective January 1, 1876.

39. Cudahy, *Destination Loop,* 19, attributed much of the problem to the Adams Law (after State Senator George E. Adams, of Chicago, a reformer).

40. *Yerkes System,* 24–25.

41. The measure apparently was included in an ordinance temporarily extending the street railway franchises.

42. Bullard, *Illinois Rail Transit,* 99.

43. Weber, "Rationalizers and Reformers," 39–40, offers an analysis of Chicago City Railway Co. annual reports for the years between 1860 and 1898.

44. Ibid., 301–4.

45. Ibid., 40 (table).

46. J. Russell Jones served between 1863 and 1869, when he was appointed minister to Belgium by fellow Galena resident President Ulysses S. Grant. He was replaced at the railway on an interim basis by William H. Bradley. Jones resumed his chief executive duties at the West Division when he returned to Chicago in 1875.

47. The presidents were John B. Turner, head of the Galena & Chicago Union Railway (later the North Western), who officiated between 1859 and 1867, and his son, Voluntine C. Turner, who officiated between 1867 and 1888.

48. *Yerkes System,* 16.

CHAPTER 5: THE TRACTION BARON AND STRAPHANGERS

1. Fritz Plous, *Chicago Sun-Times,* May 27, 1973; *Midwest Magazine,* 14–17; and Yago, *Decline of Transit,* take the view that Yerkes was a robber baron. Carter H. Harrison, II, *Stormy Years* (New York, 1935), 110–208, is particularly critical of Yerkes. Weber, Rationalizers and Reformers," 250, 307–10, advances a somewhat contrary view that, at least until the end, Yerkes was more the victim of political corruption than the perpetrator of it.

2. Wayne Andrews, *Battle for Chicago* (New York, 1946), 176.

3. *Yerkes System,* 20.

4. Harrison, *Stormy Years,* 111.

5. Weber, "Rationalizers and Reformers," 306.

6. *Yerkes System,* 21.

7. Keating, *Building Chicago,* 109 10, makes the point that the annexation was not so much a land grab by Chicago as the financial collapse of the town form of government popular before passage of the Cities and Villages Act of 1872.

8 Samuel K. Gove and James D. Nowlan, *Illinois Politics and Government* (Lincoln, Neb., 1996), 75. Before adoption of the 1970 state constitution, Illinois was known as a Dillon's Rule state in which local governments had only those powers granted them by the state.

9. Pierce, *History of Chicago,* 2:326; Weber, *Outline History,* 379

10. Weber, "Rationalizers and Reformers," 21.

11. Weber, "Rationalizers and Reformers," 22.

12. Slason Thompson, *A Short History of American Railways, Covering Ten Decades* (Chicago, 1925), 201.

13. *Journal of the Senate* (1897), 272; *Chicago Tribune,* February 18, 1897.

14. Bullard, *Illinois Rail Transit,* 17.

15. George A. Schilling, *Street Railways of Chicago and Other Cities* (Chicago: Campaign Committee of One Hundred, 1896), 27–28, estimates that the replacement cost of the existing lines was $65,000 per mile, although suburban lines were considerably less expensive to build. Bullard, *Illinois Rail Transit,* 36, indicates that the 2.75-mile Evanston Electric Railway in 1896 cost $75,000, or $27,272 per mile, to build.

16. The Constitution of the State of Illinois adopted Article X, Section 6, on March 6, 1848.

17. Gove and Nowlan, *Illinois Politics,* 151–52. Illinois in 1990 had 6,677 units of local government—more than any other state—including 102 counties, 1,281 municipalities, 1,434 townships, 2,107 special-purpose districts, and 951 school districts.

18. Howard, *Illinois,* 329–30.

19. Pierce, *History of Chicago,* 2:234–35, indicates that the state legislature in the city charters of 1837 and 1851 did not empower Chicago to grant such franchises.

20. Weber, "Rationalizers and Reformers," 180.

21. Andreas, *History of Chicago,* 2:119.

22. The Constitution of the State of Illinois, Article XI, Section 4, adopted on May 13, 1870.

23. Delos F. Wilcox, *Analysis of the Electric Railway Problem* (New York, 1921), 43–46.

24. Weber, "Rationalizers and Reformers," 53–54, concluded that the fee, which raised about $22,500 from all three companies, or about one-third of what the city had sought, was imposed strictly as a revenue measure.

25. *Journal of the Senate* (1897), 943–52. Allen's original House bill, which allowed a fifty-year franchise only after approval by voters in a referendum, was amended in the Senate to eliminate the election provision.

26. Weber, "Rationalizers and Reformers," 347.

27. Yago, *Decline of Transit,* 54.

28. This technique persisted well into the twentieth century. Henry Crown acquired bonds of the Chicago, Rock Island & Pacific Railroad at a discount during a bankruptcy, then took stock in the company as part of its reorganization. *Chicago Tribune,* October 5, 1975, quoting Crown from an interview with the author.

29. Data consolidated from the 1994 annual shareholders reports of five railroads (Union Pacific, Chicago & North Western, Santa Fe Pacific, Wisconsin Central and Illinois Central) indicate that their combined earnings were 8.1 percent of revenues and their dividends were 42.7 percent of earnings but only 3.45 percent of revenues.

30. Chicago City Railway Co., *Annual Report,* 1861 (Chicago, CTA Archives).

31. Bullard, *Illinois Rail Transit,* 17.

32. Chicago City Railway Co. annual reports to stockholders for the period 1860–1900.

33. Weber, "Rationalizers and Reformers," 41–42.

34. Ibid., 231–32.

35. Harrison, *Stormy Years,* 111.

36. *Yerkes System,* 22.

37. Frank J. Piehl, "Our Forgotten Streetcar Tunnels," *Chicago History* 4, 3 (Fall 1975): 130–39; *Chicago Tribune,* May 29 and August 14 and 17, 1881; a survey showed that only 1,349 of the 54,612 persons who crossed between the central business districts and the west and north sides used the tunnels beneath LaSalle and Washington streets.

38. Piehl, "Our Forgotten Streetcar Tunnels," 130–39, indicates that the tunnel under the south branch of the river was completed in 1869 at a cost of $517,000.

39. U.S. Department of Interior, *Report on the Transportation Business in the United States at the Eleventh Census (1890)* (Washington, D.C.: Census Office, 1895), part 1, 683–85. In terms of trackage, or track miles, Chicago with 390.33 was followed by New York City with 377, Boston with 366, Brooklyn with 352, and Philadelphia with 351. In terms of route miles, however, which counts a double-track line as a single mile, Philadelphia with 277 and Boston with 238 both led Chicago with 193 and New York with 181.

40. Task Force on a Public Transportation System for Northeastern Illinois, *Legal History of Mass Transit Operations in Northeastern Illinois* (Springfield, Ill., 1972), 9; Samuel W. Norton, *Chicago Traction: A History, Legislative and Political* (Chicago, 1907), 114–17, 122–37, and 140.

41. Keating, *Building Chicago,* 69.

42. The Ogden Gas Co. was probably the most notorious of the utility shakedown schemes engineered by Chicago politicians of the time (including Roger C. Sullivan and Mayor John P. Hopkins, both of whom were stockholders). Chartered ostensibly as a competitor to the existing Peoples Gas, Light & Coke Co., it was in fact a dummy company created solely for the purpose of enriching its political stockholders when Peoples was forced to buy it out for several million dollars; see Howard, *Illinois,* 408. Altgeld and real estate developer Bernard F. Weber organized the Union Street Railway Co. to connect Lake View with Chicago but lost the bidding for the franchise to Yerkes's North Chicago Railway; see Weber, "Rationalizers and Reformers," 205.

43. Weber, "Rationalizers and Reformers," 94.

44. Bion J. Arnold, *Report on the Engineering and Operating Features of the Chicago Transportation Problem,* a report to the Committee on Local Transportation of the Chicago City Council, November 19, 1902.

45. Mayer and Wade, *Chicago,* 124–38, discuss the skyscraper phenomena begun in 1880 with Daniel H. Burnham and John Wellborn Root's ten-story Montauk Block and their sixteen-story Monadnock Building completed in 1891. The trend reached its culmination in the nineteenth century in the structures of Louis Sullivan. Also see Miller, *American Apocalypse,* 63–168.

46. *Chicago Tribune,* May 29, August 14 and 17, and November 8, 1881, reported that a survey of traffic in 1881 showed that 54,612 persons crossed the Chicago River between the central business district and the West and North sides, an indication of the size of the daytime population of the business district at that early date.

47. George M. Smerk, *The Federal Role in Urban Mass Transportation* (Bloomington, Ind., 1991), 52.

48. Hilton, *Cable Car in America,* 235.

49. Vance, *Capturing the Horizon,* 407; determining Yerkes's net worth, even in probate, proved difficult. He died in 1905 in New York, leaving an estate valued at $4 million. His widow, Mary Adelaide, however, who was willed one-third of the estate, disputed a decision by the executor to sell $4.5 million in Chicago City Railways bonds discounted to thirty cents on the dollar, and the case dragged on until her death in 1911. *Chicago Tribune,* April 3, 1911.

50. Harrison, *Stormy Years,* 206.

CHAPTER 6: THE ELEVATED TRAINS

1. Bullard, *Illinois Rail Transit,* 28.

2. Ibid., 26.

3. Cudahy, *Destination Loop,* 7, indicates that in common

usage in Chicago, the contraction "L" is preferred over "El."

4. Moffat, *The L*, 12. The first electric elevated railroad in Chicago was a 3.5-mile, narrow-gauge freight line built entirely within the 39-acre Armour & Company packing plant near the Union Stockyards. It opened in September 1892.

5. The words "rapid transit" appeared in the 1880s in connection with elevated railways, apparently to distinguish them from the slower street railways.

6. Bullard, Thomas R., "Columbian Intramural Railway" (Oak Park, Ill., 1987), 7, identifies the winning bidder as the Western Dummy Railway Co., organized by Bernard E. Sunny, president of the Chicago Arc Light & Power Co. Moffat, *The L*, 15, states that Western Dummy was backed by Thomson-Houston Electric Co., of which Sunny was a vice president.

7. Bullard, "Columbian Intramural Railway," 17.

8. Moffat, *The L*, 17. The earliest use of a third rail on an elevated railway was by the Liverpool (England) Overhead Railway on February 4, 1893, three months prior to the Intramural's commencement of service on May 1 (p. 12). The earliest electrified elevated railway was the North Hudson County Railroad in Hoboken, New York.

9. Cudahy, *Destination Loop*, 22.

10. Ibid., 11.

11. The issue of the life cycle of the original elevated structures was settled in 1992—one century later—when the Chicago Transit Authority decided to shut down the Jackson and Lake lines for reconstruction, the most important part of which consisted of replacing the concrete and brick footings on which the steel columns rested.

12. Bullard, *Illinois Rail Transit*, 27.

13. Weber, "Rationalizers and Reformers," 36. The elevated company agreed to give the street railway company one share of common stock for each $100 in bonds, plus one seat on the two-member committee formed to oversee construction.

14. Ibid., 195–96.

15. The first three-mile segment from Congress to 39th Street commenced service on June 6, 1892, and was completed to Jackson Park on May 12, 1893.

16. Bullard, *Illinois Rail Transit*, 27.

17. *Chicago Tribune*, September 17 and 30, 1896.

18. Calculations based on data culled from the annual reports of the Chicago City Railway Co. and the Chicago & South Side Rapid Transit Co. for the years 1894 through 1896.

19. Chicago City Railway Co. annual reports, 1896 through 1898.

20. Cudahy, *Destination Loop*, 14. Among other things, the original charter was for only twenty-five years—half the time prospective bondholders considered the minimum.

21. Weber, "Rationalizers and Reformers," 251–53.

22. The Columbian Intramural line technically claimed that distinction, but it was torn down after the 1893 fair.

23. Moffat, *The L*, 123–39.

24. Weber, "Rationalizers and Reformers," 39, 263.

25. The name Northwestern became a misnomer as Chicago grew and the Northwest Side migrated further west beyond the L tracks. The Northwestern eventually became the Howard

Street and Ravenswood lines that served the North Side.

26. Moffat, *The L*, 187–94.

27. *Yerkes System*, 97–98. This anonymous 1897 work published at Yerkes's behest, the closest thing available to a sanctioned biography, makes no mention of his reasons for building the Loop, but subsequent transit historians have no difficulty discerning the reasons. Cudahy, *Destination Loop*, 18; Moffat, *The L*, 167–68.

28. Bullard, *Illinois Rail Transit*, 27–28.

29. Weber, "Rationalizers and Reformers," 254–56; Cudahy, *Destination Loop*, 18–21.

30. Ibid., 257, 262.

31. Cudahy, *Destination Loop*, 27–31, discusses the opening of the Loop in some detail.

32. Charles T. Yerkes, letter to G. H. Wheeler, July 1, 1891; *Yerkes System*, 10.

33. Charles K. Mohler, *Report on the Union Elevated Railroad of Chicago* (Chicago, 1908), 13.

34. Schroeder, "Metropolitan Transit Research Study," 38, provides data on Chicago Rapid Transit Co. ridership on which estimates of the Loop use are based; Chicago Transit Authority, OP x79069 (annual bulletin on rail system ridership by route and station) for November 1978 and April 27, 1979.

35. Moffat, *Forty Feet Below*, 12–14.

36. Ibid., 7–8; Weber, "Rationalizers and Reformers," 71–73.

37. Moffat, *Forty Feet Below*, 9.

38. *Chicago Tribune*, April 22, 27, and 28, 1902.

39. Ibid., April 27, 1902.

40. Ibid., June 15, 1992, quoting estimates of the Chicagoland Chamber of Commerce.

CHAPTER 7: SUBURBAN TRANSIT

1. White, *American Railroad Passenger Car*, 478. The fastest passenger train in the United States in 1874 operated on the 979-mile New York–Chicago run, averaging only twenty-five miles per hour.

2. Lawrence Grow, *On the 8:02: An Informal History of Commuting by Rail in America* (New York, 1979), 13–14; Michael H. Ebner, *Creating Chicago's North Shore* (Chicago, 1988), 22–23.

3. Keating, *Building Chicago*, 74.

4. Everett Chamberlin, *Chicago and Its Suburbs* (Chicago, 1874), 204–5.

5. Keating, *Building Chicago*, 23.

6. Ibid., 24.

7. Patrick C. Dorin, *Everywhere West: The Burlington Route* (Seattle, 1976), 91. The scheduled running time of Chicago, Burlington & Quincy Railroad commuter trains for the twenty-one-mile run from Downers Grove to Chicago was forty-three minutes in 1895.

8. Bion J. Arnold, *Report on the Re-arrangement of the Steam Railroad Terminals in the City of Chicago* (Chicago, 1913).

9. Robert Fishman, *Bourgeois Utopias: The Rise and Fall of*

Suburbia (New York, 1987), 39–72; Jackson, *Crabgrass Frontier*, 30–33; Grow, *On the 8:02*, 25; Binford, *First Suburbs*, 126–27.

10. Mayer, "Railway Pattern of Metropolitan Chicago," 114–15n.; Ada Douglas Harmon, *The Story of an Old Town— Glen Ellyn* (Glen Ellyn, 1928), 54; Ebner, *Creating Chicago's North Shore*, 22–23.

11. Mayer, "Railway Pattern of Metropolitan Chicago," 112–13n.

12. Corliss, *Main Line of Mid America*, 347–48.

13. Ibid., 350.

14. Illinois Central Railroad, *Annual Report to Shareholders* (1857), tables of ridership and revenues.

15. Illinois Central Railroad, *Annual Report to Shareholders* (1858), 16 and 21–22, tables of ridership and revenues.

16. Ibid.

17. Ibid., 16.

18. Grow, *On the 8:02*, 25.

19. Illinois Central Railroad, *Annual Report to Shareholders* (1884), tables of revenues and passenger traffic.

20. Corliss, *Main Line of Mid America*, 356.

21. Illinois Central Railroad, *Annual Report to Shareholders* (1884), 15.

22. Dorin, *Everywhere West*, 91.

23. Mayer and Wade, *Chicago*, 183–86.

24. Chamberlin, *Chicago and Its Suburbs*, 399.

25. George, *Forty Years on the Rail*, 136–38.

26. Ibid., 138–39.

27. Larry Plachno, *Sunset Lines: The Story of the Chicago, Aurora & Elgin Railroad* (Polo, Ill., 1986–1989), 2:233.

28. Illinois Central Railroad, *Annual Report to Shareholders* (1900), 16.

29. White, *American Railroad Passenger Car*, 133. A 1903 series of similar cars had twelve doors on each side.

30. Ibid., 35, 106–32, 379–419.

31. Jennifer Sieroslawski, *Suburban Transit History* (Arlington Heights, Ill., 1996), 60.

32. Bullard, *Illinois Rail Transit*, 43; Sieroslawski, *Suburban Transit History*, 65.

33. Bullard, *Illinois Rail Transit*, 42.

34. Sieroslawski, *Suburban Transit History*, 61.

35. Bullard, *Illinois Rail Transit*, 43.

36. Ibid., 39.

37. Sieroslawski, *Suburban Transit History*, 50.

38. The Constitution of the State of Illinois adopted Article III, Section 34, on May 13, 1870.

39. The Constitution of the State of Illinois, Article XI, Section 1, adopted on May 13, 1870.

40. The Cities and Villages Act established population standards of one thousand for incorporation as a city and three hundred for incorporation as a village.

41. Keating, *Building Chicago*, 83, 92–105; Keating indicates that Hyde Park's financial problems were the primary reason for annexation.

42. Ibid., 114.

43. Illinois Secretary of State, *Blue Book* (1905), 438–55.

44. May Estelle Cook, *Little Old Oak Park, 1837–1902* (Oak Park, 1961), gives an account of the episode.

45. Illinois Secretary of State, *Blue Book* (Springfield, Ill., 1905–1935), tables of incorporated municipalities of Illinois.

46. Charles Warren, *The Supreme Court in United States History* (Boston, 1922) 2:578–79. The commission was the subject of the historic *Munn v. Illinois and Granger* cases rulings in the 1870s that legalized the economic regulation of railroads within their borders in the absence of any federal regulation.

47. George Krambles, *The Great Third Rail*, CERA Bulletin 105 (Chicago, 1961), 1–7. The conversion to one-operator Birney streetcars, which Chicago politicians successfully resisted on most of that system, was accomplished in Aurora in 1922 by the receiver for the bankrupt Fox River lines with little political interference.

48. Illinois Secretary of State, *Blue Book* (Springfield, Ill., 1905), 438–55.

49. Illinois Secretary of State, *Blue Book* (Springfield, Ill., 1933), 643–60.

CHAPTER 8: REGULATION AND COMPETITION

1. Chicago City Railway Co., *Seventieth Annual Report to the Stockholders* (January 31, 1930): 5. Nonfare revenues included $4,586 for charters, $2,019 for hauling newspapers, $1,560 for transporting patients between hospitals, $311,792 for advertising, $163,294 for rental of buildings, $99,983 from the sale of power, $175,026 for interest, and $8,611 classified as miscellaneous.

2. Chicago Rapid Transit Co., *Annual Report to Shareholders*, 1930.

3. Norton, *Chicago Traction*, 164–68, claims that the 1903 Union Traction company receivership was orchestrated by the company and a friendly creditor to protect them during renegotiation of the expired franchises.

4. Lind, *Chicago Surface Lines*, 400. The calculations were based on data from the rosters of the Chicago Railways and Chicago City Railway.

5. Schroeder, "Metropolitan Transit Research Study," 38.

6. Ibid. Chicago Motor Coach, an independently owned and operated bus company, increased ridership from 3 million rides in 1917 to just over 69 million in 1929.

7. Weber, "Rationalizers and Reformers," 326.

8. *Journal of the Senate* (Springfield, Ill., 1897), 272; *Chicago Tribune*, February 18, 1897.

9. Weber, "Rationalizers and Reformers," 323–24.

10. Weber, *Outline History*, 30.

11. *Blair v. Chicago*, 201 U.S. 400 (1906).

12. *Lobdell v. Chicago*, 227 Ill. 218 (1906).

13. Paul Barrett, *The Automobile and Urban Transit: The Formation of Public Policy in Chicago, 1900–1930* (Philadelphia, 1983), 82. Traction settlements in Cleveland, Detroit, San Francisco, Toledo, Seattle, Toronto, and Des Moines were modeled on the Chicago Settlement Ordinances.

14. The vote on April 2, 1907, was 167,367 to 134,281 in favor of ratification.

15. An Ordinance Authorizing the Chicago City Railway Co. to Construct, Maintain, and Operate a System of Street Railways in Streets and Public Ways of the City of Chicago (an identical ordinance dealt with the Chicago Railways Co., and both were known collectively as the Traction Settlement Ordinances), City of Chicago, February 11, 1907, Sec. 24. They were ratified in a referendum on April 2, 1907.

16. Weber, *Outline History*, 61–79; Traction Settlement Ordinances, Sec. 1–42, 1–90.

17. Traction Settlement Ordinances, Sec. 20–21.

18. Chicago City Railway Co., *Seventieth Annual Report to the Stockholders* (1930), 2.

19. Annual reports of the Chicago City Railway Co., 1886–1898; North Chicago City Railway Co. and successors, 1887–1898; and the Chicago West Division Railway and successors, 1888–1898.

20. Reports of the Chicago City Railway Co., the Chicago Railways Co., the Calumet & South Chicago Railway Co., and the Southern Street Railway Co., to the Chicago Board of Supervising Engineers, 1908–1917.

21. Weber, *Outline History*, 91–92.

22. Schroeder, "Metropolitan Transit Research Study," 11–12. The debt loads of the street traction companies in 1930 were as follows: Chicago Railways Co., $80,720,546; Chicago City Railway Co., $27,644,550; Calumet & South Chicago Railway Co., $3,332,550; and Southern Street Railway, none. An Ordinance Authorizing Unified Operation of the Surface Street Railways in the City of Chicago, City of Chicago, November 13, 1913.

23. When it took operating control of the system on February 1, 1914, the Chicago Surface Lines operated 3,975 cars—1,067 from the Chicago Railways Co.; 1,810 from the Chicago City Railway Co.; 29 from the Southern Street Railway Co.; and 59 from the Calumet & South Chicago Street Railway.

24. Albro Martin, *Enterprise Denied: Origins of the Decline of American Railroads, 1897–1910* (New York, 1971), 12–18.

25. U.S. Department of Labor, Bureau of Labor Statistics, 1914–1947.

26. Chicago Surface Lines, *Tenth Anniversary Report* (1926), 30, and Board of Supervising Engineers, Chicago Traction, *Twenty-Fourth Annual Report* (1931), 74–81, tables.

27. Martin, *Enterprise Denied*, 309, notes that the Interstate Commerce Commission study of the financial condition of steam railroads in 1915 reported the operating ratio of those companies that year at an unacceptably high 79.3 percent, up from 68.6 percent in 1901.

28. Chicago Railways Co., *Annual Report to Stockholders* (1925).

29. Wilcox, *Analysis of the Electric Railway Problem*, 327, notes that on May 31, 1919, about six thousand of the nation's forty-four thousand miles of electric railroads were in the hands of receivers, although those figures included interurban as well as street railways.

30. McDonald, *Insull*, 113.

31. *Public Utilities Commission v. Quincy*, 290 Ill. 360 (1919); *Chicago Railways Co. v. Chicago*, 292 Ill. 190 (1919).

32. Schroeder, "Metropolitan Transit Research Study," 98.

33. Illinois Public Utilities Commission Case no. 8721, order of August 6, 1919.

34. *Chicago Railways Co. et al. v. City of Chicago*, 292 Ill. 190 (1920).

35. McDonald, *Insull*, 181–82.

36. Weber, *Outline History*, 120–230, is the most complete synopsis of the case outside of the court transcripts.

37. *Chicago Tribune*, December 16, 1926.

38. Edmund F. Bard, "Accountant's Report," in *The Street Railways of Chicago: A Report of the Civic Federation of Chicago* (New York, 1901), 25–26, 112, 150. The report also said the Chicago City Railway Co., which was separately owned, had assets of $11.6 million and liabilities of nearly $16.9 million.

39. *In re. Chicago Railways Co.*, 160 Fed. 2d, 59, 61; case no. 9057 Consolidated Causes, brief of the Chicago Transit Authority, 3–4, and brief of the Securities and Exchange Commission, 4.

40. *Harris Trust & Savings Bank v. Chicago Railways Co.*, 56 Fed (2d) 942.

41. Krambles and Peterson, *CTA at 15*, 44.

42. Lind, *Chicago Surface Lines*, 351.

43. Schroeder, "Metropolitan Transit Research Study," 38, table; Barrett, *Automobile and Urban Transit*, 175.

44. Gilbert Gorman and Robert E. Samuels, *The Taxicab* (Chapel Hill, N.C., 1982), 39–49.

45. *Chicago Tribune*, July 15, 1924.

46. He sold his Yellow Cab Manufacturing Co. to General Motors Corp., which got that company into the business of building transit buses.

47. *Chicago Tribune*, February 16, 1932; Chicago Surface Lines, *Annual Report, 1932*, 7; and Moffat, *The L*, 99, 105–6, 178, 183, 189, 192, and 235–37; Vance, *Capturing the Horizon*, 407.

48. Lind, *Chicago Surface Lines*, 353.

49. Barrett, *Automobile and Urban Transit*, 173.

CHAPTER 9: THE LIMITATIONS OF PRIVATE ENTERPRISE

1. Schilling, *Street Railways*, 27–28; Bullard, *Illinois Rail Transit*, 27; Moffat, *The L*, 139.

2. Barrett, *Automobile and Urban Transit*, 11.

3. A. E. Burnett, *Sixteen Year Record of Achievement*, Chicago Board of Local Improvements (Chicago, 1931), 80.

4. T. A. Heppenheimer, "American Prometheus," *Audacity* (Summer 1994): 28–29.

5. McDonald, *Insull*, 83–86.

6. Andrews, *Battle for Chicago*, 176–85, 257–82.

7. McDonald, *Insull*, 96–97; Harold L. Platt, *The Electric City: Energy and the Growth of the Chicago Area, 1880–1930* (Chicago, 1991), 120.

8. Heppenheimer, *Audacity*, 35.

9. Moffat, *The L*, 235–37; McDonald, *Insull*, 156–58.

10. Commonwealth Edison Co., annual report to shareholders, December 31, 1914, 1–3. Insull justified the loan to Commonwealth Edison shareholders by saying he was acting to protect an estimated $100 to $125 million in revenues the company expected to receive over an unspecified period from the street and elevated traction companies for electric service. The Collateral Trust was a voluntary association that ultimately secured $7 million in loans from Edison by pledging 200,996 shares as collateral and $1.27 million in debentures.

11. It was eventually extended to Marengo Avenue in Forest Park in 1910.

12. *Central Trust Co., of New York, v. Chicago & Oak Park Elevated Railway Co.,* case #30578, April 25, 1912; petition by the Central Trust Co.; and Report of the Receiver of the Chicago & Oak Park Elevated Railway, U.S. District Court, July 23, 1918, which indicates that for the years 1916 and 1917 $300,718, or 14.2 percent, of the C&OPE's operating expenses of $2,113,496 were for power.

13. *Central Trust Co., of New York, v. Chicago & Oak Park Elevated Railway Co.,* case #30578, December 28, 1911, order of Kohlsaat; January 30, 1924, final report of the receiver; July 24, 1918, biennial report of the receiver. Fare revenues in 1916 were $857,467 and expenses were $906,541; fare revenues in 1917 were $921,658 and expenses were $1,206,955.

14. *Chicago Tribune,* July 6 and 11, 1919.

15. Moffat, *The L,* 237, citing the engineering study.

16. Charles K. Mohler, *Report on the Union Elevated Railroad of Chicago* (Chicago: Loop Protective Association, 1908), 13–25.

17. Bullard, *Illinois Rail Transit,* 31.

18. Chicago Rapid Transit Co., *Annual Report,* 1925, 6; CERA, *Rolling Stock, 1892–1947,* 10–189, car rosters. The roster of wooden motor cars numbered 3147 through 3166 (p. 179) ordered by the Chicago & Oak Park Elevated Railway in 1909 indicates that car number 3151 was the last wooden car still equipped for revenue service when it was scrapped in March 1959, although several wooden cars rebuilt for work service in 1950 survived in that role as late as 1968. Chicago & South Side Rapid Transit Co. car number 1, built in 1892, survives as a museum piece maintained by the CTA.

19. R. F. Kelker Jr., *Report on a Physical Plan for a Unified Transportation System,* to the City Council Committee on Local Transportation, May 22, 1923.

20. Later developments in through routing permitted substantial increases in efficiency. By 1955 the average speed on the heavily traveled Howard Street line, which used the new State Street subway, was more than twenty-two miles per hour. The construction of the subways and the elimination of one hundred stations on the L system had resulted in average speeds that made fewer cars necessary. The Chicago Transit Authority was able to reduce the size of the rapid-transit fleet from 1,623 cars on October 1, 1947, when it took over the system, to 1,297 on April 17, 1955. Schroeder, "Metropolitan Transit Research Study," 164, 181–82.

21. *In the Matter of the Chicago Rapid Transit Co.,* no. 65037, report of A. A. Sprague and Bernard J. O'Fallon, trustees, 1953, 5, 7, 9; McDonald, *Insull,* 156–58, 202.

22. John Hogan, *A Spirit Capable: The Story of Commonwealth Edison* (Chicago, 1986), 79–80, 90, 134, 141.

23. William D. Middleton, *North Shore: America's Fastest Interurban* (San Marino, Calif., 1964), 25–26, indicates Insull had been interested in acquiring the North Shore as early as September 1911. At the time he was the receiver of the Lake L, but he had not yet acquired the other elevated companies. Concerning the other two acquisitions, William D. Middleton, *South Shore: The Last Interurban* (San Marino, Calif., 1970), 34–35, reports that purchase was related to an acquisition by Insull of utilities in Indiana. Plachno, *Sunset Lines,* 2:303–7, states that the CA&E sale resulted from the owners' wish to sell in order to concentrate on other railroads they owned.

24. U.S. Department of Labor, Bureau of Labor Statistics, 1913–1954, indicates a CPI of 69.4 on November 31, 1918, and 86.6 on August 31, 1920.

25. Schroeder, "Metropolitan Transit Research Study," 38. Rapid transit (elevated) ridership increased from 162,866,136 originating rides in 1906 to 228,812,766 rides in 1926 before beginning a long decline that ended just before World War II.

26. Ibid., 38.

27. Chicago Department of Streets and Sanitation, cordon count for 1926. The counts were generally conducted between 7:00 A.M. and 7:00 P.M., generally during one week in May.

28. Steven Michael Rock, "The Redistributive Effects of Mass Transit in the Chicago Area" (Ph.D. diss., Northwestern University, 1975), 66, 109–10. The study identified three profitable routes (with the cost to revenue ratio, or operating ratio, in parentheses)—the Howard (0.91), Skokie (0.83), and Ryan (0.75); three that essentially broke even—Jackson-Englewood (1.11), Douglas (0.98), and Milwaukee (1.01); and four that lost money—Evanston (1.35), Ravenswood (1.29), Lake (1.17), and Congress (1.29).

29. George Krambles, retired executive director of the Chicago Transit Authority, suggested the factors in a series of conversations with the author concluding June 9, 1995.

30. Data calculated from the Chicago Area Transportation Study estimates of population for small area units, CATS, January 1968.

31. Krambles, conversations with the author, June 9, 1995.

32. CERA, *Rolling Stock, 1947–1976,* 226.

33. Krambles, conversations with the author, June 9, 1995.

34. Chicago Board of Supervising Engineers, trackage map of Chicago Surface Traction Companies, January 1907. Chicago Railways Co. streetcar lines were (from north to south) Grand Avenue, Lake Street, Madison Street, Van Buren Street, Harrison Street, Taylor Street, 12th Street, 14th Street, 18th Street, and 21st Street.

35. Moffat, *The L,* 141.

36. Wilcox, *Analysis of the Electric Railway Problem,* 183, 201.

37. Chicago Rapid Transit Co., *Annual Report,* 1924, 6; Chicago Rapid Transit Co., *Annual Report,* 1925, 7; Chicago Rapid Transit Co., *Annual Report,* 1928, 6.

38. Chicago Rapid Transit Co., *Annual Report,* 1932, table of liabilities.

39. McDonald, *Insull,* 252.

40. Heppenheimer, *Audacity,* 40, suggested Insull was a pioneer in the mass marketing of securities; Andrews, *Battle for Chicago,* 273–76, suggested Insull was paranoid about Eaton's holdings and believed Eaton was trying to get control of his companies.

41. An enormous amount has been written about Insull's fall, but Heppenheimer, *Audacity,* 37–41; Andrews, *Battle for Chicago,* 273–77; and McDonald, *Insull,* 300 et seq., provide a range of perspectives on the end of the Insull empire.

CHAPTER 10: THE CAMPAIGN FOR PUBLIC OWNERSHIP

1. Yago, *Decline of Transit,* 159; Cudahy, *Destination Loop,* 63. The city's contribution to the subway project was not all it seemed to be, however. Of the $64 million cost of the two subways, $23 million was from a depression era federal Public Works Administration grant, $40 million was provided by the city traction fund that was maintained by tax on street railways, and the balance was in the form of an interest-free loan from the city to the Chicago Rapid Transit Co. to furnish the subways with track and signals.

2. Miller, *City of the Century,* 506, quoting Chicago Record of November 30, 1892.

3. Rudyard Kipling, *American Notes: Rudyard Kipling's West,* edited by Arrell Morgan Gibson (Norman, Oklahoma, 1981).

4. Campaign Committee of One Hundred, *Street Railways of Chicago and Other Cities* (Chicago, 1897), 27–28.

5. *Report of the Special Committee of the City Council of Chicago on Street Railway Franchises and Operations* (Chicago, 1898), 63.

6. Edmund F. Bard, *The Street Railways of Chicago: Report of the Civic Federation of Chicago,* Accountant's Report (New York, 1901), 25–26, 112, 150, calculated the liabilities of the street railway system at $82.2 million and its assets at $42.9 million. The other half of the report was the Analysis of Financial Operations by Milo Roy Maltbie.

7. The vote was 142,826 to 27,988 in favor of public ownership.

8. *Illinois Revised Statutes,* chap. 131a, sec. 1–7, adopted May 18, 1903.

9. The Mueller Certificates were approved 153,223 to 30,279.

10. The April 4, 1905, vote was 64,391 to 150,785 against the extension.

11. Barrett, *Automobile and Urban Transit,* 32; Arthur F. Bentley, "Municipal Ownership Interest Groups in Chicago: A Study of Referendum Votes, 1902–1907" (Chicago: University of Chicago, ca. 1910), concluded that the middle class constituted the largest class of riders and voted for regulation when municipal ownership seemed impossible and municipalization when regulation seemed unattainable.

12. *Blair v. Chicago,* 201 U.S. 400 (1906).

13. Weber, *Outline History,* 51; the vote was 121,916 to 110,323 in favor of municipal operation of the street railways.

14. The vote was 167,367 to 134,281.

15. Condit, *Chicago, 1910–1929,* 40.

16. Chicago Department of Public Works, *32nd Annual Report,* 1907, 403.

17. Schroeder, "Metropolitan Transit Research Study," 38.

18. Chicago Department of Streets and Sanitation, cordon count, 1926; Schroeder, "Metropolitan Transit Research Study," 38.

19. Bion J. Arnold, *Report on the Engineering and Operating Features of the Chicago Transportation Problem,* 22, 49.

20. Bullard, *Illinois Rail Transit,* 93; Barrett, *Automobile and Urban Transit,* 95–96.

21. Report of the Chicago Traction and Subway Commission, December 16, 1916.

22. Henry A. Blair, "Outline of a Plan for a Comprehensive Unified System of Local Transportation, March 3, 1922," *Journal of Council Proceedings* (1921–1922), 2143.

23. Kelker, *Report on a Physical Plan.*

24. William E. Dever, "Outline of a Plan for the Solution of Chicago's Traction Problem, July 2, 1923," *Journal of Council Proceedings* (1923–1924), 672.

25. William E. Dever, "Letter of October 22, 1924," *Journal of Council Proceedings* (1924–1925), 3713–21. Dever estimated the cost of subway construction at $5 million per mile of double-track line in the downtown area and $4.3 million per mile elsewhere.

26. "An Ordinance Providing for a Comprehensive Municipal Local Transportation System, adopted February 27, 1925," *Journal of Council Proceedings* (1924–1925), 4840.

27. The vote was 227,554 to 329,228 against municipal ownership and 226,681 to 327,543 against a companion issue for municipal operation of the system.

28. *Journal of Council Proceedings* (1930–1931), 2978–79. The vote was 325,837 to 56,837 in favor of the Terminable Permit Ordinance.

29. Chicago City Railway Co., *Seventieth Annual Report to Stockholders,* 1930, 4; the fourth CSL member, The Southern Street Railway Co., had no indebtedness of its own but was wholly owned by the Chicago City and Connecting Railways Collateral Trust, which had $20.6 million in bonds outstanding.

30. *Chicago Tribune,* September 21, 23, 25, 26, 27, 28, and 29, 1933.

31. Ibid., November 1, 1933. They were to receive series A bonds in the new corporation and a slightly better position than rapid transit creditors, who were to get a series B bond.

32. Ibid., March 24, 1934.

33. Ibid., October 28, 1935.

34. Ibid., May 29 and 30; July 24; August 6; and November 21, 1936.

35. Schroeder, "Metropolitan Transit Research Study," 136–39.

36. Ibid.

37. *Report to Federal Court on Plan of Reorganization,*

Securities and Exchange Commission, 1945, Consolidated Case no. 63057, National Archives-Great Lakes Region, Chicago.

38. Schroeder, "Metropolitan Transit Research Study," 164.

39. "Chronology of The Traction Situation," 1947, archives of Chicago Transit Authority, Chicago.

40. Schroeder, "Metropolitan Transit Research Study," 11–13, citing *In re. Chicago Railways Co.*, 160 Fed. 2d, 59, case no. 9057 Consolidated Causes; and Trustee's Final Report and Account in the Matter of the Chicago Rapid Transit Co., case no. 65037, filed November 30, 1953.

41. Schroeder, "Metropolitan Transit Research Study," 143.

42. Illinois Revised Statutes, chap. 111 2/3 (1945).

43. Schroeder, "Metropolitan Transit Research Study," 155. The transaction included the purchase of $24 million in cash in a CSL deprecation fund, so the actual price paid was $51 million.

44. Ibid., 11–13, citing John E. Sullivan, Chicago Surface Lines Constituent Companies, report for the period October 1, 1947, to January 31, 1954, case no. 9057 Consolidated Causes; Trustee's Final Report and Account, case no. 65037, November 30, 1953.

45. Schroeder, "Metropolitan Transit Research Study," 172.

CHAPTER 11: STEAM TECHNOLOGY TO INTERNAL COMBUSTION

1. Jensen, *American Heritage History of Railroads,* 264.

2. Philip Van Doren Stern, *A Pictorial History of the Automobile as Seen in "Motor Magazine," 1903–1953* (New York, 1953), 252–53.

3. Flink, *America Adopts the Automobile,* 31.

4. G. N. Georgano, *The Encylopedia of American Automobiles* (New York, 1971), 21–25; Flink, *America Adopts the Automobile,* 240.

5. Stern, *Pictorial History of the Automobile,* 17.

6. Georgano, *American Automobile,* 94.

7. Ibid., 63–64.

8. Stern, *Pictorial History of the Automobile,* 245; Georgano, *American Automobile,* 37.

9. James A. Wren et al., *The Automobile—The Unwanted Child,* SAE Technical Paper Series (Detroit: International Congress and Exposition, 1989), 20.

10. Undated record of the Department of Public Works. The first use of concrete was on a two-block section of Schlitz Avenue between 111th and 113th Streets.

11. Chicago Bureau of Public Efficiency, *Street Pavement Laid in the City of Chicago,* 1911, 40.

12. Ibid., 24–25.

13. Chicago Daily News, *Almanac and Year Book* (Chicago, 1936), 951; Howard L. Willett, *Willett and the March of Time* (Chicago, 1959), 13.

14. Motor Vehicle Manufacturers Association of the U.S., *MVMA Facts and Figures '92* (Detroit, 1992), 30, extrapolated from U.S. Department of Commerce, Bureau of Census, *1987 Census of Transportation, Truck Inventory and Use Survey* (Washington, D.C.: Bureau of Census, 1987).

15. Schroeder, "Metropolitan Transit Research Study," 38.

16. Condit, *Chicago, 1910–1929,* 250.

17. Ibid., 32, 250–52.

18. Chicago Department of Public Works records.

19. Carl W. Condit, *Chicago, 1930–1970: Building, Planning, and Urban Technology* (Chicago, 1974), 236; Chicago Department of Public Works records.

20. *Chicago Tribune Sunday Magazine,* June 25, 1989, 10–17.

21. Gary M. LaBella, *A Glance Back: A History of the American Trucking Industry* (Washington: American Trucking Associations, 1976), 7.

22. Schroeder, "Metropolitan Transit Research Study," 204–11.

23. George M. Smerk, *Urban Mass Transportation: A Dozen Years of Federal Policy* (Bloomington, Ind., 1974), 237.

24. Krambles and Peterson, *CTA at 45,* 47.

25. Denis N. Miller, *Passenger Vehicles, 1893–1940* (London: Olyslager Auto Library, 1973), 13, 39; Ross D. Eckert and George W. Hilton, "The Jitneys," *The Journal of Law and Economics* 15 (1972): 293–325; George W. Hilton, testimony on the Industrial Reorganization Act, S. 1167, before the Subcommittee on Antitrust and Monopoly, Judiciary Committee, U.S. Senate, 93d Cong., April 1974, 2233.

26. Krambles and Peterson, *CTA at 45,* 44.

27. George Krambles, interview with the author on August 9, 1996.

28. Krambles and Peterson, *CTA at 45,* 43.

29. Ray Hebert and Harre W. Demoro, "The Big Bend Bus," *Mass Transit* 6, 10 (December 1979): 12 et seq.

30. John B. Rae, *The American Automobile* (Chicago, 1965), 102.

31. Schroeder, "Metropolitan Transit Research Study," 208–9; Barrett, *Automobile and Urban Transit,* 177.

32. Schroeder, "Metropolitan Transit Research Study," 208–9.

33. Krambles and Peterson, *CTA at 45,* 39, 44.

34. Maury Klein, "The Diesel Revolution," *American Heritage of Invention & Technology* 6, 4 (Winter 1991): 17.

35. The name *Zephyr 9900,* as the train was originally known, was changed to *Pioneer Zephyr* after it entered revenue service. The three-car motor train was 196 feet long and seated 72 passengers. It was donated to Chicago's Museum of Science and Industry after being retired in 1957 after 2,735,600 miles of service. Steve Glischinski, *Burlington Northern and Its Heritage* (Andover, N.J., 1992), 10.; Chicago, Burlington & Quincy Railroad, *Chicago-Aurora Centennial* (Chicago, 1964), 19–22; and *Chicago Tribune,* May 27, 1934.

36. White, *American Railroad Passenger Car,* 618–24. The *Pioneer Zephyr,* principally because its six-hundred-horsepower diesel engine was so efficient, paid for itself ($200,000) in revenue service in thirty months, and the M10000 version bought by the Illinois Central Railroad as its *Green Diamond* train between

Chicago and St. Louis in 1938 produced a profit of $110,000 on an investment of $425,000.

37. Klein, "The Diesel Revolution," 19; David P. Morgan, *Our GM Scrapbook* (Milwaukee: Kalmbach Publishing Co., 1971), 48–55.

38. Klein, "The Diesel Revolution," 19.

39. Glischinski, *Burlington Northern and Its Heritage*, 10–11; Chicago, Burlington & Quincy Railroad, *Chicago-Aurora Centennial*, 21. The commuter division was converted to diesel in the fall of 1952, several years after the railroad began converting its commuter fleet to modern bilevel cars. Chicago & North Western Railway, *95th Annual Report*, 4; Chicago & North Western Railway, *96th Annual Report*, 33.

40. Klein, "The Diesel Revolution," 19.

41. White, *American Railroad Passenger Car*, 35, 178, and 195.

42. Ibid., 193, points out that bilevel cars date back to the nineteenth century, including two triple-deckers used on the East Indian Railways in the 1890s, but that the revival of the bilevel in the last half of the twentieth century dates from the commuter experience in Chicago. Michael R. Weinman, "High Rollers: The Bilevel Evolution," *Passenger Train Journal* 21, no. 2 (February 1990): 28–32, notes that the Long Island Railroad even earlier, in 1932, developed a hybrid bilevel with staggered trireme seating to increase the passenger capacity of commuter coaches that stayed within the height limits (13 feet, 6 inches) mandated by the tunnels and catenary system in New York. The cars, which seated 120, were cramped and therefore never popular with riders.

43. *Chicago Tribune*, July 8, 1945.

44. Weinman, "High Rollers," 31, indicates that the primary concern about a taller car was the risk of roll motion. It was solved by the addition of a bolster roll stabilizer added to the truck.

45. Railway Age, September 4, 1903, reports that the Illinois Central built a number of one-hundred-seat, side-door coaches for suburban service in 1903.

46. White, *American Railroad Passenger Car*, 155–56.

47. Dorin, *Everywhere West*, 91; *Chicago Union Station Company Operating Agreement*, July 2, 1915, 1–10.

48. White, *American Railroad Passenger Car*, 194–95.

49. Weinman, "High Rollers," 32.

CHAPTER 12: PUBLIC OWNERSHIP

1. Howard, *Illinois*, 554–55.

2. Gove and Nowlan, *Illinois Politics*, 22.

3. John G. Allen, "From Centralization to Decentralization: The Politics of Transit in Chicagoland" (Ph.D. diss., Massachusetts Institute of Technology, 1995), 79–84, 94–100, and 106–11.

4. Walter J. McCarter, *Report on the 1977 Budget*, report filed with the First National Bank of Chicago, December 15, 1976, 1–3.

5. Schroeder, "Metropolitan Transit Research Study," 255–68.

6. Illinois Revised Statutes, Chap. 111 2/3, Sec. 312, Para. 12, commonly known as the Metropolitan Transit Authority Act.

7. The Chicago Transit Authority audit for 1960, statement of application of revenues to fixed requirements for the twelve months ending December 31, 1960, indicates the payment of $10.4 million was $212,406 short of the 8 percent requirement.

8. Chicago Transit Authority, November 1978, report on rail system traffic, OP x79096. The weekday passenger count at all rapid-transit turnstiles on the system included 298,000 entering on full fares, 33,800 entering on reduced fares, and 204,600 entering on transfers, and 71,800 interchanging between rail routes.

9. McCarter, *Report on the 1977 Budget*, 2–3.

10. CTA Annual Reports, 1956–1966.

11. John M. Cook, *Cost and Revenue of Public Transportation in Northeastern Illinois, 1960–1995*, Technical Appendix, vol. 2, to the Report to Governor's Transportation Task Force (Springfield, Ill., 1972), 30.

12. Krambles and Peterson, *CTA at 45*, 10.

13. Albro Martin, *Railroads Triumphant* (Oxford, U.K., 1992), 299–300.

14. Krambles and Peterson, *CTA at 45*, 31–32.

15. Milton Pikarsky, who at different times headed the Chicago Department of Public Works, the CTA, and the Regional Transportation Authority, and George Krambles, executive director of the CTA in the 1970s, in several conversations with the author over the years were unwavering in their opinion that the prevailing wisdom at the CTA, supported by considerable evidence, was that fare increases would accelerate ridership losses. See also David Young, "Fares Ups & Downs," *Mass Transit* 10, 6 (June 1983): 14–44, for a discussion of the prevailing Simpson and Curtin formula used to predict the effect of fare increases on ridership. Schroeder, "Metropolitan Transit Research Study," 171. The earlier $106 million modernization had been largely financed by $59.2 million accumulated in depreciation funds, some dating back to the Settlement Ordinances; $11.5 million from revenue bonds issued in 1947 and 1952; and $32.1 million in equipment trust certificates.

16. Allen, "From Centralization to Decentralization," 96, 107–9; CTA Audit, CY 1970.

17. George Krambles, CTA director of planning at the time, in interviews with the author.

18. Allen, "From Centralization to Decentralization," 88–90.

19. Smerk, *Federal Role in Urban Mass Transportation*, 50–141, is probably the most complete account available of the growth of the federal mass-transit program.

20. Krambles and Peterson, *CTA at 45*, 125–28.

21. Condit, *Chicago, 1930–1970*, 235. Planning for Chicago's radial expressways was done during World War II by the Cook County Department of Highways and the Chicago Department of Public Works.

22. Chicago Department of Public Works, brochure, June 22, 1958, commemorating the opening of the transit line, indicates that of the $183.5 million project cost, only $2 million—

the cost of the connection to the Dearborn subway—was financed by bonds to be repaid by CTA revenues while $12.3 million was paid by the CTA from the depreciation fund to equip the transit line for service.

23. Plachno, *Sunset Lines,* 2:383.

24. Krambles and Peterson, *CTA at 45,* 120.

25. Chicago Department of Public Works internal planning documents and memoranda of April and July 1966.

26. Cook, *Cost and Revenue of Public Transportation in Northeastern Illinois,* 33n.13.

27. CTA audit, CY 1970.

28. Joseph A. Tecson, *The Regional Transportation Authority in Northeastern Illinois* (Chicago, 1976; reprint in RTA archives of articles in May–June 1975, and July–August 1975, Chicago Bar Record), 8–11 (quote on p. 9), summarized the convention's debate on the topic.

29. Illinois Secretary of State data for 1978 show 1,506,173 autos registered in Chicago, which at the time had a population estimated at 2,950,800.

30. Tecson, *Regional Transportation Authority,* 12–13.

31. Allen, "From Centralization to Decentralization," 124.

32. CTA budget, CY 1973.

33. Tecson, *Regional Transportation Authority,* 15.

34. Cook, *Cost and Revenue of Public Transportation in Northeastern Illinois,* 149.

35. Thomas J. McCracken, speech before the East-West Corporate Corridor Association, in Lisle, October 26, 1995.

36. George W. Hilton, testimony on the Industrial Reorganization Act, S. 1167, before the Subcommittee on Antitrust and Monopoly, Judiciary Committee, U.S. Senate, 93d Cong., April 1974, 2203–39.

37. Ibid., 2209.

38. Brian Cudahy, "Mass Transit in American Cities," unpublished abstract, 1981, 20–21.

39. Milton Pikarsky, "After the Dust Settles: Transit in Transition," unpublished abstract, 1981, 3, 27.

CHAPTER 13: SUBSIDIES AND REGIONAL GOVERNMENT

1. Smerk, *Federal Role in Urban Mass Transportation,* 54.

2. Ibid., 117.

3. Smerk, *Urban Mass Transportation,* 28–32.

4. Ibid., 39–49.

5. Smerk, *Federal Role in Urban Mass Transportation,* 139.

6. Booz Allen Hamilton, Inc., *Regional Transportation Authority Strategic Plan and Capital Investment Plan* (Chicago, 1987), Exhibit 2–5.

7. *Chicago Tribune,* December 11, 1994, quoting Dale Janik, bureau chief for statewide planning for the Illinois Department of Transportation. Cancellation of the expressway made $1.916 billion available for other projects, which because of an inflationary clause in federal law grew to $2.58 billion to be split equally between the city and suburbs. Chicago divided its share 67 percent for transit and 33 percent for roads, and the suburbs spent 92 percent on roads and 8 percent on mass transit.

8. Tecson, *Regional Transportation Authority,* 9–11, cites debate at the Constitutional Convention of 1970 indicating there was some doubt as to whether the state's constitution of 1870 allowed subsidies to transit carriers.

9. George A. Ranney Jr., et al., *Crisis and Solution: Public Transportation in Illinois,* Report by the Governor's Transportation Task Force (Springfield, 1973), i–v.

10. Tecson, *Regional Transportation Authority,* 21–22.

11. Allen, "From Centralization to Decentralization," 149.

12. Unpublished 1974 analysis by author of RTA vote returns in selected precincts of Du Page County.

13. Gove and Nowlan, *Illinois Politics,* 26–27; Allen, "From Centralization to Decentralization," 154–61; *Chicago Tribune,* December 24, 1995, reported that later in his life Blair hid from his former wife in the Dominican Republic to avoid paying a divorce settlement.

14. Allen, "From Centralization to Decentralization," 200–16; Tecson, *Regional Transportation Authority,* 35–36.

15. Allen, "From Centralization to Decentralization," 215; *Chicago Tribune,* August 7, 1978.

16. Krambles and Peterson, *CTA at 45,* 10 (table).

17. Pikarsky's successor as general manager of the CTA was George Krambles, a transit professional, but the post of chairman was reserved for political appointees.

18. *Chicago Tribune,* June 18, 1989.

19. *Hoogasian v. Regional Transportation Authority,* 58 Ill. 2d 117, 132, 317 N.E. 2d 534 (1974).

20. Tecson, *Regional Transportation Authority,* 37.

21. *Chicago Tribune,* July 15, 1979.

22. David Young, "Transit's Fiscal Fiasco: Looking for a Way Out," *Mass Transit* 8, 7 (July 1981): 6–24.

23. The state operating subsidy was an amount equal to 3/32nds of the state sales tax collected in the Chicago area.

24. Young, "Transit's Fiscal Fiasco" 6–24.

25. Allen, "From Centralization to Decentralization," 236–38; *Chicago Tribune,* December 21, 1979.

26. Young, *"Fares Ups & Downs,"* 14–15, 42–44.

27. *Lena Lundgren-Gaveras, RTA Reorganization,* University of Chicago School of Social Service Administration project paper, 1985, 1–9, is a synopsis of the RTA reform act, as is James A. Lesser, *The Reorganization of the RTA: A Case Study of the Changing Legal Structure of a Regional Special Purpose Public Authority,* Columbia University Law School, 1984.

28. The Illinois Central Railroad and its successors provided commuter rail service to the southern lakeshore, an area not served by the CTA's rapid-transit system, and the Chicago, Rock Island & Pacific Railroad performed the same function in the extreme southwest corner of the city.

29. Chicago Transit Authority annual rapid-transit traffic reports for 1967 (RP x 68327, August 15, 1968) and 1990 (OP x91034, April 30, 1991) indicate a decline in ridership on those lines. Entering passengers on the Jackson-Englewood line declined to 32,100 in 1990 from 115,750 in 1967 (or 75,100 in 1970 after the parallel Ryan line was opened) and on the Lake Street line to 24,800 in 1990 from 40,350 in 1967.

30. Chicago Transit Authority, Bus Cordon Counts, June 1988.

31. Federal Transit Administration and City of Chicago, *Chicago Central Area Circulator Project Final Environmental Impact Statement,* 1994, I-4; M. K. Ludgin, *Downtown Development: Chicago 1987–1990,* Chicago Department of Planning, July 1989.

32. Federal Transit Administration and City of Chicago, *Chicago Central Area Circulator Project Final Environmental Impact Statement,* 1994, I-6-8.

33. Ibid., I-3-12, 33; Friends of Downtown, *The 1988 Downtown Chicago Parking Survey,* Chicago, September 1988.

34. David Young, "Chicago: Stuck on the Loop," *Mass Transit* 7, 1 (January 1980): 30–34.

35. Cudahy, *Destination Loop,* 85–88.

36. Young, "Chicago: Stuck on the Loop," 30–34.

37. *Chicago Sun-Times,* January 2, 1984.

38. Ibid., October 19, 1995.

39. Chicago Transit Authority, annual rapid transit traffic reports for 1967 (RP x 68327, August 15, 1968) and 1990 (OP x91034, April 30, 1991).

40. Regional Transportation Memorandum, November 7, 1995. The memo is based on data from the Federal Register or Federal Transit Administration tables.

41. Smerk, *Federal Role in Urban Mass Transportation,* 147–52.

42. *Chicago Sun-Times,* August 14, 1995.

43. Anthony M. Pagano, "The Private Transit Industry: Public Service or Profiteers," paper presented to the 35th Annual Meeting of the Transportation Research Forum, N.Y., October 1993. For discussions of privatization of mass transit elsewhere, see Ian Savage, "Deregulation and Privatization of Britain's Local Bus Industry," *Journal of Regulatory Economics* 5 (May 1993): 143–58.

44. Regional Transportation Authority, *Review of the Hearings on the Privatization of CTA Bus Services,* Chicago, November 2, 1995, 1–13.

45. Regional Transportation Authority annual budget and appropriation ordinance, 1995.

46. Isaiah Thomas, president of Amalgamated Transit Union Local 241, and Jerry Williams, president of ATU Local 308, letter to Regional Transportation Authority Chairman Thomas J. McCracken Jr., July 7, 1995.

47. William H. Hudnut III, president of the Civic Federation, statement at the RTA hearing, August 2, 1995.

48. Chicago Transit Authority Announcements of Service Changes of September 25, 1997; December 19, 1997; and April 3, 1998.

CHAPTER 14: SUBURBAN TRANSIT

1. George S. Rogers, "Chicago Area Interurban Systems (1892–1963): A Brief History" (Chicago: Regional Transportation Authority), 1980, 1–5.

2. Bullard, *Illinois Rail Transit,* 42, puts the population of the near west suburbs at 4,500 people in 1880, or about 450 people per square mile, and ascribes the failure of the Chicago & Western Dummy Railway in 1885 to the lack of patronage.

3. Pace, *1996 Operating and Capital Program* (Chicago, 1996), 74. The population density of suburbia in 1995 was 1,293 persons per square mile.

4. David Young, "Nortran Rises from the Ashes of Chicago's Transit Crisis," *Mass Transit* 9 (October 1982): 34; and Pace, *1996 Operating and Capital Program,* 12.

5. *Chicago, South Shore and South Bend Railroad: Perspectives on the Transit Crisis in Northern Indiana* (Michigan City, Ind.: Northern Indiana Commuter Transportation District), 1986, 3–7.

6. Bullard, *Illinois Rail Transit,* 12–50.

7. Ibid., 39, 42–43, 56.

8. Sieroslawski, *Suburban Transit History,* 35–36.

9. Middleton, *North Shore,* 42–43.

10. Plachno, *Sunset Lines,* 2:295.

11. Bullard, *Illinois Rail Transit,* 42–43; Sieroslawski, *Suburban Transit History,* 62, 67.

12. Bullard, *Illinois Rail Transit,* 12; George Krambles, *The Great Third Rail,* Central Electric Railfans Association Bulletin 105 (Chicago, 1961), I-4-19; and Sieroslawski, *Suburban Transit History,* 34–45.

13. Bullard, *Illinois Rail Transit,* 55–56; and Sieroslawski, *Suburban Transit History,* 74.

14. Sieroslawski, *Suburban Transit History,* 77–84.

15. Pace, *1996 Operating and Capital Program,* 74.

16. George W. Hilton and John F. Due, *The Electric Interurban Railways in America* (Palo Alto, Calif., 1960), 7–8.

17. Middleton, *North Shore,* 46.

18. William D. Middleton, *The Interurban Era* (Milwaukee, 1961), 393.

19. A. A. Sprague and Bernard J. O'Fallon, income account of the receivers of the CA&E for the period between 1926 and 1944, as cited by Plachno, *Sunset Lines,* 2:368–69; Chicago & North Western Railway, *Seventy-Third Annual Report,* 1932, 5.

20. Chicago, South Shore & South Bend Railroad, *Annual Report,* 1965, 11, and Chicago, South Shore & South Bend Railroad, *Annual Report,* 1971, 8, table of statistics.

21. Hilton and Due, *Electric Interurban Railways,* 208–39, note that the typical interurban, unable to compete with the automobile, had disappeared by 1933. The industry's decline began before World War I. Middleton, *Interurban Era,* 396, suggests that the greater flexibility of automobiles was possibly the most important factor in their ascendancy.

22. Norman Carlson and Arthur Peterson, *Remember When—Trolley Wires Spanned the Country,* Central Electric Railfans Association Bulletin 119 (Chicago, 1980), 18–19.

23. Chicago & North Western Railway, *94th Annual Report,* 1953, 7; Chicago & North Western Railway, *96th Annual Report,* 1955, 7. Note diversions of interurban traffic to C&NW commuter lines.

24. Middleton, *South Shore,* 22–47.

25. Chicago, South Shore & South Bend Railroad, *Annual Report*, 1971, 8 (summary of various statistics). Ridership in 1971 was 2,030,993.

26. Chicago, South Shore & South Bend Railroad, *Annual Report*, 1975, reported freight revenues at $9,252,969 and passenger revenues at $2,865,072.

27. David Young, "End of the Line for the South Shore?" *Mass Transit* 3, 8 (September 1976): 38–39.

28. David Young, "Success for 'The Little Train that Could,'" *Mass Transit* 10, 2 (February 1983): 36–48.

29. Middleton, *North Shore*, 14–19, 25–31.

30. Ibid., 94, 111.

31. Ibid., 64–72.

32. Hilton and Due, *Electric Interurban Railways*, 226–29.

33. Plachno, *Sunset Lines*, 2:169–77.

34. Ibid., 2:405, 427, indicates that ridership declined from twenty-two thousand per day in 1952 to eleven thousand to twelve thousand per day in 1957, and the railroad lost $1.96 million in the first thirty-nine months after loss of access to downtown Chicago.

35. Various filings with the Illinois Commerce Commission indicate that the carrier lost $36,129 on revenues of $3.5 million in 1948, $140,637 on revenues of $2.97 million in 1953, and $884,216 on revenues of $1.35 million in 1956.

36. U.S. Department of Commerce, Bureau of Census, *Statistical Abstract of the United States: 1967*, 88th ed. (Washington, D.C.), 569; *Chicago Tribune*, April 8, 1967.

37. Bureau of Census, *Statistical Abstract of the United States: 1967*, 230; Automobile Manufacturers Association, *Automobile Facts and Figures* (New York, 1966), 18, 65; Illinois Secretary of State, historical table of auto registrations. There were almost 5 million cars registered in Illinois in 1966, although there was no breakdown by county to indicate the number in Chicago's suburbs.

38. American Public Transit Association, *1987 Transit Fact Book* (Washington, D.C., 1987), 32, table 9.

39. David Young, "Commuter Buses: A Transit Phenomenon," *Mass Transit* 5, 7–8 (July–August 1978): 20–21, 24, 64, 80; Joseph DiJohn III, "The Profitability of Rail Commutation in Chicago," DePaul University marketing research report (Chicago, 1968), 27.

40. Lind, *Limiteds Along the Lakefront*, 56–77.

41. Regional Transportation Authority, *ICG Fare Demonstration Study* (Chicago, 1981), tables of ridership, fare tables.

42. Association of Western Railways, *Yearbook of Railroad Facts* (Chicago, 1966), 14, 34–35.

43. Chicago & North Western Railway Co., *97th Annual Report* (Chicago, 1956), 24–27, in ten-year revenue and expense summaries, indicates that freight revenues grew from 85.2 percent of total revenues in 1947 to 90.6 percent in 1956, and commuter revenues grew from 2.3 percent of the total in 1947 to 4.5 percent, mainly at the expense of the declining share of intercity traffic.

44. DiJohn, "Profitability of Rail Commutation," 12–13, 26.

45. David Young, "The Rock Island: Back from the Brink," *Mass Transit* 5, 10 (November 1978): 16–18.

46. Regional Transportation Authority ridership data indicate 66.5 million riders used the system in 1970 and 72.7 million in 1990.

47. Railroad and Warehouse Commission of Illinois, *Thirtieth Annual Report* (Springfield, Ill., 1900).

48. Illinois Revised Statutes, 111 2/3, 351–59.

49. Sieroslawski, *Suburban Transit History*, 79; Lind, *Limiteds Along the Lakefront*, 76–77.

50. Ted Schuster, *History of the West Suburban Mass Transit District* (Batavia, Ill., 1996), 1–8.

51. Sieroslawski, *Suburban Transit History*, 52.

52. Ibid., 17, 25, 52, 79; Young, "Nortran Rises from the Ashes," 26–36.

CHAPTER 15: THE AUTO AGE

1. Rossiter Johnson, ed. *A History of the World's Columbian Exposition Held in Chicago in 1893* (New York, 1897–98), 3:236. "In the German section was a road carriage driven by the Daimler petroleum motor which made occasional trips around the grounds. An electric carriage also made its appearance at the Electric Building and made frequent trips around the grounds."

2. Flink, *America Adopts the Automobile*, 169, 175.

3. James J. Flink, *The Automobile Age* (Cambridge, Mass., 1988), 5.

4. Barrett, *Automobile and Urban Transit*, 45.

5. Flink, *America Adopts the Automobile*, 174–77.

6. Barrett, *Automobile and Urban Transit*, 6 (from the Chicago City Council Journal, 1908), 3829.

7. Chicago Department of Public Works, *Bureau of Streets Report*, 1913, 367.

8. Flink, *America Adopts the Automobile*, 171.

9. Ibid., 12.

10. Beverly Rae Kimes et al., *Standard Catalogue of American Cars, 1805–1942*, 3d ed. (Iola, Wis., 1996), 154.

11. Ibid., 674, 680, 932, 977, 1276, 1408.

12. *Chicago Tribune Sunday Magazine*, November 30, 1975.

13. *The Horseless Age*, February 9, 1910, 233.

14. *Chicago Tribune*, October 26, 1997.

15. Data on Chicago manufacture of automobiles was compiled from Kimes et al., *Standard Catalogue of American Cars*.

16. David A. Kolzow, "William O. Worth: The Forgotten Automobile Pioneer," *Antique Automobile* 56, 4 (July–August 1992): 29–39.

17. *Motocycle* was an early term for automobile.

18. Kimes et al., *Standard Catalogue of American Cars*, 248.

19. Ibid., 123, 1331, 1357; Flink, *America Adopts the Automobile*, 71.

20. Kimes et al., *Standard Catalogue of American Cars*, 1259–60; Flink, *Automobile Age*, 68; and *Chicago Tribune*, July 1, 1969.

21. *Chicago Tribune*, August 7, 1988, and July 3, 1994.

22. Kimes et al., *Standard Catalogue of American Cars*, 526–27.

23. Ibid., 453, 712, 770, 1335, 1386. Kimes et al. places Holsman production (1903–1910) at 6,348 vehicles (p. 712), but Franklin B. Tucker, *Holsman History: 1901–1910* (Decorah, Ia., 1993), places production at only 2,295 cars.

24. Tucker, *Holsman History*, 5–7.

25. Kimes et al., *Standard Catalogue of American Cars*, 1253, 1570.

26. Gorman and Samuels, *Taxicab*, 49–53; Kimes et al., *Standard Catalogue of American Cars*, 279, 367, 1153.

27. Gilbert and Samuels, *Taxicab*, 40–49; Kimes et al., *Standard Catalogue of American Cars*, 30–31, 279, 701, 1344–45.

28. Kimes et al., *Standard Catalogue of American Cars*, 1566; Flink, *Automobile Age*, 41.

29. Flink, *America Adopts the Automobile*, 73.

30. Schroeder, "Metropolitan Transit Research Study," 38.

31. Vance, *Capturing the Horizon*, 390.

32. Harvey Wish, *The American Historian* (New York, 1960), 181–208.

33. David V. Herlihy, "The Bicycle Story," *American Heritage of Invention & Technology* 7, 1 (Spring 1992): 58.

34. Flink, *Automobile Age*, 3 6.

35. Jacques Damase, *Carriages*, translated by William Mitchell (New York, 1968), 106.

36. Ibid., 106; Kimes et al., *Standard Catalogue of American Cars*, 1335.

37. Data culled from Federal Coordinator of Transportation, *Passenger Traffic Report* (Washington, 1935); U.S. Census Bureau decennial reports; Frank A. Smith, *Transportation in America* (Washington, D.C.: Eno Transportation Foundation, 1992), 47.

38. Barrett, *Automobile and Urban Transit*, 62, citing the proceedings of the Chicago City Council Committee on Local Transportation, June 30, 1915, 48–53.

39. Flink, *Automobile Age*, 137–38, 359–76, discusses the auto as a competitor to public transportation.

40. Wilfred Owen, *Transportation for Cities: The Role of Federal Policy* (Washington, D.C., 1976), 5–6.

41. Schroeder, "Metropolitan Transit Research Study," 55–74.

42. Northeastern Illinois Planning Commission, "Gridlock without Growth," *Planning in Northeastern Illinois* 31, no. 1 (Summer 1991): 1, 4.

43. Chicago Area Transportation Study, *2010 Transportation System Development Plan* (Chicago, 1990), 5.

44. *Chicago Tribune*, March 10, 1977, quoting the Crystal Lake report by Real Estate Research Corp., indicates that a new five-bedroom ranch home in that suburb required $8,027 in capital improvements and $1,314 in annual public operating costs thereafter, resulting in a tax deficit of $2,950. David Listokin et al., *Fiscal Impacts of and Responses to Growth: Naperville, Ill.* (New Brunswick, N.J.: Rutgers University Center for Urban Policy Research, 1988). Du Page County Planning Department, *Impacts of Development on Du Page Property Taxes* (Wheaton, Ill., 1991).

45. James A. Dunn, *Miles to Go: European and American Transportation Policies* (Cambridge, Mass., 1981), 73–91; Yago, *Decline of Transit*, 49–76; and Bradford C. Snell, "American Ground Transport," *Hearings before the Subcommittee on Antitrust and Monopoly of the Committee on the Judiciary, United States Senate on S. 1167* (The Industrial Reorganization Act), 93d Cong., February 1974, Part 4A (Appendix to Part 4), 1–77.

46. John R. Meyer and Jose A. Gomez-Ibanez, *Autos, Transit, and Cities* (Cambridge, Mass., 1981), 15.

47. Mayer, "Railway Pattern of Metropolitan Chicago," 48–69.

48. Ibid., 45–50, 55–56; Corliss, *Main Line of Mid America*, 361–68.

49. Fishman, *Bourgeois Utopias*, 121–33, 182–207; Jackson, *Crabgrass Frontier*, 61–67

50. Chicago Area Transportation Study, *Transportation Facts* (Chicago, 1996), 13(4): 14.

51. Barrett, *Automobile and Urban Transit*, 74–75, 147–48; Condit, *Chicago, 1910–1929*, 31–37.

52. Mark H. Rose, *Interstate: Express Highway Politics, 1941–1956* (Lawrence, Kans., 1979), 15–40.

53. Phil Patton, *Open Road: A Celebration of the Open Highway* (New York, 1986), 74; U.S. Department of Transportation, *America's Highways*, 136.

54. U.S. Department of Transportation, *America's Highways*, 151.

55. Yago, *Decline of Transit*, 173–74.

56. The name was changed to the Illinois State Toll Highway Authority in 1968.

57. The population figures were computed by the author from U.S. Census Bureau data.

58. U.S. Census, 1980, Statistical Abstract Data, Counties, Commuting.

59. U.S. Census Bureau and Metra, Weekday average ridership reports, July 1990–June 1991.

60. Robert Cervero, *Suburban Gridlock* (New Brunswick, N.J., 1986), 42–58, discusses floor area ratios included in zoning laws to reduce traffic congestion.

61. Sorkins Directory of Largest Enterprises, St. Louis, Mo., October 11, 1996, computer data compiled for author showing the location of corporate offices of Chicago area companies with annual revenues of $100 million or more.

62. Ruth Sheldon Knowles, *The First Pictorial History of the American Oil and Gas Industry, 1859–1983* (Athens, Ohio, 1983), 33; Daniel I. Vieyra, *Fill 'Er Up* (New York, 1979), 4; Paul H. Giddens, *Standard Oil Co. (Indiana): Oil Pioneer of the Middle West* (New York, 1955), 175–76.

63. Flink, *Automobile Age*, 185; Randolph McAusland, *Supermarkets: 50 Years of Progress* (Washington: Food Marketing Institute, 1980), 14; Jackson, *Crabgrass Frontier*, 257.

64. Jewel Tea Co., *The First Thirty Years, 1899–1929* (Chicago, 1929), 9–11.

65. Jewel Companies Inc., *Sharing* (Fall 1974): 15.

66. Ibid., 14; Jewel Tea Co., *First Thirty Years,* 20–21.

67. Jackson, *Crabgrass Frontier,* 268.

68. *Chicago Tribune,* May 17, 1992, sec. 19, 18.

69. Newell Corp., *The Sanford Story* (Freeport, Ill., 1993), 11, 14; and June 24, 1994, interview by the author with Robert Parker, president of Sanford Corp.

70. *Chicago Tribune,* "Chicago's Top 100," special supplement, May 14, 1995; and interview by author with Robert W. Racic, vice president and treasurer of Federal Signal Corp., February 7, 1994.

71. W. W. Grainger, Inc., *Sixty Years of Growth* (Skokie, Ill., 1987), 5–6; June 30, 1993, interview by author with David W. Grainger, chairman and president of the company.

72. Flink, *Automobile Age,* 157; Philip M. Klutznick, *Angles of Vision* (Chicago, 1991), 168.

73. *Chicago Tribune,* November 11, 1991, sec. 4, p. 1.

74. *Chicago Tribune, Shopping Center Report* (Chicago, 1988), 20–21.

75. Ibid., 18–87.

76. *Chicago Tribune,* January 20, 1992.

77. Chicago Association of Commerce and Industry, "Final Report and Recommendations of the CACI Downtown Parking Task Force" (Chicago, 1990), 6; and *Chicago Tribune,* August 1, 1990,

78. City of Chicago, Department of Streets and Sanitation, *Cordon Count 1980* (Chicago, 1980), table 2.

EPILOGUE

1. Chicago Area Transportation Study, *Draft 2020 Regional Transportation Plan* (Chicago, 1997), 24–26.

2. Illinois Secretary of State, Table of Auto Registrations by Chicago and Counties, Springfield, 1995.

3. Chicago Area Transportation Study, *Draft 2020 Regional Transportation Plan,* 112, projects spending $17.2 billion on highway capital projects between 1996 and 2020 and $12.7 billion on rail and bus systems. The CATS *2010 Transportation System Development Plan* (Chicago, 1990), 47, in its "cautiously optimistic" forecast projects that $8.5 billion will be spent on highways and $6.3 billion on transit between 1988 and 2010.

APPENDIX B: MASS TRANSPORTATION DISASTERS

1. Moffat, *The L,* 42, 77, 109, 136–37. The accidents occurred on June 20, 1896, when a Lake train derailed at Rockwell Street, losing one car; December 23, 1896, when a motorman asleep at the controls of a single-car Garfield Park train at 48th Avenue ran past the 48th Avenue terminal and off the elevated; April 7, 1908, when a powered (motor) car derailed and fell to the ground at 43rd Street on the South Side; and January 8, 1913, when the motorman of a three-car train took the Loop curve at Van Buren Street and 5th Avenue too fast, losing the unoccupied third car, which crashed to the street.

2. Illinois Department of Transportation, data on traffic accidents for Cook, Du Page, Kane, Lake, McHenry, and Will Counties, Springfield, Ill., 1991.

3. Robert B. Shaw, *A History of Railroad Accidents, Safety Precautions and Operating Practices,* 2d ed. (Potsdam, N.Y., 1978), 99–103.

4. Shaw, *History of Railroad Accidents,* 180–81.

5. Middleton, *South Shore,* 23–24.

6. Shaw, *History of Railroad Accidents,* 176–78.

7. Middleton, *North Shore,* 105.

8. Interstate Commerce Commission, *Accident on the Line of the Chicago Rapid Transit Company,* investigation no. 2121 (Washington, D.C., 1937).

9. Interstate Commerce Commission, *Chicago, Burlington & Quincy Railroad Co. Report in re Accident at Naperville, Ill., April 25, 1946,* investigation no. 2988 (Washington, D.C., 1946).

10. National Fire Protection Association, *Fire News,* Chicago Street Railway Car Fire Preliminary Report (Boston, Mass., 1950), 2–4; report to James O. Dwight, CTA general attorney, June 30, 1950, on the testimony before and findings of the Cook County coroner's inquest concluding June 29, 1950.

11. *Chicago Tribune,* November 28, 1956.

12. Ibid., September 8, 9, 1967.

13. Shaw, *History of Railroad Accidents,* 361–63.

14. National Transportation Safety Board, *Report NTSB-RAR-77-10: Railroad Accident Report: Rear End Collision of Two Chicago Transit Authority Trains, Chicago, Ill., February 4, 1977* (Washington, D.C., 1977).

15. National Transportation Safety Board, *Report NTSB/HAR-96-02: Collision of Northeast Illinois Regional Commuter Railroad Corporation (METRA) Train and Transportation Joint Agreement School District 47/155 School Bus at Railroad/Highway Grade Crossing in Fox River Grove, Illinois, on Oct. 25, 1995,* October 29, 1996 (Washington, D.C., 1997).

The following is a list of books in general circulation, government reports widely circulated, and a few of the more significant research papers by scholars on the topic of Chicago mass transit. For the most part, statistical summaries, periodicals, and unpublished academic papers are cited in footnotes.

Allen, John G. "From Centralization to Decentralization: The Politics of Transit in Chicagoland." Ph.D. diss., Massachusetts Institute of Technology, Cambridge, 1995.

Andreas, A. T. *History of Chicago from the Earliest to the Present Time*. 3 vols. Chicago, 1884.

Andrews, Wayne. *Battle for Chicago*. New York, 1946.

Barrett, Paul. *The Automobile and Urban Transit: The Formation of Public Policy in Chicago, 1900–1930*. Philadelphia, 1983.

Binford, Henry C. *The First Suburbs: Residential Communities on the Boston Periphery, 1815–1860*. Chicago, 1985.

Bullard, Thomas R. *Illinois Rail Transit*. Unpublished manuscript, Oak Park, Ill., ca. 1987.

Casey, Robert J., and W. A. S. Douglas. *Pioneer Railroad: The Story of the Chicago & North Western System*. New York, 1948.

Central Electric Railfans Association. *Chicago's Rapid Transit: Rolling Stock, 1892–1947*. Bulletin 113, vol. 1. Chicago, 1973.

Central Electric Railfans Association. *Chicago's Rapid Transit: Rolling Stock, 1947–1976*. Bulletin 115, vol. 2. Chicago, 1976.

Cervero, Robert. *Suburban Gridlock*. New Brunswick, N.J., 1986.

Chamberlin, Everett. *Chicago and Its Suburbs*. Chicago, 1874. Reprint. New York, 1974.

Chandler, Alfred D., Jr. *The Visible Hand: The Managerial Revolution in American Business*. Cambridge, Mass., 1977.

Chicago Area Transportation Study. *1987 Chicago CBD Parking Survey*. Chicago, 1986.

Chicago Area Transportation Study. *Transportation Facts*. Vol. 13, No. 4. Chicago, 1996.

Clarke, Thomas Curtis, et al. *The American Railway*. New York, 1888. Reprint. New York, 1972.

Clutton-Brock, Juliet. *Horse Power: A History of the Horse and the Donkey in Modern Society*. Cambridge, 1992.

Condit, Carl W. *Chicago, 1910–1929: Building, Planning, and Urban Technology*. Chicago, 1973.

———. *Chicago, 1930–1970: Building, Planning, and Urban Technology*. Chicago, 1974.

Cooke, Alistair. *Alistair Cooke's America*. New York, 1973.

Corliss, Carlton J. *Main Line of Mid-America, The Story of the Illinois Central*. New York, 1950.

Cronon, William. *Nature's Metropolis*. New York, 1991.

Cudahy, Brian J. *Destination Loop. The Story of Rapid Transit Railroading in and Around Chicago*. Brattleboro, Vt., 1982.

Currey, J. Seymour. *Chicago: Its History and Builders*. 2 vols. Chicago, 1912.

Damase, Jacques. *Carriages*. Translated by William Mitchell. New York, 1968.

Davis, James Leslie. *The Elevated System and the Growth of Northern Chicago*. Northwestern University Studies in Geography, no. 10. Evanston, Ill., 1964.

Douglas, George H. *Rail City: Chicago USA*. San Diego, 1981.

Dunn, James A. *Miles To Go: European and American Transportation Policies*. Cambridge, Mass., 1981.

Ebner, Michael H. *Creating Chicago's North Shore*. Chicago, 1988.

Fishman, Robert. *Bourgeois Utopias: The Rise and Fall of Suburbia*. New York, 1987.

Flink, James J. *America Adopts the Automobile, 1895–1910*. Cambridge, Mass., 1970.

———. *The Automobile Age*. Cambridge, Mass. 1988.

Foster, Mark S. *From Streetcar to Superhighway: American City Planners and Urban Transportation*. Philadelphia, 1981.

Giddens, Paul H. *Standard Oil Company (Indiana): Oil Pioneer of the Middle West*. New York, 1955.

Gove, Samuel K., and James D. Nowlan. *Illinois Politics and Government*. Lincoln, Neb., 1996.

Grant, H. Roger. *The North Western: A History of the Chicago & North Western Railway System*. DeKalb, Ill., 1996.

Harrison, Carter H. *Stormy Years*. New York, 1935.

Hart, Val. *The Story of American Roads*. New York, 1950.

Heise, Kenan, and Michael Edgerton. *Chicago: Center for Enterprise*. 2 vols. Woodland Hills, Calif., 1982.

Hilton, George W. *The Cable Car in America*. San Diego, Calif., 1982.

Hilton, George W., and John F. Due. *The Electric Interurban Railways in America*. Palo Alto, Calif., 1960.

Hindley, Geoffrey. *A History of Roads*. New Jersey, 1972.

Hokanson, Drake. *The Lincoln Highway: Main Street across America*. Iowa City, 1988.

Jackson, Kenneth T. *Crabgrass Frontier: The Suburbanization of the United States*. Oxford, U.K., 1985.

Jensen, Oliver. *The American Heritage History of Railroads in America*. New York, 1975.

Johnson, James D. *A Century of Chicago Streetcars*. Wheaton, Ill., 1964.

Johnson, Rossiter, ed. *A History of the World's Columbian Exposition Held in Chicago in 1893*. 5 vols. New York, 1897–98.

Keating, Ann Durkin. *Building Chicago: Suburban Developers and the Creation of a Divided Metropolis*. Columbus, Ohio, 1988.

Kimes, Beverly Rae, et al. *Standard Catalogue of American Cars: 1805–1942*. 3d ed. Iola, Wis., 1996.

Klutznick, Philip M. *Angles of Vision*. Chicago, 1991.

Knowles, Ruth Sheldon. *The First Pictorial History of the American Oil and Gas Industry: 1859–1983*. Athens, Ohio, 1983.

Krambles, George. *The Great Third Rail*. Central Electric Railfans Association, Bulletin 105, Chicago, 1961.

Krambles, George, and Arthur H. Peterson. *The CTA at 45*. Chicago, 1993.

Lind, Alan R. *Chicago Surface Lines*. Park Forest, Ill., 1974.

———. *Limiteds Along the Lakefront: The Illinois Central in Chicago*. Park Forest, Ill., 1986.

Martin, Albro. *Enterprise Denied: Origins of the Decline of American Railroads, 1897–1910*. New York, 1971.

———. *Railroads Triumphant*. Oxford, U.K., 1992.

Mayer, Harold M. "The Railway Pattern of Metropolitan Chicago." Ph.D. diss., University of Chicago, 1943.

Mayer, Harold M., and Richard C. Wade. *Chicago: Growth of a Metropolis.* Chicago, 1969.

McDonald, Forrest. *Insull.* Chicago, 1962.

McKelvey, Blake. *The Emergence of Metropolitan America, 1915–1966.* New Brunswick, N.J., 1968.

———. *The Urbanization of America, 1860–1915.* New Brunswick, N.J., 1963.

Meyer, John R., and Jose A. Gomez-Ibanez. *Autos, Transit, and Cities.* Cambridge, Mass., 1981.

Middleton, William D. *The Interurban Era.* Milwaukee, 1961.

———. *North Shore: America's Fastest Interurban.* San Marino, Calif., 1964.

———. *South Shore: The Last Interurban.* San Marino, Calif., 1970.

———. *The Time of the Trolley.* Milwaukee, 1967.

Miller, Donald L. *City of the Century.* New York, 1996.

Miller, Ross. *American Apocalypse.* Chicago, 1990.

Moffat, Bruce G. *The L.* Chicago, 1995.

Moses, John, and Joseph Kirkland. *The History of Chicago.* 2 vols. New York, 1895.

Norton, Samuel Wilber. *Chicago Traction: A History, Legislative and Political.* Chicago, 1907.

Overton, Richard C. *Burlington Route.* New York, 1965.

Owen, Wilfred. *Transportation for Cities: The Role of Federal Policy.* Washington, D.C., 1976.

Parmelee Transportation Company. *An Essential Link in American Transportation, 1853–1953.* Chicago, 1953.

Patton, Phil. *Open Road: A Celebration of the Open Highway.* New York, 1986.

Pierce, Bessie Louise. *A History of Chicago.* 2 vols. Chicago, 1937.

Plachno, Larry. *Sunset Lines: The Story of the Chicago, Aurora & Elgin Railroad.* 2 vols. Polo, Ill., 1986–1989.

Quaife, Milo M. *Chicago and the Old Northwest: 1673–1835.* Chicago, 1913.

———. *Chicago's Highways Old and New: From Indian Trail to Motor Road.* Chicago, 1923.

Rae, John B. *The American Automobile.* Chicago, 1965.

Ranney, George A., Jr., et al. *Crisis and Solution: Public Transportation in Illinois.* Report by the Governor's Transportation Task Force, Springfield, Ill., 1973.

Richman, William A. *The Sweep of Time.* Elgin, Ill. 1961.

Ripley, William Z. *Railroads: Finance and Organization.* New York, 1915.

Rogers, George S. "Chicago Area Interurban Systems (1892–1963)." Chicago, 1980.

Rowsome, Frank, Jr. *Trolley Car Treasury.* New York, 1956.

Schlessinger, Arthur M. *The Rise of the City, 1878–1898.* New York, 1933.

Schofer, Joseph L. "Passenger Transportation for the Chicago Region: Today and Tomorrow." 1896. Northwestern University Transportation Library, Evanston, Ill.

Schroeder, Werner W. "Metropolitan Transit Research Study." 1954. CTA archives, Chicago.

Schuster, Ted. *History of the West Suburban Mass Transit District.* Batavia, Ill., 1996.

Shaw, Robert B. *A History of Railway Accidents, Safety Precautions and Operating Practices.* 2d ed. Potsdam, N.Y., 1978.

Sieroslawski, Jennifer. *Suburban Transit History.* 1996. Pace files.

Smerk, George M. "200 Years in Transit." *Mass Transit,* July–August 1976.

———. *The Federal Role in Urban Mass Transportation.* Bloomington, Ind., 1991.

———. *Urban Mass Transportation: A Dozen Years of Federal Policy.* Bloomington, Ind., 1974.

Smith, Frank A. *Transportation in America: A Statistical Analysis of Transportation in the United States.* 10th ed. Westport, Conn., 1992.

Stennett, W. H. *Yesterday and To-day.* Chicago, 1905.

Stilgoe, John R. *Borderland: Origins of the American Suburb, 1820–1939.* New Haven, Conn., 1988.

Stover, John F. *American Railroads.* Chicago, 1961.

———. *History of the Illinois Central Railroad.* New York, 1975.

———. *The Life and Decline of the American Railroad.* Oxford, U.K., 1970.

Suttles, Gerald D. *The Man-Made City: The Land Use Confidence Game in Chicago.* Chicago, 1990.

Tarr, Laszlo. *The History of the Carriage.* Translated by Elisabeth Hoch. New York, 1969.

Thompson, Gregory Lee. *The Passenger Train in the Motor Age.* Columbus, Ohio, 1993.

Thompson, Slason. *A Short History of American Railways, Covering Ten Decades.* Chicago, 1925.

Tucker, Franklin B. *Holsman History, 1901–1910.* Decorah, Ia., 1993.

Turner, Frederick Jackson. *The Frontier in American History.* New York, 1920.

Vance, James E., Jr. *Capturing the Horizon: The Historical Geography of Transportation since the Sixteenth Century.* Baltimore, 1986.

———. *The North American Railroad.* Baltimore, 1995.

Vieyra, Daniel I. *An Architectural History of American Gas Stations.* New York, 1979.

———. *Fill 'Er Up.* New York, 1979.

Wade, Richard C. *The Urban Frontier: The Rise of Western Cities, 1790–1830.* Cambridge, Mass., 1959.

Waitley, Douglas. *Roads of Destiny.* Washington, D.C., 1970.

Wallis, Michael. *Route 66: The Mother Road.* New York, 1990.

Weber, Harry P. *Outline History of Chicago Traction.* Chicago, 1936.

Weber, Robert David. "Rationalizers and Reformers: Chicago Local Transportation in the Nineteenth Century." Ph.D. diss., University of Wisconsin, Madison, 1971.

White, John H., Jr. *American Locomotives: An Engineering History, 1830–1880.* Baltimore, 1968.

———. *The American Railroad Passenger Car.* Baltimore, 1978.

Willett, Howard L. *Willett and the March of Time.* Chicago, 1959.

Yago, Glenn. *The Decline of Transit: Urban Transportation in German and U.S. Cities, 1900–1970.* Cambridge, U.K., 1984.

INDEX